In *Whose* Steps?

One Man's Search for Answers
Inspired by true-to-life stories

A Novel by Cathy Wiseman

In *Whose* Steps?

One Man's Search for Answers
Inspired by true-to-life stories

Copyright © 2010 by Cathy Wiseman

All rights reserved in all countries. No part of this material may be reproduced, stored in a retrieval system, or transmitted in any form or by any means electronic, mechanical, photocopying, recording, or otherwise without prior written permission of the author, publisher and/or copyright owners, except as provided by USA copyright law.

Published and Printed By Dare 2 Dream Books
Mustang, Oklahoma
405-642-8257

Publisher's Cataloging in Publication

Wiseman, Cathy: In Whose Steps?
1. Counseling 2. Psychology 3. Christianity 4. Discipleship

ISBN 978-0-9779693-8-8

One Man's Search for Answers

TABLE OF CONTENTS

Chapter 1. 5
Chapter 2. .27
Chapter 3. .36
Chapter 4. .49
Chapter 5. .60
Chapter 6. .68
Chapter 7. .76
Chapter 8. .86
Chapter 9. .92
Chapter 10. 103
Chapter 11. 114
Chapter 12. 126
Chapter 13. 136
Chapter 14. 144
Chapter 15. 152
Chapter 16. 163
Chapter 17. 172
Chapter 18. 181
Chapter 19. 191
Chapter 20. 200
Chapter 21. 217

Chapter 22..................227
Chapter 23..................231
Chapter 24..................242
Appendix....................281
References..................334
A Word from the Author......346
Endnotes for Chapter 24.....352

One Man's Search for Answers

Chapter One

Dr. David Cunningham stared out the window, mesmerized by the sight and sound of the steadily falling rain.

What a dreary, depressing day—although it matches the heck out of my mood. Then he remembered he'd felt the same numbness the day before when it wasn't raining. Actually, more often than not he was feeling—*well, what am I feeling?* Although he wasn't used to verbalizing his feelings, he knew he needed to figure them out before he did something he'd strongly regret. *Is it depression? No!* His response came back quickly. *That's not possible. I'm a pastor. I'm the one who has the answers to all of life's problems!*

Well, then, since you're the one with all the answers, Pastor, why don't you tell me what they are—especially the answer for your own problem? He was sweating. A prosecuting attorney couldn't have cornered him more effectively than he had trapped himself.

"Because I don't know the answer!" he exclaimed loudly, answering his own thoughts. He was angry and upset because he couldn't figure out the answer and feeling ridiculous because he was having a conversation with himself. And now that he was starting to answer himself, he wondered if this was how it felt to lose one's mind. Desperate for an answer (although sure he wouldn't get it), he pleaded with God to give him some sign—a rainbow, a loud peal of thunder, writing on the wall—anything to explain why he was feeling so bad that he felt like quitting his perfect job.

In Whose Steps?

I have absolutely no reason to feel this way. He lectured himself sternly. *I'm still young and healthy; I love my wife and kids; I pastor one of the largest churches in the city; I'm continuously asked to speak at conferences and seminars; and hey, I'm even pretty good looking for a forty-five year old!* But the positive self-talk didn't help. He diverted himself from his questions by wrestling with whether his last thought about being good-looking meant he was vain. A quick check in the mirror seemed to be in order. All the while telling himself that it was going to be the same exact face he'd just seen in the mirror while shaving this morning, he forcefully shoved his chair back, slamming it into the paneled walls of his elegant office. Quick steps took him to face his image in the ornate gold-framed mirror. He had to admit; he liked what he saw. *No, it's not vanity; it's just honest to acknowledge that I have the image of a leader.*

As he continued to stare at himself, his face faded into the background as the colors of his study slowly came to the forefront. The congregation had given David carte blanche to redecorate the previous pastor's office after his resignation. They wanted David to feel at home in an office that fit *his* taste. And, he did feel comfortable with his (and his decorator's) choices. His office was filled with expensive leather and mahogany; it proclaimed elegance and importance. His impressive library let everyone know he must be well-read.

The room was large enough that David could easily have an elders' meeting around his conference table, but it also lent itself to comfortable one-on-one counseling sessions in the corner of the room—not that he actually used his office for counseling anymore. He sighed. In the beginning of his ministry, he loved being the counselor to his flock and loved sharing scripture with those in need of help. However, after just a year or two, he was more than ready to refer them to a professional counselor. He thought he had been equipped to counsel while in seminary but finally came to the realization that the congregation's problems were just too hard for him to handle. *Did people just get worse over the years?* David sighed again. He just didn't know.

He turned from the mirror and walked back to his desk, absent-mindedly running his fingers across its sheen. As he yanked his chair back over to the desk, he sat down hard. Swiveling toward the windows, although it was still cloudy, he noticed the rain had stopped. He was oblivious to the signs of new life that were noticeable outside the window: green leaves were sprouting on the trees while perky yellow daffodils and purple wisteria bloomed all over the well-manicured church grounds. But all *he* saw was the last of the rain dripping from the trees. *Great, just great. This really helps me feel better!* The sarcasm didn't help, either.

An attorney again, he put himself back on the stand; again he started asking questions. *Why and how could I possibly feel down* (he couldn't make himself say the word "depressed")? *The elders and deacons look up to me, deferring to my leadership.* Actually, they came close to rubber-stamping anything he wanted to do. The previous pastor Dr. Burns had stayed on as an elder, but had made it clear to David and the other elders that he also would defer to David; he stated that he never wanted to be the cause of dissension. David admired Dr. Burns for being willing to submit to the leadership of a much-younger man.

Although young, David had just confirmed in his mirror that he certainly looked like a leader. Tall, with just enough gray sprinkled in his dark hair to give him an air of maturity, his presence was immediately noticed in any gathering. Clear gray-green eyes that appeared to pierce others' souls added to his charisma. He knew his good looks and stature had contributed to his desirability as a leader. But he wasn't kidding himself. He knew it was his Ph.D. from one of the most prestigious seminaries in America that had secured him this coveted position—as well as a political connection, perhaps? He couldn't deny it: there *was* a powerful connection. Nor could his peers; they had a difficult time not being outright envious when David landed this pastorate right out of seminary. Even though he was a little older than the average graduate, they still wondered why God would bless him with this mega church at the beginning of his career. After all, he hadn't paid his dues yet. Actually, David did contemplate whether being chosen by the church had more to do with his father-in-law being president of the denomination's convention and a life-long friend of Dr. Burns than it had to do with his abilities or God blessing him. Just as he was graduating, Dr. Burns just happened to retire? David was sure that his friends believed those were the politics that played a big part in his calling. *Well, so what if they did? I have done an excellent job at this church and everyone knows it. Even me, if I do say so myself.*

As soon as arrived at the church, not wasting a single minute, David had hit the ground running. Although they loved Dr. Burns, the congregation immediately fell in love with their new pastor and his innovative programs that helped the church grow exponentially. Now, after ten years of presenting sermons on the important topics of the day (delivered with increasing political correctness), along with attending Chamber luncheons and befriending business leaders of the city, he was firmly entrenched as someone with whom to be reckoned.

First Christian Community Church, *his* church, had become the one that important people attended. Not only that, it was known as a seeker-friendly church, a place where those turned off by traditional churches could visit and not feel threatened. The drama and music in the Sunday seeker services were outstanding. And the church was also known throughout the city for its ability and willingness to meet the felt needs of anyone who came asking. David's toleration was well-known; he knew he seldom ruffled anyone's feathers the way he had when he was younger (he chalked his ability to be more tolerant and accepting up to experience and maturity).

I have absolutely no reason not to be happy and so maybe if I say it enough, I'll believe it? Maybe it's that I've been so busy trying to meet others' felt needs that mine have not been met! As he contemplated further, he decided perhaps the thought had some merit. What were his felt needs? Did he need a better marriage? He guessed his relationship with his wife, Nikki, was good, at least when he compared it to the marriages he knew among his congregation. Still, he did not look forward to going home every day. It wasn't anything he could put his finger on—it just seemed as though, over the last few years, coolness and then coldness had begun to emanate from Nikki. But she said *he* was distant and that *he* didn't listen to her. Well, all he knew was that the initial passion was gone; he supposed that just happened as couples got older.

And his kids, both teens, didn't seem any more disobedient than other teens. Sometimes they seemed just to tolerate him, but he knew that was what he did with them too. His oldest son, Neil, seventeen, was like him—tall, black hair, greenish eyes, preppy-looking. David was proud of Neil's natural leadership abilities. He didn't run with a bad crowd, and David was sure *(am I sure?)* that if someone offered Neil drugs, he would not only say no, but he would encourage his friends to say no also. Appearance—people-pleasing—was terribly important to Neil. David sighed. *Neil's a performer. Just like me. I've taught him well—probably too well.*

Blue-eyed, with different-colored hair from day to day, his daughter Alyssa was the opposite of Neil. Although she was fifteen, a normal time to want the approval of one's peers, she seemed to be oblivious to anyone's approval other than her own. David used to think that she looked like her mom, but when it came to hair and clothes, she was so unconventional that he wasn't sure who she looked like anymore. In his opinion—definitely not hers—she tended to cover her good looks with solid black clothing, blue fingernails (sometimes even blue hair!), bright red or black lipstick, and earrings up and down her earlobes. Her boyfriend's hair, clothes, and earrings were almost identical to hers. David did not like her choice of clothes or boyfriends. Even though she didn't seem to care what they thought of her, David was worried about what the congregation thought. One thing he knew for sure: he didn't want to harm Alyssa's self-esteem and that made it even harder to know whether to please the congregation or Alyssa.

At least both kids were members of the youth group, and David liked and trusted the youth pastor Tim. He knew that Tim was a young man with strong views, and David was especially glad Tim had plenty to say to the teens about the dangers of drugs and premarital sex. Tim had taken an interest in his kids, even meeting personally with them a couple of times. *Well, at least I can count on the kids staying clear of drugs and sex!*

So what is my problem? He demanded of himself yet once again. *I'm sick of whining and feeling sorry for myself.* Restlessly, he shoved his chair back again, jumped up, and started pacing. He was talking to himself again—only this time he spoke out loud! "Life just doesn't seem to have any meaning anymore. But isn't that one of the symptoms of depression?" He gasped; now he'd applied the word to himself. "Well, what was that weird word I heard Carl say was a symptom of depression? Anhedonia? I need to ask him—maybe I am depressed because I can't think of any other answer except depression! Maybe I've been in denial, and I just need to admit it."

Quickly, before he could change his mind, he walked to his office door, stuck out his head, and asked his secretary Linda, "Have you seen Dr. Jamison this morning?" She shook her head no without looking up.

"Well, would you please ask him to come to my office when you see him?" She continued typing, still not looking up, nodding her head yes.

Carl was a friend as well as a counselor. David felt blessed that the leadership in the church knew the value of having a Christian psychologist on its staff. He and Carl Jamison became good friends in seminary. Carl had been working on his Ph.D. in clinical psychology when they met in the student center. They had struck up a conversation on philosophy and had enjoyed bantering with each other since their first meeting. When the church leadership suggested they add a Christian counselor to the staff, David jumped at the chance to get his friend, Dr. Carl Jamison. He'd already become tired of doing the counseling himself and he needed someone he felt was better equipped. Carl was the guy.

Under Carl's able direction, the church added support groups and self-help groups of every description to minister to the congregation and visitors alike. David chuckled to himself at his own joke as he thought that at First Christian Community Church, they'd "aced" the recovery movement because they had a group for "**Adult Children of Every Dysfunction.**" David was proud to say that his church offered at least 30 support or self-help groups to minister to hurting people. Many who now attended came to the church because they had first attended one of the many groups offered at First Christian. Adding Carl to the staff had been of great benefit and had brought even more credibility to their ministries. Only Dr. Burns was against adding Carl, but he acquiesced in the end so as not to undermine David's leadership.

In Whose Steps?

Carl was a valuable staff member and continued to be a good friend. David and Nikki had become close friends with Carl and his wife Susan. David knew Nikki and Susan had formed a "lonely hearts club" since their husbands were gone all the time. The men thought it was a joke and had yet to learn it wasn't a joke at all to their wives.

What's keeping Carl this morning? David was anxious to get some feedback from him, hoping and praying he could help him figure out this mysterious malady of the soul. He thought of another possibility for his uneasiness: maybe it was just normal Monday morning quarterbacking of the Sunday sermon? Maybe, but it was Thursday, and he was still in the dumps. To make matters worse, it was only two weeks until Easter and he should have a stellar message on the resurrection almost finished by now—and he hadn't even started! Besides, he felt dead inside, like he needed some kind of resurrection himself. He'd read about guys in their forties having mid-life crises. *Ahhh. Now that seems to ring some bells. Is it possible I'm having a mid-life crisis?*

David turned his back on the still-gray skies as his eyes swept his office again. For some strange reason, they caught on a book he'd read years before—at least he thought he'd read it. Walking to the bookshelves, he took down a worn copy of <u>In His Steps.</u> 1937!! David couldn't remember if it was his book and he'd read it, or whether Dr. Burns left it for him. *Well, there couldn't possibly be anything helpful in a book so outdated, definitely nothing that will apply to my church.* As he leaned against the shelves, he opened it at random and fanned the pages.

"Hmmm, what would Jesus do?" David read, vaguely remembering the phrase and deciding he had read it long ago. As he pondered the words, he realized with a start that the phrase sounded odd to him. More often than not, he thought about what *people* would want him to do, not what *Jesus* would want him to do. As he continued to read, barely realizing what he was doing, he eased himself into one of the side chairs. <u>In His Steps</u>' Reverend Henry Maxwell's church actually sounded much like his own First Christian Community Church. *Not only the church, their pastor even sounds like me.*

David read to himself. "As Henry Maxwell delivered his striking sentences with impassioned and dramatic utterances, there was a mutual feeling of satisfaction between the pastor and his congregation." Suddenly David realized that he was standing, hand in midair, as if he had just given an "impassioned and dramatic utterance." He had to admit that he was familiar with that "mutual feeling of satisfaction between the pastor and his congregation" because he often experienced it. He loved it. Yet, somehow, as he saw it in print, he realized how smug it—*he?*—sounded. Was that what he was? Smug?

Although he hated to acknowledge it, he reflected that "smug" was probably an adjective that did fit him. *But I think it's more than that; I must have some unconscious unmet need. Some kind of deep ache down in my heart, something eating at me that just won't go away, something I'd love to find out; it feels like it's hanging right at the edge of my consciousness. It couldn't just be smugness.* A huge sigh escaped. Maybe it wasn't an ache after all; maybe he could more accurately call it numbness. Thoughts of a mid-life crisis returned.

He heard himself ask out loud, "What's keeping Carl?" then quickly glanced around to see if Linda had heard him. As he craned his neck, he could see around the corner of the door that she was engrossed on the phone. *Saved from exposure!* Then he sighed, but even that scared him. *Uh, oh, isn't sighing a symptom of depression?* The "depression" word seemed to haunt and stalk him. One of his elders had actually been hospitalized for depression, and was still on medication for it.

If it could happen to him maybe it was contagious! That's stupid, of course it's not contagious—I must be getting paranoid—next I'll be obsessing.

Noticing the book was still in his hand, he thought he might as well continue to read to keep his mind from dwelling on thoughts of depression. Strangely enough, Reverend Maxwell's story seemed to speak to him. Soon he was engrossed—absorbed in the story that seemed so much like his own. He read on, oblivious of the time.

As he walked unannounced through David's open office door, Carl asked, "David! What's going on? Linda said you wanted to see me?"

David looked up, almost guiltily, as if he'd been caught doing something wrong. He jumped up with a quick glance at his watch—he'd been reading for more than two hours. Incredible! Not so much that two hours had passed as that he'd gotten his rainbow, his sign. *Thank you, God! I've found the answer to my apathy. It's all right here in this book.* Although he now felt fine and wanted to shout it out loud, of course he didn't. *Why don't I just tell Carl I'm feeling great?.*

David looked at his friend, thinking once again how much he reminded him of the caring therapist Robin Williams played in the movie <u>Good Will Hunting</u>. *Come to think of it, Carl even looks like Robin Williams, beard and all.*

Carl seemed to ooze the fruits of the Spirit: gentle, kind, patient, good, loving—you name it. It was beyond David how Carl could always be such a good guy; he guessed it was from his training. He was always tolerant and accepting. David knew he could share anything with him. *Then why haven't you?*

"Hellllooo, David, are you going to answer me? Have you done some self-hypnosis? Maybe I left you in a hypnotic trance the last time we were together and never snapped you out of it." Laughing, Carl snapped his fingers close to David's face, as if to bring him out of a trance. "You are *really* engrossed."

"I can't wait to tell you why, Carl!" exclaimed David. "I was so anxious to see you this morning, thinking I actually needed a session with you . . ."

Carl interrupted quickly. "I can't . . ."

David cut him off. "I know, I know, you can't see a friend professionally. I was only kidding. Well, kind of; I wanted to talk to you about some weird feelings I've been having to see what you thought I should do. Actually, I was afraid you might even refer me to one of your therapist friends. But not now. Carl, I've been reading this old book, In His Steps, and. . ."

Carl interrupted again. "Yeah, I read it about twenty or so years ago—think I was a teenager when I read it. Didn't the pastor of that church, along with a bunch of his congregation, decide not to do anything for a year without first asking, 'What would Jesus do?' Pretty interesting concept. And, it would be neat if it would work, but of course, it won't. Too idealistic. Too simple."

"Why not, Carl? Really, I think it would. As I've been reading about it, my heart has been stirred and challenged. This is actually the answer I was looking for," David said excitedly, beginning to pace again as he continued talking.

"Here's what's been going on with me. I've been having some depressing thoughts over the past, oh, month or so—especially the last couple of weeks, thinking I'd lost my purpose in living—lost any real meaning in life. If you can believe it, I've even thought of quitting the pastorate! I was thinking I didn't seem to care about anything anymore. And, I wouldn't admit this to anyone but you, but, but—oh, boy, is this embarrassing—I've even lost a lot of interest in—well, you know . . ." he stammered, stopped, his face turning slightly red. He looked at Carl to see his reaction.

"Lost interest in . . ." Carl said gently, waiting patiently for David's answer.

"Don't do that therapist stuff on me, man. I'm your friend, not your client, remember? Lost interest in intimacy with Nikki—as if you didn't know. You just wanted me to admit it!" David glared at Carl, waiting for an answer. *Or a diagnosis.*

"Just asking, that's all, just asking," Carl pacified David. He said nothing else as he waited patiently for David to continue.

"The church seems to run by itself!" David exclaimed. "My sermons are getting drier, and it's getting harder and harder for me to come up with something good. God has seemed really far away. But right now, after reading most of this book, I'm getting an inkling of what it's like to really live for God—to love God. And, Carl, I'm excited about finding out more!"

Finally Carl spoke, choosing his words carefully. "You do seem excited, David, very excited. No doubt you've read some provocative things that have started your heart racing. Certainly it's good to be excited about godly things. I'd like to check out just a couple of other things that you've touched on, though, if that would be okay with you."

"Sure it's okay, Carl. Right now, though? I'm dying to tell you about this book and how learning to think about what Jesus would do in any given situation changed these peoples' lives. You won't believe the difference He made in their everyday lives! It's incredible!"

"Won't take but a minute, David," Carl interrupted in his kind, calm voice. "Take a deep breath, okay? First things first. How is your sleep? Are you sleeping okay?"

"Well, pretty much. Sometimes I wake up early in the morning and can't go back to sleep for quite a while, if at all. It's as if I can't turn my thoughts off. But not nearly as much as it is now! Let me tell you . . ."

"Slow down, David. I think your mind is racing right now. Just a couple of other things, buddy. How about your appetite? Have you gained or lost any weight recently?"

"I don't know, I haven't thought about it. I do remember Nikki saying it seems like I've been picking at my food and that I didn't seem hungry. So what?" David stuck his hands in his pocket, purposely slowing his excitement, wondering where Carl was headed with the conversation.

"Any problem with fatigue, tiredness, like it's hard to take the next step sometimes?"

Bingo. Those drizzle—or whatever they were called—feelings were back again, just like that. David sat down on the edge of his desk. "Well, before you came in I was thinking maybe I was headed for a mid-life crisis. Is that what you mean?"

"Some of the feelings might be the same," Carl told him. "Do you ever have difficulty concentrating, or do you ever feel confused?"

"Yeah, I did feel confused, and I have had a hard time concentrating. But listen, Carl," David said, beginning to pace again. "I don't want to go there. I'm telling you, it's like God lit a fire in my heart! I started having hope that he could truly change my life; that I could learn to walk in His steps, think like He thinks—the Bible says we have the mind of Christ!" He turned and looked at Carl, throwing out his arms with as much emphasis as if he were passionately entreating his whole congregation to believe him.

"Listen! Do you have any idea what it's like to think that I've been a pastor these last several years and it's just this hour beginning to dawn on me what it means to walk with God? Having hope is exciting! Carl, I have hope in what Christ can do in my life!"

Carl ignored David's outburst and continued with his assessment. David wasn't the only man on a mission. "You say these 'down' kind of feelings have been going on at least two weeks? Have you gotten so low you've thought of harming yourself? Maybe even had suicidal thoughts?"

In Whose Steps?

What was this guy, a mind reader? David didn't want to answer but finally did. "Yeah, at least two weeks. Probably longer. And the thought 'of harming' myself entered my mind, fleetingly. But, the down feelings are leaving, even now—listen to me! I'm telling you they're leaving. And I know you're probably asking me questions related to depression. I've been around you too long not to know what you're asking me. I'm not trying to evade your questions, Carl, but I believe I've found the solution. Aren't you listening to me?"

Carl's eyes saddened. Searching David's eyes with his own, he asked, "You know I want the best for you, don't you?" David stood very still, watching Carl, knowing Carl's concern for him, but feeling his hope draining out of his heart. Maybe the feelings hadn't been real after all; feelings are just that—feelings. Slowly, David nodded his head. "Yes, Carl, I know you want the best for me. I would never doubt that."

"Then I need you to consider something else. We both know that God can do miraculous things and that He is all-powerful. But we also know that He's given us some incredible insight about the human condition through the discipline of psychology. You know that we've discussed before that all truth is God's truth, whether it's from His Word or from the psychological world."

Looking at David to make sure he was listening to him and not headed off on his spiritual wild goose chase, Carl continued. "What I'm wondering right now, David, is whether you might have a pattern in your life of running from painful feelings. It sounds a little like you've hit a distressing time in your life. But, rather than walk through it and work through whatever feelings this pain and suffering is bringing up, you've grasped hold of the first thing you could find that helps you feel better." Carl held eye contact with him until David looked at the floor.

One Man's Search for Answers

David's knees actually buckled, and with a long, slow sigh, he seemed to sink into his chair. Confusion invaded his heart and it began to pound. It was almost as if some monster had suddenly jerked open the door to the hiding place he had found deep in the dark closet of his heart. Vaguely he wondered if he'd ever had to hide in a dark closet to escape his dad's rages. He was sweating now, and his tongue seemed stuck to the roof of his mouth. With great effort he whispered thickly, "I don't want to talk about this anymore."

David didn't want to look at Carl's face even though he knew he would see nothing there but compassion and patience. Carl respected David's pain, but after a few moments of silence, he said gently, "David, would you please just think and pray about whether what you have read in this book might have become your 'drug of choice' to escape your pain? I know that you are hurting right now and it hurts me to pursue it with you. But, David, you have finally gotten in touch with your real pain. Instead of dealing with it, however, you want to use this book's ideas in the same way an addict would to keep from facing the aching reality of life and the deep sufferings that brings. Often hitting midlife brings these things up for us men, you know," Carl said, stopping to take a breath, and continuing to look at David with kindness and understanding in his eyes.

David kept his eyes on the floor as he rubbed his forehead. Finally, with another deep sigh, he said, "I hate to admit that I was thinking I had this deep ache inside, and I had no idea where it was from. Carl, this is hard for me, but I trust you and I trust your relationship with God. You really think this is something I need to work through? You really think that this book is—well, what you're saying is that it's an escape from my real pain. Please tell me what you think my 'real pain' is."

"You're going to have to go deep and find out for yourself, David. And yes, I do have an idea that the book's ideas do present an addict's way out of pain, an escape, if you will, for you. Even religion can be an addiction."

David was listening intently to Carl but as he heard the words, "a way out," I Corinthians 10:13 flashed through his mind: ". . . but when you are tempted, he will also provide a way out so that you can stand up under it." He shook his head as if to clear it so that he could continue to hear Carl rather than his own thoughts. He was beginning to realize how much he must have used God's Word as a way out of his own real pain—and who knew what pain lurked in the depths of his heart better than his good friend Carl?—especially since he was a therapist. Carl must be "the way out" that God was providing for him. He sat up in his chair, straightened his shoulders, and with great effort, renewed eye contact with Carl. David gave him sort of a "give-it-to-me-I'm-a-man-and-I-can-take-it" look.

A look which Carl ignored because he didn't want David, once again, trying to escape his feelings of sadness and pain with either a tough-guy approach or a super-spiritual attitude. Instead, he continued to pursue David's dysfunctional patterns of handling discomfort and conflict. "When you've discovered why you are hurting because your own personal inner longings for meaning and significance have not been met, you can always come back and look at the book again. But right now, I think—as you yourself have acknowledged—you have the classic symptoms of depression. Actually, I would like to refer you to a good friend of mine. She's a great therapist, very gentle and godly."

David's head jerked up. "Wait a minute, now! See a woman? Are you kidding? I don't care what kind of therapist she is, that's not a good idea. Maybe I need to think right now, 'What would Jesus do?' and the answer is, I don't think he'd see a woman therapist. Actually, he wouldn't see a male therapist either—or any therapist—for that matter."

Again Carl ignored David's sad attempt at humor to sidetrack him and calmly stated the facts. "Dr. Wilkerson is excellent. After you think about it, I think you'll agree; you said you trust me to have your best interests at heart. I think I know what your issues are, and I think that she can help you get through them faster than anyone I know. Then, you can be well faster and better able to help others."

David felt the hair rising on the back of his neck. What unknown things had Carl been able to see in him that he couldn't see himself? He crossed his arms, leaned even further back in his chair, and asked, "Just what do you mean, you 'know what my issues are,' Carl?"

"Hey, buddy, don't get defensive. I'm just thinking that you've probably never learned to 'love yourself' the way God intended so that you can truly love your neighbor. Your self-esteem is based on performance rather than on being. I know your parents, remember? Your dad didn't teach you much other than how to perform to stay out of trouble, and your mom taught you to be a pushover for others." As David continued to stare at Carl, Carl patiently waited for David's response. David's eyes, once again, shifted back to the floor, engulfed with shame. His defensiveness diffused.

Without looking up, he finally quietly acknowledged, "Well, it's true, 'performance' *is* my middle name—maybe even first and last, too," he finished, thinking of his son, Neil's efforts to do the same. "I guess you've got me there. I'm beginning to see what you mean." But then with a hint of defiance, he looked up and challenged Carl: "I'm not accepting that I'm a pushover, doormat, or whatever you call it. You've got a long way to go to convince me on that one. But, if you think it's really necessary, well, okay," he said in resignation. "I still think it would be better to see a male therapist, though, Carl. Think about it." David got up from the chair, and stood, looking down at Carl. He needed to get some control back.

In Whose Steps?

Carl calmly looked up into David's face, matching his stare. Unperturbed, he replied to David, "This lady is totally ethical, David. Totally. You've read too many romance novels or seen too many movies. Don't be so suspicious." Carl chuckled. "I promise you, she won't bite. You won't have to get behind your desk or stand up to try and control her, either."

"You don't miss a lick, do you?" asked David, backing away and sitting back down. "I can't do anything, even stand up, without your reading something into it; your analyzing it!"

"Hey, that's what I do. I see you needing protection from the big, bad, lady therapist so, if you like, I'll protect you. I'll pave the way by calling her and telling her I'm referring a very special client to her, and she better darn well take good care of him."

"I'd better let Nikki know first, don't you think?" David was already looking for a reprieve, considering he hadn't had a serious conversation with Nikki in forever. Certainly not a conversation serious enough to discuss seeing a therapist!

"Why don't you wait until you've had your first session with Dr. Wilkerson? If you decide you guys can work together, then you can let Nikki know. Besides, Dr. Wilkerson will probably want to bring in Nikki and even Neil and Alyssa before she's finished. And a couple of other things . . ."

"*Other* things?" David exclaimed, his attention fully on Carl again. Not only was he not getting a reprieve, now he was being told there was even *more* to dig into.

"Yes," Carl continued unashamedly, "other things."

So I admit my problems and Carl's running with them. He's not going to turn lose till it thunders! Which thankfully it might do any moment, what with this weather. David half-smiled at the thought but then immediately was reminded that none of this was very funny, not in the least. But it didn't stop Carl.

"One, getting into a 12-step group for Adult Children of Alcoholics would probably be helpful. In the group you can learn to verbalize your feelings about growing up in a very dysfunctional, destructive family. As you know, we have 12-step groups meeting at our church. Praise God for that! You've been open and understanding about the importance of meeting the congregation's felt needs. But there are some 12-step groups just for pastors—actually there's one downtown. I think you'd probably be more comfortable in it rather than one at our church."

"You've got that right. Finally, something we can agree on. The last thing I want is having a bunch of church members see me letting it all hang out. So what else? I'm sure there's more."

Sure enough, Carl continued with more. "Okay, secondly, I think you need to see your family doctor—or, if you like, I can refer you to a psychiatrist I know—for a physical checkup. It might be that you can profit from an anti-depressant. You probably know that it requires an M.D. to prescribe medication, so that means neither Dr. Wilkerson nor I can prescribe them for you. The anti-depressant could possibly help you though the pain and hurt you're going to encounter. It can help you to function better since things usually get worse before they get better. Need to check it out with an M.D., though."

"I think I'll just go to my family doctor." David folded his arms across his chest. He was feeling super defensive. He would not see a psychiatrist; Carl would not talk him into doing that! *My gosh, he must really think I'm loony, if he thinks I need medication.* But he replied to Carl, "I like my family doctor a lot, and he's seen my whole family for a number of years. I trust him. I don't think I need medication, Carl. Look at Jack. He's on medication and it hasn't seemed to help him."

"Just think how bad he'd be if he weren't on medication," was Carl's matter-of-fact answer.

Darn, the guy has an answer for everything! "Well, I guess I never looked at it that way." Still, David had a question. "You don't believe there's anything wrong with taking medication, Carl? That it's not godly? I mean, shouldn't I be able to handle things on my own without medication? What if I asked what Jesus would do about medication?"

"I sure hope you don't buy into *that* guilt trip, buddy. Obviously, Jesus could handle anything without medication. He was the Son of God; you're not. You're only human, you know—even if you don't always act like it with all the expectations you have of yourself. Please. Just give yourself a break."

For the first time in their interaction, Carl appeared to be having some feelings; he even appeared agitated. In one motion, he pushed back his chair, got up, and walked quickly to stand in front of David. He placed both his hands on the armrests, leaned over, and looked David square in the eye.

"I cannot tell you how many Christians have been harmed either by not taking an anti-depressant in the first place or by believing it's God's will that they should get off their anti-depressant, even if they are suicidal! I have seen people die!" Carl was angry, but he backed out of David's face.

"Okay, okay, I hear you." Actually, David was glad to see that Carl could get angry, too—kind of nice to see that he was human enough to lose it. That was a side of Carl he didn't see often. Then it hit him—Carl's anger was probably righteous anger. All he wanted to do was protect David. He was afraid other people might make destructive comments about medication which would hurt him and keep him from taking it if he needed to do so.

"I'll talk to the doctor about it, Carl. You've convinced me at least that I should get checked out for medication. I'll take it if he says I need to—especially if you're going to get mad about it," David teased, then added seriously, "Obviously, you think it's a good idea and as I said, I trust your judgment. I'll talk to him."

"You know I wouldn't steer you wrong, but of course it's your decision. And yeah, I guess I do feel some anger when I think how many Christians have been hurt by the shame and guilt they heap on themselves—or allow some supposedly well-meaning Christians to heap on them. Taking an antidepressant for emotional health is no different than a diabetic's taking insulin, or someone with an infection taking an antibiotic—there's certainly no shame in that."

"I think I understand the concept; I just never thought about it the way you've explained it, No wonder you get ticked." *Yeah, it's righteous anger.* David finally conceded to Carl. *It's obvious that Carl is concerned about the spiritual and emotional health in the body of Christ—and mine! He loves me enough to tell me the truth.*

"So. The lady shrink. I *guess* one appointment won't hurt anything. Do you have her card?" David asked. Couldn't help it. He was still apprehensive.

"Yep, I think I do." Carl took out his wallet and began digging. "Yeah, here it is," he said as he found the card and handed it to David. "Shelby Wilkerson, Ph.D."

David held it as if it were a spider. "It's only a card, David. It won't bite," Carl laughed. "You hold it like it's a snake or something."

David put down the card on his desk and stared at it for a few moments. Suddenly he grabbed the phone. "Okay, I'll call right now while you're here, before I lose courage. I'm not sure I want to look at myself as closely as you think I should, though. Lots of children were beaten up by alcoholic fathers. This just really isn't necessary." David continued to stare at his phone.

He tried another excuse. "Maybe you need to hypnotize me, Carl, so I'll make the call." Carl didn't laugh at David's effort to make a joke. Obviously, it was serious business to him. He continued to hold David's eyes, willing him to pick up the phone and call for an appointment.

Finally, David picked up the receiver, slowly and methodically punching each number. Maybe no one would answer! He thought he heard a faint, "What would Jesus do?" and chastised himself for looking for a painless way out—a way to avoid the deep, searing pain caused by living through an abusive and traumatic childhood. His thoughts were invaded by a kind voice asking, "May I help you?"

"You may," David found himself saying. "I need to make an appointment with Dr. Wilkerson."

CHAPTER TWO

David's feet seemed to drag as he walked wearily into his beautiful home. As he stepped into the gleaming marbled entry, his steps sounded hollow. *Matches the hollowness echoing in my heart; how can I feel so low?* His life had changed incredibly after he and Nikki had been flown in to candidate at the church and one wonderful thing after another happened. They had made a short excursion into the neighborhood around the church to look for a house. He had thought it was a pipe dream that he would even be considered to candidate for the position of pastor for one of the largest churches in the denomination. To think that one of the elegant homes in this neighborhood could belong to him had seemed beyond his wildest dreams. When the position was offered to him, he thought his heart would burst with happiness and excitement. Then, thinking it could be no better, he and Nikki brought Neil and Alyssa to see the church, the city, their schools, and this house at 1013 Meadow Lane. All of them fell in love with the gorgeous home. What had happened to all of the excitement?

He felt a catch in his throat as he heard Nikki call, "Is that you, David?" Was it deceitful not to tell her what was going on with him? Was it better, like Carl said, first to get an idea of what he was dealing with before he shared it with Nikki? She walked into the hall as he was hanging up his jacket.

"David! My gosh, your jacket is wet," she scolded. Think about it! If you hang your jacket in the closet, don't you realize everything else will get wet, too!" Then she scowled at him as if he were a disobedient child.

"Okay, honey, sorry. I wasn't thinking," he said, thinking that he didn't think much about anything anymore. *Here's evidence of what Carl said. I do feel confused. Lethargic. Apathetic.* His mind was wandering again.

"David! Where are you? Hellllo. Earth to David. Welcome home, spaceman," Nikki said, waving her hand in front of his face.

Looking at Nikki's pained expression, David acknowledged to himself that at thirty-eight, in spite of her scowl, Nikki was a beautiful woman. Suddenly, he pictured her the way she'd looked when he first laid eyes on her. A gorgeous, slim brunette with a mouth that seemed to always be smiling and whose compassionate blue eyes—almost on a level with his own—said, "talk to me." And he had. She'd listened and responded like no other woman he had ever dated. They had talked and talked for hours on end. They shared a love for Christ and doing ministry. They also shared a love for hiking, bicycling, swimming, and sailing.

Most importantly, they shared a deep love for one another. When Nikki walked down the aisle to become his bride, he thought he couldn't be happier. Startled, he realized that was true, because it had been downhill since their honeymoon. He was carrying a heavy load in seminary and working part-time. Nikki worked full-time to help support them through seminary. As soon as he graduated, he'd gotten this wonderful church. But how devastatingly sad to think that he was, after all, in a marriage like the pathetic marriage his parents had. He'd said it would never happen to him—to Nikki and him. But that same big wall he'd always felt between his parents, whatever it had been, seemed to be there for them, too. They no longer hiked or biked, much less talked to each other, not even on a surface level. Actually, they seemed to find it hard even to be civil to one another.

Sometimes David thought Nikki had found a store that took trade-ins: perpetual smiles for perpetual frowns. Where had that gorgeous, welcoming smile gone? That sparkling light in her eyes? It seemed she was never happy anymore. At least not happy to see *him*. Could it have anything to do with him? He wasn't sure since they didn't talk about anything of any consequence anymore and certainly not about their relationship. Who had time? But wasn't that normal? What couple continued to spend hours talking after two kids, a dog, and eighteen years of marriage? He probably wanted too much from a relationship. *Sadly, this is probably as good as it gets.* Another sigh followed.

"Hey, Nikki, how was your day?" he attempted asking, hoping to make communication and deflect her anger. *Like trying to distract a firing squad. Useless.*

"No better than yours was, evidently," she snapped. "Why are you always so tired when you get home? You never have any time for me or the kids. You seem to have time for every lousy person in the whole church except us! And I'm sure you have somewhere to go tonight, right?" she demanded.

"I reminded you this morning I have a conference I have to go to tonight, remember? I did tell you it was on my agenda. It's not like I'm surprising you." David had determined on the way home he wouldn't react angrily to Nikki, but frustration quickly rose as he heard her impossible demands on his time.

"I'm the pastor, remember? I stay the pastor because I do my job, and part of my job means I've got to go to the conference tonight. Just lay off me, will you? Why couldn't you just say you're glad to see me?" Good intentions were gone. Angrily, he started down the hall.

"Glad to see you?" she retorted loudly. "Well, I would be except I know it's just long enough for you to throw your supper down—when you even eat at all—and drag back out the door. Why get excited over spending half an hour with you— especially when you're not really here at all? No words for me; I'm just your wife. Why would you possibly want to spend any time with me?"

"Forget it," David said flatly, his shoulders drooping as he walked back down the hall where Nikki stood, arms crossed and eyes flashing. "I'm sorry I said anything. Let's eat and then I'm going to grab a quick shower before I go."

Nikki marched into the kitchen ready to sling supper onto the table. David gulped, then said, "Nikki, do you suppose we might ever . . ."

Quickly she whirled around and interrupted him with a cool, "What? Might ever what?"

He hated her cold response. *What's the use. It's impossible, why the heck should I be vulnerable when she acts like this?* His cold reply matched hers: "Never mind."

"Fine. Supper's ready. It's just us. The kids have gone out with their friends. We can have a nice romantic dinner."

"Sarcasm will get you nowhere."

"Neither will anything else, will it?"

"I guess not."

David went into the kitchen, sat down at the table opposite Nikki. They sat in cold silence. He tried to eat even though the way he felt the food may as well have been sawdust. But, Nikki had made the effort to cook a good dinner, so after gulping it down, he mumbled, "Thanks for dinner," and walked upstairs to get ready for the conference. Nikki didn't reply; she continued to sit and stare—seemingly at nothing—as he ran up the stairs.

Oh, boy, going to be a long night, I better prepare for the tears. She's going to want to sit and rehash how hurt she was tonight at dinner and then how mad she'll be because I'm home so late. Can't wait for this one.

But after a quick shower and change of clothes, David felt better, at least physically. *If only I didn't have to put up with Nikki's moodiness I'd feel better, I think, but I guess grumbling about her will get me nowhere.* He ran down the stairs and out the door, calling as he went, "Going to be late; don't wait up." He hoped she'd get the hint and go to bed, but he didn't hear a response. Well, the last thing he wanted to do when he got home was to talk about their dead marriage and his numb heart.

Funny, though, I sure got a spark of passion reading that old book in my library. Huh. Why am I thinking about that now? Oh, well. At least Carl's helping me to understand what's going on with me. And, he was beginning to see the pattern Carl was talking about; how quickly he tried to escape his pain.

It was a short trip to the hotel where the conference was to be held. As David entered the large ballroom, he immediately glimpsed a woman with several men gathered around her. He wondered who she was. He stared at the title of the conference, for a moment not even remembering why he was there. Then it hit him: Carl had asked last week if he would attend a conference in his place since he had another engagement.

"It's already paid for and I think you'll enjoy it," Carl had encouraged him.

Yeah, right. Obviously Carl had ulterior motives. David couldn't help but think that as he glimpsed the title of the conference: "Healthy Christian Communication," the sign read. *Was this a set-up?* Then he started feeling guilty for his recent and very unhealthy communication with Nikki. *Well, it's not like she makes any attempt to have 'Healthy Christian communication' with me, either.* Rationalism and denial often worked for him.

Just then he was hit with the now-familiar stab of pain where he thought his heart was. *What is wrong with me? I know I'm in good physical shape, just had a physical. What the heck is wrong with me*? Well, he knew at least he wasn't running from the emotional pain any longer. He had an appointment with the doctor. He turned from the sign to enter the conference room where the meeting was to be held.

Walking over to the rest of the crowd, again he saw the striking-looking woman. Yes, she was professional-looking in her tailored black suit, and she was pretty—but not as pretty as Nikki. *A lot shorter than Nikki, and not nearly as slim as Nikki.* He couldn't help but notice her long, shiny brown hair and her twinkling brown eyes. In fact, he couldn't take his eyes off her. He just couldn't figure out what he found so attractive about her. Not really sexually attractive; he was sure of that. Nevertheless, he was undeniably drawn to her presence. Just then, she looked up at him and smiled. Her brown eyes were smiling too. He felt uncomfortable.

"Are you David?" She asked. He did a double take. How on earth could she know his name? He hoped his staring hadn't shown too much.

"Well, yes," he said, trying not to stammer. "David Cunningham. How did you know?"

"Carl asked me to keep an eye out for you. He described you well. I picked you out almost immediately," the lady said.

"You have the advantage, I'm afraid," he managed to say. Why was he feeling so strange? Almost exhilarated. "But, Carl didn't tell me to keep an eye out for you. So, I don't know who you are."

"I'm Shelby Wilkerson."

"No way. Isn't that strange? I mean, well, what I mean is . . . " he couldn't seem to get the words out.

"Yes, what do you mean? Cat got your tongue?" Shelby Wilkerson cocked her head to one side, smiled at him, waited for an answer.

"No. I mean yes. Actually, I don't know what I mean." He was stammering now. *What is wrong with my brain? My gosh, I meet and talk with new people all the time; I never meet a stranger.* He tried again. "Well, you see, I just came to this conference for Carl and I didn't realize it was—I guess it's a Christian Psychology conference?" David finally got it out.

"It is. You are very perceptive." She was still looking at him.

Is she making fun of me? Does she know that just today I made an appointment with her? I am so embarrassed. Well, this is ridiculous. Two can play at this game.

"That's what I'm known for, perceptiveness," he blurted out, "and I perceive you are an attractive lady." *Oh, dear Lord, did I actually say that???*

"Why, thank you, David—may I call you David? Should I call you Dr. Cunningham?"

"No, no, not at all. David is fine." She seemed to be totally unaware he had an appointment with her. *Okay, that's good; I can get to know her without her having on her therapy hat.*

"Would you like to sit down?" he asked.

With a contagious laugh, she said yes, she would, and they sat down on a sofa outside the conference room. She patted the seat next to her. David sat down beside her.

Before he knew it, two hours had passed. He shook his head, as if coming out of a trance. They had never even gone in to the seminar. *What just happened?* He realized he had talked with this wonderful woman and then remembered the long talks he and Nikki used to have—except talking with this woman *was* different. She seemed to listen so well, so non-judgmentally; she was totally understanding and accepting of everything he said. Nikki was always on his case and this lady—okay, Shelby!—didn't get ruffled about anything he said. He knew they'd just met, but still . . . Maybe this therapy thing wouldn't be so bad after all. When he finally told her he had made an appointment to see her as a therapist, she just laughed and said, "Bad boy. You should have told me sooner. I guess we'd better go, then."

He hated for the evening to end. And if he had dragged his steps when he got home earlier, David knew he felt even more hesitant about going in the house and talking with Nikki. As earlier, he hoped she'd be asleep. Quietly, he opened the garage door, parked the car, walked into the kitchen, and tiptoed up the stairs. *No lights on. Great. Maybe I'll make it with no conflict.* So, even more quietly, he started undressing but then he heard Nikki say sleepily, "David? How was the evening?"

"It was okay, Nikki. Go back to sleep. We'll talk about it in the morning." *Unbelievable. She doesn't sound angry at me. Boy, I hate her anger.* Although he seldom admitted it to himself, he hated angry people like his mom and dad had been. He wanted to run and hide when Nikki was angry, just like he had as a kid when his parents were yelling at each other. Now she turned over and actually went back to sleep.

Creeping into the covers beside Nikki, he immediately thought of Shelby. *Uh, oh. This isn't going to work,* he told himself. But he couldn't get her out of his mind! *Definitely, this is not okay. Guess I need to do some praying.*

Carefully, he pulled the covers back and got up. *Time to read and pray. I'm getting into trouble in my thought life. I know it's not okay to be thinking about another woman!* David began reading every passage he could remember about immorality and sexual purity. Then he prayed as he beseeched God to take away his thoughts about Shelby. Even though he was only dwelling on his time with her, he knew it was just a starting place. He knew of no other recourse . . . but it wasn't working.

God! Aren't you going to do anything? Aren't you going to take away these feelings? I'm confessing; I'm repenting. It's time for you to do your part. I know it isn't pleasing to you that I would think of Shelby. But God seemed silent. David took a deep breath. He acknowledged and assured himself again that his thoughts about Shelby and his attraction to her weren't sexual. Yes, they were there, to a certain extent, but they weren't the main attraction he had to her. What was it then? Whatever it was, it seemed to touch that deep part of him that he was just now acknowledging and that Carl had been talking about.

That was it! She seemed like Carl, a soul mate, a real friend. That was the attraction he had to her. She accepted him; he could tell that she genuinely liked him. Her quiet, gentle spirit was also attractive. *She's like a female Carl! Well, of course I like her too. Who wouldn't be drawn to people like Carl and Shelby? What is it about these therapists? It's like moths to a flame, but in a good way. I'll have to tell her tomorrow when I see her that I am attracted to her as a person and so I don't think I should be her client. God, you answered my prayer.*

Pleased by his decision, David thought that it should take care of everything. And it would probably even be better to call and cancel instead of going to the office to see her. *Well, I guess going one time won't hurt. It would be rude to call and cancel without explaining after the great talk we had tonight. Okay. One time only.* Resolving his dilemma made him feel better and he was able to go back to bed. However, he slept fitfully while he dreamed of Shelby.

CHAPTER THREE

Friday morning. Staff meeting with the elders. The litany of the day started in David's head. *Please not today.* He could hardly drag himself out of bed. Seemed he'd hardly gone to sleep and it was already time to get up. He suddenly remembered he was going to see a shrink today. *Me? See a shrink? Surely I'm dreaming.* Then he remembered he'd dreamed of the shrink—Shelby. *God help me,* he prayed again. Nikki was still asleep; the alarm hadn't fazed her. Guiltily, he looked at her as if she were able to read his mind. Thankfully, she couldn't. Cautiously, he crept from the bed, just as he had done the night before. Showering, then dressing quickly and quietly, he was able to leave home before Nikki got up. A sigh of relief escaped his lips as he backed out of the driveway on the way to church. Thankfully, Linda would have coffee prepared and he was more than ready for it.

"Morning, Dr. Cunningham," Linda said cheerfully. She was always glad to see him. Widowed, kids grown and gone, she had been at the church much longer than he had. He understood she had also kept the former pastor, Dr. Burns, in line. But he didn't mind. If anyone ever fit the description of "sweet, little, gray-headed lady," it was Linda. She was a dear.

"Coffee's almost ready. Shall I bring in a cup?" she asked him. Morning ritual.

"Yes, please." He always said yes. He started into his office.

"Doctor?"

"Yes, Linda?" he answered.

Looking closely at him, she asked, "If you don't mind my asking, are you feeling okay this morning?"

"Just tired. I didn't sleep well last night." Maybe she wasn't a therapist, but just like Carl, it was hard to let anything get past her. She picked up on his every mood. Quickly he changed the subject. "Is everyone going to be here this morning?"

"Yes, sir; everyone's confirmed. Shall I send them in as soon as they arrive?"

"Sure. Thanks." David was already exhausted. He noticed In His Steps was still open in his chair where he'd left it the day before. Picking it up once more, he opened to yesterday's turned-down page and started reading. For some reason he didn't understand, it captivated him. He knew now what Carl would say—and that he was probably right. The book created emotion in him—emotion generated by reading about people willing to sell their lives out for Jesus Christ. People who were willing to base every decision, as best they could, on what they believed Jesus would do in their circumstances. People who lived life "Coram Deo,"—before God. He started sighing again as he read. *Here I go again. Dying for a way out, looking for a quick escape. I'm back into denial. Thank God I have Carl to keep me focused.*

Hearing male voices, he slid the book into his top drawer. Carl entered first. "How're you doing this morning, David?"

"Okay, I guess. Did you set me up to meet Shel--Dr. Wilkerson last night?"

"No, honest, I didn't. She was there? What did you think of her?" Carl peppered him with questions.

"I think she's a nice lady, and I'm not going to see her as a client," David answered, turning his head so Carl couldn't see his eyes.

"Why? What happened? What's the deal? I thought we hashed this out already!"

"Tell you later; the others are coming in." Quieter, David asked Carl, "Do you think I should let the elders know I'm going to see a shrink?"

"No! Not all of them. Not yet, anyway. Eventually you'll need to so you can get your visits covered financially. We've educated them a lot, David, but they wouldn't all understand, especially Paul. He'll pull out his big, black Bible and disapprove for sure. And Dr. Burns would have a cow."

The seven elders straggled in, each with a steaming cup of coffee as Linda brought in her homemade coffee cake. It smelled cinnamony as she placed it, still warm, on the conference table.

"Help yourselves," she said, smiling at them as she turned and left the room.

"How on earth is that woman so cheerful this early in the morning?" Jack asked. "It never fails; she's always happy."

Carl glanced at David; David knew what his look said. Carl had often suggested that Linda was in denial. She was much too happy after all the tragedies she'd experienced in her life. David knew that Carl thought she should have some psychological testing. If she were hired at this point, she would have had to go through it for sure. Everyone hired on staff for the last several years had to take a battery of psych tests. That way, Carl said, they could be sure they had healthy people working at the church.

But David always remembered hearing someone's joke about the psychological profiles on each of the twelve apostles. Turned out Judas was "the only one with promise." He thought it was funny, but Carl had been offended. David had to admit that it was a blessing that Carl had been able to educate the staff on the importance of psychological testing in order to get quality people working at the church.

One Man's Search for Answers

Elder Paul Fletcher, along with retired pastor Dr. Burns, had problems with psychological testing for those who were hired. Dr. Burns told Carl that he thought psychological tests were poor substitutes for Biblical standards. In no uncertain terms, and more than once, Dr. Burns stated emphatically that selecting people for leadership should entail a thorough evaluative process, but one that would be done by the church, not some "new technology." It was his belief that those under consideration for a staff or elder position could be evaluated more comprehensively and honestly by their own families and peers than by a supposedly objective psychological test. Paul was the only elder who had an opinion about testing; the others weren't sure what to think. Soon elders would have to be tested, also. They might have an opinion then.

Beyond a doubt, however, Dr. Burns and Paul were thorns in Carl's side and vice versa. Carl thought they were stuck in the dark ages and unwilling to use modern, scientific tools that God had allowed men to discover and continually asked God for patience in his dealings with them.

That's a fight for another day. David realized he'd have to do some research on the issue himself before making up his own mind. He trusted Carl greatly but hated to rubber stamp the issue without checking into it. Unbidden, *What would Jesus think? What would Jesus do?* flashed through his mind because he just couldn't imagine Jesus giving a psychological test to his prospective disciples before choosing them. What also came to his mind were the directions Paul gave to Timothy: he was to choose elders and deacons by their godly character and reputations. *And that's a different kind of test for sure.* As he continued to ponder those profound differences, he suddenly noticed that everyone was seated around the table and had stopped talking.

In Whose Steps?

With a start, he realized they were waiting for him to begin the meeting. Some of the elders had to be at work later this morning; two of them were retired. All in all, they were actually a good bunch of men. Prayer always came first so David asked elder Jack Grimes to open the meeting. *Poor Jack.* Depressed to the point of suicide, he'd been in a psychiatric hospital and had been released only recently. *He tries way too hard to act spiritual, as if everything is okay.* Jack had offered to step down from leadership, but David had told him to wait. Carl had been seeing Jack for quite some time before he'd suggested hospitalization for Jack's nearly-continuous suicidal feelings—*what had Carl called it? Suicidal ideation; same thing he asked me yesterday!* Carl believed it would be best for Jack to go to the psychiatric hospital so he could be monitored while he was starting on some new medication.

Evidently the medication was working; Jack definitely seemed more cheerful. *Prozac, was it? Well, it sure seems to be helping.* Then David was struck with a sobering thought: *Were people going to be saying the same about him soon? "Pastor David finally got the medication he needed. Have you noticed how much more peaceful he seems?" And what would Nikki say?* David shuddered at the thoughts he was having.

At forty-two, Jack looked much older than David's forty-five partially because his hair was already totally gray. Although Jack was outgoing like David, he had become withdrawn during his depression. David wondered if Jack ever exercised to help his depression—*as well as his beginning weight problem. Something I should do more of, myself.* That thought took him to wondering if Shelby liked to ride bikes. *She doesn't look very athletic—knock it off! I'm not going there again!* But the feelings didn't go away. *These thoughts and feelings are just crazy! Am I going to be the next psych ward patient from around this table?* And then David realized he was just plain scared of what was happening to him.

He realized Jack had finished praying and they were looking at him again. *Okay, okay, I know I'm acting crazy. I'm just trying to get my thoughts in order. God help me.* Quickly, he glanced at the agenda, very thankful for its order. He started the meeting and happily, it went like clockwork. They were through within the hour. *Thank God it's over. No disagreements or conflicts. That is the last thing I need today.* David breathed a long sigh of relief.

It was a good decision not to let the guys know how badly I've been feeling. I'm the Senior Pastor and it wouldn't be right to let them down. They look up to me and I need to be strong for them. And like Carl said, especially I shouldn't tell Paul and Dr. Burns. No telling what they would say to me. Even though he was relieved the meeting was over, David's thoughts were racing.

"Pastor."

David looked up and saw Paul Fletcher and guiltily wondered if Paul could read his mind. He tried to stifle his sigh. *Great. Just when I thought it was safe . . . and where's Carl when I need him?* David glanced around the room to see if perhaps Carl was still around, thinking he would need moral support for anything Paul brought up to him.

"Yes, Paul? What is it? Did you need something else?"

"Well, Pastor, I've been noticing that you seem to be listless-like, you know, just kind of not yourself lately." He looked searchingly at David. "Pastor, are you okay?"

You'd be the last person I'd let know if I weren't okay, that's for sure. He answered quickly, "No, Paul, I'm just fine. Thanks for asking."

"I'd like to tell you what helped me when I was feeling down-in-the-dumps, if you're willing," Paul said hesitantly.

"I said I'm fine, Paul, so perhaps you could tell me another time." David was frustrated that Paul wouldn't leave.

In Whose Steps?

"You know, Pastor, I feel funny telling you this," Paul continued as if David had said yes. "You're the Bible teacher and all, but the Bible does have the answers to life's problems. We can know Scriptures in our heads but not know how to apply it to our lives. So then we think it doesn't work. You know what I mean?"

David stared at him for a moment. Paul was sixty-eight and in extremely good health. Actually, he was still a handsome man; David hoped he'd look that well when he was that old. Strong, too, both physically and spiritually. At times, he'd been like a father to David. Then Carl had warned him about the danger of getting too close to someone so simple; someone who believed the answers to life's problems were all in God's Word and who refused to join the modern scientific world with its medication and searching questions about life.

Continuing to look at Paul's kind but simple face, David had a sudden desire to grab him by the shoulders and say, "Tell me, Paul, because I think you'd know: What would Jesus say about my situation?"

But David knew he was probably looking for easy answers—an escape, like Carl said. If he did ask Paul that question, David knew from Carl that Paul would—what had he called it before?—"Bible-bash" him. "Bible-bashing is like hitting someone with Scripture when they're down, David," Carl had patiently explained. *That's probably what Paul is going to do to me right now, and that's the last thing I want for me or for my flock, either, for that matter. But I know Paul means well, even if he is uneducated.*

"I do know what you mean, Paul, and I'm sure you're right. Thank you again for your concern. I'll see you next week, okay?"

"Alright, Pastor, sorry if I was out of line. It's hard not to remind folks of what really works when you see them suffering."

For all Paul's innocuous ways, David wasn't fooled. He knew the minute he admitted he did not know what to do, Paul would say the Bible had the answer, and he'd start shoving it in his face. Okay, not shoving, exactly; he'd just say it strongly, and it would feel like shoving. David didn't doubt Paul's motives. Obviously, Paul was just too old and too darn stubborn to consider new discoveries. He thought searching the Scriptures was enough truth for him.

David didn't reply, hoping Paul would finally leave. Sensing a reply wasn't coming, Paul finally left. David quickly picked up his briefcase and headed out of his office where he saw Linda looking at him.

She generally made his appointments, but he'd been too embarrassed to tell her he had an appointment with Shelby, much less ask her to make one. So, certainly she was surprised to see him leaving already. Curiously, she asked him where he was going, since she always kept his schedule and knew exactly where he was almost all the time. Even Nikki would call Linda to find out where David was.

"Linda, I have a doctor's appointment," he said as he walked through the entry. "Nikki made it for me yesterday," he lied.

"Sure thing, Pastor," she replied, but looked at him with a question in her eyes. *Why did I do that? Why did I think I had to lie to her? What is wrong with me to lie without even thinking about it? What am I scared of? Or maybe I'm just paranoid—must be, if I'm lying.* He couldn't answer his questions to himself but he still didn't go back and ask Linda's forgiveness for lying. *What she doesn't know won't hurt her, and besides, it's really none of her business. Maybe I'll ask her forgiveness later.* The justification seemed to work so he got into his Volvo, slammed the door, and headed to the shrink's office.

In Whose Steps?

As David drove up to the suite of offices where Dr. Wilkerson practiced, he was impressed with the landscaping. He was even more impressed when he found her office to be calm and welcoming. He felt very at home as he looked around, forgetting this was to be his one and only visit. As he sat down, the receptionist asked his name and told him it would be only a few minutes before the doctor would see him.

"Thanks, no problem," he said. Usually he hated to wait, but he couldn't resist telling the receptionist, "I don't mind sitting for a few minutes in this restful place." Subtle and cool blue, green, and violet striped wallpaper set the tone for the healthy, shiny green plants that were everywhere. It truly felt like a haven, a place of escape. *Wonder if the people who come in here look as healthy as the plants. Of course it's possible they do. I look pretty healthy on the outside, myself. It's just my brain's that's messed up. Probably most people who have messed up brains don't look or act like raving maniacs or serial killers.* He was brought out of his reverie as he heard his name called.

"Dr. Cunningham, Dr. Wilkerson will see you now," the young receptionist said. "Please follow me." He couldn't resist looking into other rooms that seemed to be empty. Then he turned into one of the most relaxing rooms he'd ever seem. It seemed to envelop him in peace as he walked in and saw Dr. Wilkerson behind her desk. As he took in the ethereal pale blue, green, and white wallpaper, he thought it matched the waiting room until he noticed sunny little yellow flowers in the forefront. Just then he saw Dr. Wilkerson and held out her hand. *She looks like a sunny flower herself.*

"David! It's good to see you again," she said. "Please have a seat wherever you think you'll be comfortable." She motioned to her overstuffed white sofa or a couple of plaid pastel Queen Anne chairs around a glass-topped table. White ceramic lights gave off a dim, warm light. Plants abounded.

It would be so relaxing to sink into one of those sofas while someone listens to every word I say with no condemnation whatsoever. Hey, get a grip, David! You have to tell her you just came to say you wouldn't see her." Shelby's sunny, welcoming smile followed him as he sat down in one of the Queen Anne chairs and she took the other.

"Well, David, where do we start? What brings you in to see me?" She was preparing for work as she crossed her legs, placed a tablet on her lap and poised her pen to write. "Oh!" she said. "Would you be comfortable if I begin with prayer?"

"Yes. Yes, I would," David said, thinking he would wait a few minutes before he told her he wasn't returning. After all, he didn't want to hurt her feelings. Obviously, if she wanted to start with prayer, she wanted their sessions to be spiritual. And, it looked as if she was going to take notes—well, that made it seem more clinical. Maybe it would be okay after all.

Bowing her head, Shelby asked God's blessings on their time together. As soon as she said, "amen," she began, "Okay, now we're blessed, so let's get started. Again, what brings you to see me?"

David was hesitant. Now was the time to say, "Forget it." but it would be so good to talk about what had been going on with him. Shelby was obviously very competent and capable to assess what that might be. *What should I do?* David wasn't sure what to say so he sighed.

"Big sigh, David. Have you been doing a lot of that lately? Do you know what the sighs are about?" she asked gently.

Okay, I'm taking the plunge and if there is any continuing problem with attraction, I'll ask her or Carl for a referral to someone else. David assured himself all would be well.

In Whose Steps?

Noticing his obvious hesitation, Shelby said, "I don't think you'll find it's as bad as you think, David. Getting started is always the hardest part. I know Carl referred you; he must have said something to you about why he thought you needed to see me. Why don't you start with that? You certainly didn't seem to have a problem talking last evening," Shelby grinned, but spoke encouragingly.

David wanted to talk about the great evening he'd had last night. However, he responded to her question. "It does sound simple when you put it like that. I told Carl I'd been feeling down for a while, worse in the last few weeks. I've recently had a physical and so I don't believe it has anything to do with my physical health. Just seems as if I don't care about anything anymore; nothing makes much sense. I just don't care about the things I always have." The words seemed to rush from his mouth.

"'Things,' David, or people? Or both?"

He wanted to tell her that it was none of her business, but of course it was. He also wanted to run. But it was hard to walk away from her listening, accepting eyes focused totally on him. So he told her: "Yes, people, too."

But Shelby made no judgmental comments and so he continued to lay the whole mess out on the table. He surprised himself as he talked about how angry he'd been as a kid at his dad when he came home drunk to yell and beat up his mom, him, and his little brother, and sister. Over the years, he'd tried to get the picture out of his mind of his dad's face contorted in rage as he crashed through the front door, grabbed the hammer and smashed everything in his way. After he'd finished destroying the house, he'd come after them. Usually they cowered in the corner, crying and screaming.

David hadn't realized he was clenching his fists as he talked to Shelby about the trauma of his childhood years. When any of them had failed Dad, well, it was bad news because it meant another beating. Even though Dad was messy and careless himself, he had high expectations of everyone else in the family.

As an adult, David had never allowed himself to feel the anger that evidently still burned in his heart toward his dad. Although he had asked God to forgive him for the bitterness in his heart toward his dad, he knew he'd never forget the pictures in his mind. Now, with Shelby's help, maybe he could do something about his feelings. David also told her he'd given Carl his word he would also see his family physician about possible medication for depression, if she thought it was necessary. He feared, yet knew, she would confirm the diagnosis of depression.

"I think you know you're depressed, David, and yes, I do believe it would be good for you to get assessed for medication. It would help you keep functioning until we can get some of these problems resolved. I think it will help your anger level immensely. A chemical imbalance is nothing to be ashamed of. It's like a diabetic ."

"I know, I know. Carl told me. It's like a diabetic taking insulin. I'll go for an assessment. And I truly can't thank you enough for the time today. I feel better already, just talking about these things. But I don't think I have an anger problem. Even my kids would say that I'm not an angry person." *At least I don't think they would say I'm an angry person.*

"It's pretty normal to feel better at first," Shelby said, ignoring his comment about not being angry. "Most people find therapy isn't as threatening and scary as they thought it would be and often end up enjoying it! Maybe you'll be one of the ones who enjoy it. It does sound as if you have some bitterness toward your dad, though, and possibly some anger at mom, too, for not leaving the situation and protecting you and your siblings. I might warn you, though, after the initial 'feel better,' sometimes people feel scared or have bad dreams because they realize they've verbalized their feelings for the first time."

She continued. "I think, David, that as you become aware of how the abuse has harmed you, it will be hard. It will hurt. But the outcome will be worth it because you'll no longer run from your feelings. You'll no longer be in denial—such as denying you are angry," she slipped in. "Actually, as you get older, the harder it becomes to hold all those bad feelings in, and your unaddressed feelings finally catch up with you."

"So the prognosis is good, then?" David queried.

Shelby laughed her contagious laugh. He loved it. "Oh, yes; I'd say it's very good," she said. "Just be prepared for things to get worse before they get better. See you next week at this same time? Or would you like to do two sessions a week so you'll be able to work more quickly through your issues?"

David thought about it, but not for long. "Let's do two and get it over with. Do you want to see Nikki and the kids, too?"

"Definitely, but later on in your therapy. We'll look at your family-of-origin issues first. So talk to my receptionist and she'll give you another time. See you again soon, David."

And David was out the door. *That wasn't so bad, now, was it? It's really no big deal. People do therapy all the time. Like Shelby said, I think I may even like it.* But he wondered how much of doing "therapy" actually had to do with spending time with Shelby. But, as long as they were praying about the therapy, surely only good could come from it.

CHAPTER FOUR

When David got in his car, he noticed he had a call on his cell. He'd left it in the car because he hadn't wanted it ringing in Shelby's office. It was the church number. He didn't want to take time to listen to the message first so he dialed his office. "It's me, Linda. Did you call me?"

"Yes, Pastor, I did. Carl is very anxious to talk with you as soon as possible. He's in his office now. Is it a good time for you?" she asked David.

"Sure, put him on," he replied, navigating his way out of Shelby's tree-lined parking lot and turning toward the church.

"David!" Carl exclaimed into his ear.

"Yeah, what's up? Sounds like there's a fire."

"You might say that there is. Can you meet with me as soon as you get back? I've got some bad news. It's about Jack."

Instantly concerned, David asked, "What? Is he hurt? Is he okay?"

"Yes and no. I mean, physically he's okay. But you know I've been seeing his daughter Ann in therapy for a couple of years—you remember she gave me permission to talk with you about her therapy? Anyway, we've been trying to get to the bottom of her depression, anorexia, and suicide attempts. I finally found out today what the problem is. Under hypnosis, she finally confessed."

"Confessed what?" David asked quickly, then continued on before Carl could answer. "You've persuaded me about a lot of psychology's techniques and helps, but I'm still not sure about hypnosis. Guess that's a discussion for another day, though—what's the problem? Is it bad?"

"I'll tell you when you get here." Carl evaded his question.

"I'm pulling into the parking lot right now." He hadn't realized the church was so close to Shelby's office.

"Okay, I'll meet you outside." Carl quickly put down his office phone and headed outside to meet David, who was already at the door. Carl invited him into his office, slightly smaller than David's but just as plush. David sank into a chair.

"No preliminaries. Let's have it. I don't want to guess."

"Just as a reminder, David, I have signed permission from Ann to speak with you about this. We're not sure what we're going to do next and we thought it would be good to have some input from you."

"Carl! Just tell me, please."

"Ann is a victim of years of verbal and sexual abuse, David."

"I'm really sorry to hear that. My heart goes out to her. How old is she, nineteen? That's a really lousy thing to happen to a girl. Is it recent?"

"It has gone on for years but she just now remembered it. She's been having bad dreams for months and then flashbacks started after we began discussing her dreams. Today, though, she saw the face of her abuser. And, she remembered she'd been abused from the time she was two until she was thirteen. But that's not the worst part. David, it was Jack."

"What do you mean, 'It was Jack'? That's preposterous. He may have some problems, but he'd never abuse his daughter, sexually or otherwise. That can't be true. Just how reliable is hypnosis, anyway? I've seen some TV programs debunking stuff like this. I don't think I believe it."

"That is the absolute worst thing you can do, David. Not believe her. Slow down. Think about it. Why on earth would Ann—would anyone!—make up something so horrible? Why would she want to go through the pain of looking at the awfulness of these years? Having to experience the trauma all over again? And it may be—we're not sure—the memories aren't clear on this yet—but her mom may have been involved also. At the very least, she didn't protect Ann from her dad. Believe me, it's true. And I think there are a lot of other memories that will surface now that she has clearly recognized and accepted that her abuser is her father."

David's face was ashen. "I don't think I can accept this."

"I thought that might happen, David. I asked you to come into my office because I have a videotape of the session with Ann. I have her permission to show it to you. Are you willing to watch it?"

"Not really. Do I have a choice? I mean, yeah, I'll watch it. I know I need to."

Carl picked up the remote. He had a TV in his office and he had it ready to go. Dimming the lights in his office, he turned on the TV.

David looked closely at the screen. That was Ann? It was hard to recognize her; Carl, of course, looked the same. They were having a session at the psychiatric hospital where Ann had been for the last several months. Her dad had been at the same hospital but not on the same unit, for the last month.

In Whose Steps?

Ann was curled into a fetal position and sitting in the corner of the room. David was shocked because the last time he had seen Ann she had looked nothing like this. She'd always been thin, but now she looked as if she were starving in a concentration camp. When she raised her head, dark circles were under her eyes. Her short blonde hair, normally shiny and well-kept, was sticking in all directions as she continually ran her fingers through it.

"I don't believe it," she was wailing.

"Don't believe what? Ann?" Carl asked softly.

"The face I see when I shut my eyes. It's my dad. And there are others in the background that I can't see."

"You are safe, Ann, here with me. You're safe. It's okay to look and see who it is."

"I CAN'T. I CAN'T. I'm too scared to see," she continued to wait. She started gagging.

"What's going on now, Ann? What is it?"

"They're trying to put a snake in my mouth? Stop! Stop!" she cried piteously. Then, in terror, "There are snakes everywhere. Help me, someone, please help me!" she screamed.

"You're safe, Ann. No one can ever put snakes in your mouth again. Try and see who is doing that to you."

Ann's eyes stayed closed the whole time. She squinted even more as she continued to gag. "I can't see well enough. The candles aren't bright enough." She slid further into the corner. "Go away, please go away," she pleaded. "Please don't burn me again with that stick. I'll be good. I'll let you put the snake in my mouth and I won't tell."

"STOP THE TAPE," David demanded. "I've seen enough." He felt sick to his stomach. Carl clicked off the TV.

"How can you do this, Carl? It hurts me to see Ann in such pain," he said.

"Certainly it isn't easy, especially when you care so much for your client. And I care for her dad, too. But he has to look at the truth. As you know, 'the truth will set you free,' and that's what will set Ann and Jack both free."

"So what do you suggest I do about Jack?"

"That's why we wanted you in on this, David. When we get ready to confront him, we think he will deny everything so I'd like for you to be there when we do confront him. Certainly he will need to step down from leadership. Ann is considering suing him. I'd like you to help Ann make a biblical decision about that. Certainly we do want him to admit it. All the symptoms of abuse are blatant and she started showing them soon after we started therapy. Almost immediately, I was sure she had been abused. Classic case. Eating disorders are nearly a foolproof symptom of childhood incest, you know. We just never knew which member of the family did it to her."

Carl continued, "I haven't told Ann, yet, but I believe it was an alter that told me about the abuse because Ann can't face the trauma of what happened. I don't want to scare her with a 'Dissociative Identity Disorder' diagnosis. You probably know it as 'MPD' or 'Multiple Personality Disorder.' And if there are alters, we may find she's even experienced Satanic Ritual Abuse."

"What do you mean, 'alter'?" David demanded. "Are you telling me you think she has more than one personality? That she may have been in a satanic cult like the ones you were telling me about after you went to that SRA Conference last year?"

"Looks that way. We'll know more in further weeks. We are definitely making some progress in therapy! It's exciting that we are finally getting to the bottom of her issues. I can't tell you how helpful that conference was to me. It has helped me understand Ann's behavior much better, and now I am more aware what to look for. David, she's been cutting and burning herself for over a year—she probably has other self-destructive behaviors I'm not even aware of yet. I don't think she's even aware of some of them, either. That's why I believe she has alters doing some of the self-abuse. I've been trying for months to recognize what's going on in her. Only today did she find a safe place." At that point, Carl choked up. "Isn't that sad she had nowhere safe to go? But today she was able to visualize herself in Jesus' healing presence and He gave her the courage to go on looking at what she was seeing."

"You mean you hypnotized her."

"It's more like visualization or guided imagery. At first, patients like Ann are aghast at what they find out and refuse to believe it. As they stay with the process, however, the memories, and sometimes flashbacks, become more real. I think that while she's in the hospital, I'm going to talk with her psychiatrist about also doing a sodium amytal interview with her."

"And what is that?" David asked.

Carl was happy to explain the process to David. "It's like a truth serum. An anesthesiologist puts her under and we do an interview while she's under the drug's influence. I've done several of these interviews and they are sometimes helpful. I knew something had to break soon because her antidepressant is no longer helping her to continue to function. Even the Xanax, which is an anti-anxiety drug, is not keeping her from being anxious and wanting to self-destruct."

"Let me get this straight. I thought I was buying into this when I saw the pain Ann was in, but it's getting a little farfetched. You are saying that Ann is taking several drugs and that she's possibly an MPD who was sexually abused by her father—we're talking Jack here!—and maybe her mother, too. Please. Ann's mother? Carl, there isn't a sweeter lady than Anita! No way. This strains the imagination. Please tell me this can't be true. Can you imagine what it will to do to our church?"

Carl's eyes narrowed. "Let ME get something straight, okay? Are you interested in hiding the secret, David? I'm surprised at you, really I am. You saw the agony Ann was in; I thought you'd want to help her. And are you slamming prescription drugs? You know, we had this conversation yesterday and I explained to you about the psychotropic drugs. I hope you're not going to read a few Scriptures to Ann and tell her she needs to ask, 'What would Jesus do if He were in my place,' are you?" he asked sarcastically.

"I didn't say I wanted to hide it or ignore it or look at it too simply. I'm just not sure I believe it, Carl. And what about what Jack believes? We have to ask him about this first—confront him with the evidence. The Bible says there should be witnesses. And there is evidence, isn't there?"

"Ann said it; you saw it with your own eyes and heard her with your own ears. Why or how could anyone make something like this up? Just believe, her, David. And you can be sure that Jack will deny what's happened. The perpetrators almost always do. And people involved in SRA cults are able to do away with the evidence, anyway. Poor Jack. Perhaps he was dissociated himself when he was abusing her."

"I give up. You know much more about this than I do. You've made my day impossible. What am I going to do with this, Carl?"

"Quit worrying about yourself, I should think, and care about Ann."

"Wasn't it just yesterday you were telling me I needed to take care of myself and go to a therapist? Now I've gone— just got back—and you're telling me to think of someone else."

"Priorities, David. By the way, I'm sure it went well with Shelby?" Carl didn't wait for an answer. "She can help you understand what's happened with Ann, by the way. I hate to tell you how much it happens. In a church this size, I'm surprised we haven't heard about it before. Perhaps Ann's bravery in being open about her abuse will encourage others to be truthful about any abuse they may have experienced. Anyway, while she's safe in the hospital, I'd like to bring in her parents for family therapy. That way, if it's too much for her, we can put her on suicide watch if we need to do so. It's going to be difficult for her to get through this. She's going to be very sensitive to the opinions of others."

"I'm glad Ann is safe; truly, I am. It frightens me to no end to think she would attempt suicide. But are you actually saying we may have a whole church full of abusers?" David exclaimed angrily. He'd had almost all the new information he could handle at one time.

"Yes, I think it is entirely possible. David, what's wrong with you? I'm beginning to think you want to protect the abusers for the sake of your reputation."

"That's ridiculous. I can't believe you'd say that. I'm just shocked, that's all, and I was already feeling lousy before this all started." David rubbed his head. *What would Jesus think about this? What would Jesus do now? I haven't the faintest clue. Oh, me, in spite of Ann's pain, this might cause a split in the church. How will the members react? Can I keep this quiet, and just handle it among the elders? How will Paul deal with Jack when he finds this out? Will he literally hit him over the head with his huge Bible? What else can go wrong now?* He was afraid to even think about it.

Carl interruped. "You're still going, aren't you? You'll get lots of information about addictions, abuse, and co-dependency and how they relate to your own issues."

"Yeah, okay, I said I'd go when I get time." He sighed deeply. He just thought he was depressed before. "Listen, Carl, thanks for telling me, really. I know you needed and wanted some support from me. Let me think about this and pray about it before I give you any feedback, though, okay?"

"Sure. Just don't take too long because we're planning on a family meeting as soon as we can get it scheduled. Ann wants to bring in her sister Carol and her brother Steve. She thinks they may have been abused also and she wants to ask them about their experiences growing up."

"Any more good news?" David asked, thinking he didn't care if he was sarcastic. Nikki was always telling him he was anyway. *At this point, I may as well be sarcastic as anything else. I can't imagine that even the fruit of the Spirit can get everyone through this mess.*

"That's it for now. We'll talk more later today or tomorrow." Carl stood up and opened his door for David. David walked out feeling like a whipped puppy. It occurred to him he could call Shelby and ask her for some input. Since this whole thing was confidential, he decided it would be better to talk to Shelby than to Nikki.

He pulled out Shelby's card as he walked into his office and shut the door behind him. Dialing quickly, before he could change his mind, he asked the receptionist if it would be possible to speak with Dr. Wilkerson.

"Just a moment and I'll see if she's available, Sir."

I'm sure she's probably in the middle of a session. But she came on the line: "Dr. Wilkerson here. May I help you?"

He noticed his heart skipped a beat. And it wasn't with any deep pain, either. It was excitement. "Shelby. It's David Cunningham."

"Is something wrong? I wasn't expecting to hear from you for a few days. Besides, you just left."

"Carl just gave me the news that one of our elders has been in the process of molesting his daughter for several years. I don't know what to do about it."

"Oh, that is so sad. We're finding out it happens more frequently than you could imagine. And the church isn't immune, I'm sorry to say. What does Carl say?"

"He said he wants to meet with the young lady and her family and then for her to confront her dad. And maybe even the mom—Carl thinks her mom may have been in collusion with her dad. He isn't sure yet how extensive the abuse is."

"Sounds as though that's the healthy way to do it. Sometimes young women are told they shouldn't forgive their dads or their parents because the crime is too heinous. As a Christian, however, I think it's best to confront the issue and hopefully—prayerfully—her dad will ask his daughter's forgiveness."

"It seems way too traumatic for everyone concerned," David said. "Isn't there a better way?"

"Don't you trust Carl? And just think—here's a good opportunity for you to look at your own issues that are beginning to show themselves. As we touched on this morning, your family had a secret that you helped to keep. It was too scary and uncomfortable for you as a little boy to do anything about it. So I think you're probably still a little scared when it comes to difficult conflict and want to avoid it at all costs. You want to keep the secret rather than face the anger, fear, anxiety—whatever—that it generates," Shelby postulated.

"I guess you're right. That's beginning to make sense to me now. Could I ask you one other question?" Without waiting for permission, David quickly blurted, "What do you think Jesus would do in this situation?"

"That's a funny question. I think he'd do exactly what we are doing. He loved people and he wanted them to be truthful. And, that's what we are encouraging."

David thought about it a minute. "Yes, I guess you're right. Of course we're doing what He would do. Thanks for humoring me."

"Anything else?" she said. He could hear the smile in her voice.

"No. Thank you for being there, though. I greatly appreciate your willingness to do that for me."

"My pleasure, David. Please call again if you need me. I'm not always by a phone but my service can reach me. Actually, why don't I give you my home and cell numbers--just in case you have another emergency?"

David's heart lurched. *Should I take it? Of course I shouldn't have her that available to me.* That wasn't what he said, however.

"Right. That would be extremely helpful. Thanks," he mumbled as he took down her numbers. Now he had almost instant access to her at any time. He knew that probably wasn't a good idea. He didn't ask himself what he thought Jesus would do about taking Shelby's phone number. He gently put the receiver down, wondering what he was feeling.

CHAPTER FIVE

"Dad's home!" Neil yelled up the stairs to Alyssa. "You wanted to ask him about the party. He's finally home but you better make it fast before he leaves again."

Never a peaceful moment; even Neil is slamming me. He walked wearily into the house, almost bumping into Alyssa who was bounding down the stairs.

"Dad, Dad, there's a slumber party tonight with the church group. Please, please can I go? Whitney will be there." Whitney was Alyssa's best friend.

"Who's chaperoning it?"

"Tim set it up, Dad. It's at his and Cindy's house. Okay? I mean, don't you trust your own youth director? I'll be home first thing in the morning."

"Have you asked your mother?"

"Yes. She said it's okay with her if it's okay with you."

"Alyssa, I thought we agreed to no last-minute events."

"Daaad! You're such a dork sometimes. We didn't plan it until the last minute, and Tim and Cindy were nice enough to let us have it at their house. Just say yes, okay?"

"Okay, okay. How about a hug for your dad?" David wanted a hug from Alyssa. He didn't want to ask Nikki for one.

"Sure, Dad," she yelled in his ear as she hugged him. "Thanks for letting me go."

"I had a choice?" David said, looking fondly at Alyssa who was looking frantically for her cell phone. She was a little weird looking now, but he remembered Carl said she would grow out of it—that parents needed to let their teens go through these strange stages. If they didn't, they would never be empowered to make their own decisions because they wouldn't have their own identity. He said that if you could just hang on through the teen years, kids would begin to return to normal. *It's just great to have your own psychologist on staff!* He knew that without Carl's input, he would be confronting Alyssa with many of her obnoxious behaviors (he hesitated to use the word "sinful," even to himself) with the fact that they were unacceptable. But, thanks to Carl, he knew not to use words that would harm her self-esteem. Neil spoke into his reverie.

"Dad."

Now what does Neil want? Don't I ever get a chance to rest? And no telling what Nikki's going to be harping about. Oh, well. There's no way possible it could be as bad as everything else that has happened today. "Yes, Neil?" he answered.

"May I borrow the car tonight? I asked you earlier in the week and you said you'd think about it. So I asked Christina out thinking you'd say yes."

"You should have waited." David was angry at Neil's presumption.

Both kids knew David's angry looks, but Neil was angry, too. "You said okay to Alyssa after you'd told her no. And you didn't even tell me no, just wait. Besides, I asked you three times and you didn't give me a final answer. Mom said if you wouldn't let me use your car that I could use hers. But I'd rather use yours."

David was really angry now. How dare Nikki tell Neil he could use her car without his permission! He didn't want to argue with both Neil and Nikki. *Argue? Or am I avoiding conflict?* Shelby's words whirled through his head.

In Whose Steps?

"Fine. Take it. Have fun. Don't do anything I wouldn't do."

"Thanks a lot, Dad," Neil returned sarcastically, sounding just like David. But he left the room quickly before he got into trouble for saying anything else.

"Hey, Neil--" David started, but Neil kept walking, acting as if he hadn't heard. David wasn't sure what he wanted to say to him; he just didn't want the conversation ending like this. His people-pleasing, he guessed.

Now to face the rest of the firing squad. Nikki had yet to appear; he suspected that she must be in the kitchen. But when he called, no Nikki appeared. "Kids!" he yelled upstairs. "Have you seen your mom?"

Alyssa yelled back down. "Yeah, Dad; she said to tell you she's shopping and she'll be late. She said your supper's in the oven."

Fuming, David went to the kitchen and looked around. Seeing nothing, he opened the oven. There was a pot there and he grabbed a hot pad and pulled it out. *Dried-out pot roast. To eat by myself.* Suddenly, he wondered what Shelby was doing for dinner. He'd left his cell in the car so he started toward the phone, pulling out her card as he went. As he picked up the phone, Alyssa said angrily, "Dad, I'm on the phone, if you don't mind!" He'd thought she was on her cell phone and hearing his daughter's voice quickly brought him back to reality. What in the world was he thinking? He shoved Shelby's card back into his wallet and decided he'd eat leftovers in front of the TV. Maybe he would even be distracted.

Shortly after seven, David still in front of the TV, dirty dishes and all, Nikki got home. She was humming to herself as David got up to greet her.

"Whoa. A personal greeting. For your wife no less. How did I rate this?" Nikki asked.

"Will you kindly drop the sarcasm?" David asked. "Where have you been?"

"Isn't that the pot calling the kettle black? Besides, since when has it made any difference to you where I am? You don't seem to care whether I'm home or not as long as you have something to eat. Besides, you're not ever home anyway."

"I do care whether you're here. And I don't like it that you weren't here when Neil and Alyssa asked about going out tonight."

Nikki's eyes pierced David's. He looked down as she said each word very slowly: "Both of them have asked your permission to go out several times this week. You never bothered to answer them. Just like you never bother to answer me, or do anything else with them—or me. None of us are as important to you as your precious congregation."

"I can see we will get nowhere with this conversation," David said. "I'm going upstairs to watch TV and have indigestion from eating my dried-out dinner."

"Fine by me. We never have a conversation when we eat anyway; why should tonight be any different than any other?" Nikki began picking up David's dishes as he stormed upstairs, ignoring her comments.

Nikki felt helpless. David never seemed to want to listen to her or to care about her life, or the kids' either. It seemed nothing she said mattered. It was obvious to her that only his own career was important to him. This was definitely not how she had envisioned their lives together.

Alyssa came dashing down the stairs, stopping just long enough to plant a quick kiss on Nikki's cheek. Nikki touched her cheek where Alyssa had kissed her, sadly thinking that it would be the only kiss she would get tonight—or any other night.

In Whose Steps?

"See you in the morning, Mom," Alyssa called, already halfway out the door. "Dad said I could go to the slumber party at Tim's and Cindy's." Nikki waved to her, continuing to stand motionless, wondering how her life might have turned out differently if she could be Alyssa's age just starting her adult life. Would she marry David again? Sad to say, she didn't think she would. Was it so wrong to want someone to cherish her? To treat her as if she were special—or at least as important as any one of his other church members? As if she were needed in his life? She silently demanded God to tell her what she had done wrong to end up in such a dead marriage.

Alyssa slammed the front door as she ran out and jumped in the car with Whitney. "Thanks for picking me up," she said breathlessly. "I was afraid Dad wasn't going to let me go. Well, not really," she said more honestly. "I know that if I keep asking him, he'll let me do whatever I want." They both giggled excitedly. Whitney's dad took them to Tim's and Cindy's and quickly they tumbled out of the car without so much as a "thanks for bringing us." Before Whitney's dad could leave, they were banging on the front door of their youth director's home.

Obviously, even with short notice, Tim and Cindy had been busy. Cookies, chips and dips, popcorn, nachos and cokes—everything growing girls need!—were set out for them. Alyssa and Whitney grabbed a plateful of food and started talking with the others girls who'd already arrived. There were about ten of them and they all adored Cindy as their Bible Study leader. Even if she was an adult, she was young enough to remember what it was like to be young. Besides, she was married to Tim. They all wanted to be married to Tim. Well, not really Tim, but he was soooo cool and Cindy was soooo lucky. Grabbing their sleeping blankets, they all plopped in the middle of the living room floor while Tim put in a video. They thought he was handsome enough to star in a video himself.

"Whitney!" Alyssa whispered. "Look at Cindy's eyes. They're all red and swollen."

"Nuh, uh," Whitney whispered back. "It's your imagination." They both watched as Cindy went out of the room with Tim. Several of the other girls turned and looked also. When they'd had slumber parties before, Cindy usually stayed in the living room and slept with them. They heard a door shut down the hall.

Beth started talking about her boyfriend, and soon they were all comparing stories. "Isn't anybody going to be quiet so we can watch the movie?" Janice asked. "I love this part. Y'all be quiet."

"We can watch later," Alyssa said, as she picked up the remote and clicked off the TV. "Besides, Tim turned it up loud enough to wake the dead."

Janice turned quickly to face Alyssa. "Well, you coulda just turned it down. Why'd you have to turn it off? It was just getting to my favorite--"

They froze as they heard someone crying hysterically. It sounded like Cindy! And then—what was that? It sounded like a slap! And a distinct, "I said, shut up. They'll hear you wailing like that!" Then quiet. The girls stared at each other. What had happened? Their minds refused to accept that Tim could have hit and yelled at Cindy. No way could that be true. It was impossible. No one said anything. Alyssa turned the movie back on and they all watched it quietly, not hearing anything.

In a few minutes, Tim sauntered in. "Hey, you girls are awfully quiet tonight," he said. "Does this actually mean we're going to get some sleep this time?

"We're wondering, where's Cindy?" Whitney asked. "She usually stays in here with us."

"Right. She asked me to tell you guys she wasn't feeling very well and that she'll be in later if she gets to feeling

In Whose Steps?

better." Tim appeared to be telling the truth, and he was certainly calm enough. The whole thing seemed like—must have been—a bad dream. "She'll be in the back bedroom if you need anything," Tim continued. "I have to go to a meeting, so I'll see you guys later. Don't tear the house down," he teased, just like he always did.

"What should we do?" Alyssa demanded of the others as soon as Tim left the house.

"It's none of our business," said Janice. Beth shook her head in agreement.

"How can you say that! It's Cindy. She's our business. She'd help us if something was wrong," Whitney whispered, still fearful to talk out loud.

"But I'm sure it's a misunderstanding," Melissa ventured. "We don't want to get Tim in trouble. I'm sure it didn't mean anything. Cindy probably made him so mad he couldn't help it."

"What planet did you drop off of!" Alyssa hissed at her. "That's just a stupid thing to say. No matter what Cindy did, she doesn't deserve to be hit or be yelled at!"

"Well, then, you quit yelling at me," Melissa retorted.

"Not yelling, just making my point," Alyssa threw back.

Beth jumped in the argument. "Alyssa, I think you oughta tell your dad. He can do something about it because he's Tim's boss. But, I really don't think we should get him into trouble."

"Stand up and be a woman, Beth. Would you want us to be quiet if your boyfriend was hitting you? I don't think so," Whitney said.

"No, you're right, I wouldn't. Okay, I agree. But I still think Alyssa should tell her dad."

Alyssa agreed. "I will. Soon as I get home in the morning. Or maybe I should call him now?" she asked, looking at the others.

"No," Janice said. "Just wait till tomorrow. You know, I think we should pray for Cindy—and Tim. What do you think will happen to him? Will he still be our youth director?"

"Maybe we shouldn't..." Beth started to say.

"Yes, we are going to go through with this, Beth. Don't be such a wimp. Let's pray," Janice said.

A group of very solemn and saddened young girls bowed their heads to pray, all thoughts of movies and boyfriends vanished for the moment. All reached for the box of tissues which had been placed there for sad movies, not real life.

CHAPTER SIX

Nikki had gone upstairs and settled in with a book for the evening, hoping it would be interesting enough to distract her. After David had finished supper, he showered and dressed.

"Where tonight, David? I guess I would have been shocked to think you were going to stay home with me."

David was frustrated. He didn't even want to go to the stupid 12-step group for pastors, but he had told Carl he would. And even less did he want to tell Nikki he was going. But since Neil took his car, he had to let Nikki know he needed hers.

"I'm going to a meeting, as usual," David said, trying to play it down so Nikki wouldn't ask questions. "I'm going to need your car, obviously, since Neil took mine. Did you have any plans?"

"Just wishing I had some with you. Sure, take my car. Where would I be going? I'm reading a romance novel. It's the only way I have any romance in my life," Nikki retorted.

David ignored the jab and asked where the keys were. "Thanks," he mumbled, as she chunked them at him. "I'm not sure what time I'll be home."

"If I didn't know better, I'd wonder if you were having an affair," Nikki replied. "You're always gone and you never have time for me. Even if you are home, you aren't 'here.' And you never seem to desire—well, never mind." She wasn't going to humiliate herself any further, she thought. Enough rejection for one day.

"I don't think this is a conversation we need to have right this minute, Nikki. I need to go."

"Well of course you need to go. You always need to go, and we never 'need to have this conversation,' do we? Whatever."

David became more frustrated. It seemed impossible to please her. "I've got to go, or I'll be late. See you later." Leaning down, he pecked her on the cheek. Tears came to her eyes as she pulled away from his gesture. She wished it meant something; obviously it didn't.

"Fine," David told her, slamming the door as he walked out of the room, down the stairs, and into the garage. As he tried to put the keys into the ignition of her car, he realized he was trying to put his key into the ignition. As he angrily got her keys from his pocket, he jammed his back in while thinking he'd like to jam them into the side of her car. *She is so darn exasperating, so darn demanding, who wouldn't feel this way?* Then his thoughts turned. *Jesus. What would Jesus do? He'd be a servant to her just like He tells me to in His Word.* Quickly he dismissed that thought. *Nikki's impossible to serve because she's impossible to please!*

David backed out of the garage and tore out of the driveway, accidentally burning off because he wasn't used to driving a standard shift. Well, it fit his mood anyway. "God!" He shouted in the empty car as he drove down the street. "Where are You?" he demanded. "I was thinking my life was meaningless—are You just wanting to prove it to me? Why don't You do anything I ask of You? I thought that was what you were in the business of doing!" David felt as alone as he'd ever felt in his life. Just then he saw a street sign reminding him he didn't know exactly where he was going. Heading in the direction he thought it was, he decided he wasn't bad enough to go to a 12-step meeting. For the hundredth time, he wondered why he'd allowed Carl to talk him into attending.

In Whose Steps?

He'd heard these groups were notorious for the smoke-filled environment, but surely the pastors' group wouldn't be. It wouldn't be wise to go home smelling like smoke! *Ah, there it is. I guess that's it although it does look like some of those guys standing outside are smoking.* He pulled in, parked, and as he walked up, several men came to him and shook his hand. "We're so glad you're here," they said warmly. They seemed real—something he didn't know a lot about. He heard a familiar voice saying, "Come on in; would you like some coffee?" It was his youth director, Tim! They saw each other at the same time and both appeared ashamed to be seen by the other.

"Pastor. Dr. Cunningham," Tim said, as he stuck out his hand. "Could I get you some coffee?"

"Sure, Tim. I guess you know I'm a little surprised to see you here, don't you?"

The other men backed off as these two, who obviously knew each other, continued to talk.

"Yes, sir. Carl sent me here. He knows I'm here. I guess he sent you, too? Or," he said, trying to save face for his pastor, "are you the speaker tonight?"

"No, Tim, I'm not the speaker. And yes, Carl sent me here, also. I wonder why he didn't tell me you attended this group?"

"Well, I guess he didn't want to scare either of us off."

"Is this your first time?" David asked Tim.

"Oh, no. Not at all. I've been coming for two years. This keeps me sane. I don't know what I'd do without this meeting."

"Really. Does Cindy know you come?"

"Sure she does. She says she doesn't know what she'd do if I didn't."

"You and Cindy seem to have it all together, Tim."

"Well, we don't. And you're talking like it's something bad to be here. It means we are willing to get help. My mom was an alcoholic and being here helps me deal with that. She expected me to be the adult and take care of her when she was drunk. I'm an 'adult child of an alcoholic.' I send many of our teens, whose parents are alcoholic, to our church's self-help groups. They are modeled on these same 12-step principles. I come here, though, because it's specifically for pastors, ministers—church staff people like us who are willing to admit they need to recover."

"Many of our teens have alcoholic parents?"

"Of course. Obviously you do, too, or you wouldn't be here."

"True. I do."

"So, here's your first meeting. It's starting; let's go on in."

It was David's first encounter with, "Hi, I'm _____ and I'm the adult child of a _____." He learned there were many other disorders of which you could be an adult child. When it was his turn, he felt dumb, but all the rest of these grown men—pastors or leaders in their respective churches—were doing it. As the evening wore on, the camaraderie between these men was tangibly obvious. They shared their stories with a transparency that was incredibly painful. Because of their lostness as adult children, they had lost their churches, wives, and kids; witnessed or experienced family suicides; become homeless; or had become drug or sex addicts. Yet there seemed to be such a bond here. They were helping each other by listening to each other's stories. Surprisingly, he realized it actually felt good and he even liked it. He thought that he'd like to have this same level of fellowship on his church staff. No matter what the problem, it sure seemed like these men accepted and loved one another. He would be anxious to come back, he thought, as he left that evening.

In Whose Steps?

Only one thing bothered him. As he and Tim had walked out, Tim stated again that this group kept him sane and sober because, at one time, he had been a drug addict and also addicted to violence. David wondered about the group's ability to keep anyone sane. It bothered him a little that the group seemed to trust each other more than they did God. But maybe he just wasn't familiar with the Bible's "one anothers," he thought.

Hesitantly he'd asked Tim, "Don't you mean that this 12-step group is very helpful to your life? What I'm asking is, you don't mean that the group is necessary for your sanity, right? That God's Word, and His people aren't adequate without this group?"

"I hate to say it, Pastor. That is what I believe. This group is necessary to me; more necessary than self-righteous, bible-thumping church people! I credit this group with saving my life. I believe God uses 12-steps because the church isn't doing what it needs to do to help people. I continually thank God for 12-step groups!" He finished emphatically.

"Why haven't you told me this before, Tim?"

"I figured as long as I did my job well you'd be happy. Church didn't seem like the place to air dirty laundry like it's okay to do here."

"Well, you're probably right, Tim. I'm not sure I would have understood before tonight," David answered. "I have a lot to think about," David told him as they parted company.

His steps were very slow as he walked to his car. It went against his grain to say that the Bible and God's church weren't adequate to help people struggling with emotional illness and addictions. But, he had to face the truth of what he'd seen tonight. This loving and accepting group did seem to work when it came to helping people stay emotionally healthy. Was "walking in 12-steps" actually the same thing as "walking in His steps" and he'd just not seen that before?

One Man's Search for Answers

As he drove home, he considered whether or not he should tell Nikki what he was doing. These guys had all been so honest, and here he was being deceitful with his own wife. He made up his mind. If she was awake when he got home, he would talk with her about it. Sure enough, the light was on as drove up. She must still be reading. With a quick prayer that God would help him be truthful, he headed for their bedroom, as he also thought that the 12-step program was already helping him to be a more honest person.

The lights were on, but Nikki was sound asleep sitting upright in the bed, the book still in her lap. Gently, he took her book away, made her more comfortable, and covered her up. She didn't stir. Turning out the light so he wouldn't wake her, he went into the bathroom to undress. "God, I'll tell her tomorrow," he whispered under his breath. As he crept under the covers, he hoped he'd go to sleep quickly. It was late, and he had an early morning appointment. Carl had asked him, with the family's permission, to be in on family therapy with Ann and her dad and mom, Jack and Anita. He closed his eyes.

Next thing he knew, there was a knock on his bedroom door and even though it was quiet, he heard Alyssa's voice hiss demandingly, "Dad! Are you awake?"

What on earth! As he glanced quickly at the clock, he saw it was one o'clock in the morning. Grabbing his robe, he walked quickly to the door before Alyssa waked up Nikki.

"What do you want? What's wrong? Aren't you supposed to be at a slumber party?" And suddenly thought, *at Tim's?*

"Please, Dad, come and talk in my room. I called Neil and asked him to come get me from Tim's and Cindy's."

"Why? You had a fit to go over there. What happened?"

"I know. But Dad, something terrible happened tonight. And I decided I couldn't wait to tell you. It's about Tim and Cindy."

"Are you okay, Honey?"

"Yeah. They don't know we know."

"That sounds rather melodramatic. They don't know you know what?"

"Dad, listen. It's not funny. Tim actually hit Cindy tonight!"

David paused and let her words sink in. Because he'd seen and heard Tim at the meeting, he guessed it was believable. But Tim couldn't have been at the meeting and at home at the same time, he thought.

"I was with Tim tonight, Alyssa. You must be wrong. Why don't you tell me the whole story?" David desperately hoped Alyssa was mistaken.

Alyssa's words ran together as if she couldn't get them out fast enough. "It was right after we got there, Dad, about 7:30. Cindy's eyes looked like she'd been crying. And she went back to the bedroom. Tim put on a movie for us—turned the sound up real loud—and then he went back to the bedroom, too. We were all talking, and I turned off the movie because we couldn't hear each other with the movie going. I figured we'd watch it later. Anyway, when I turned it off, I—that is, all of us—heard someone crying; it sounded like Cindy—who else could it have been—and then a slap, and then someone—it sounded like Tim—told her to shut up right now! Dad, we know it was Tim. And right after that, he came in and said Cindy wasn't feeling good. And that he needed to go out for a while, but Cindy would be in the bedroom if we needed her."

David sighed heavily as he thought about it. He hadn't gotten to the meeting till 8:00 but Tim had already been there. Admittedly, it wasn't very far from Tim's house. "So, did you guys talk to Cindy?"

"We girls talked about what happened and everybody wanted me to tell you. After Tim left, we went back and knocked on her door, and she said she wasn't feeling good, but she'd come out if we needed her. We said she didn't need to 'cause we were okay, but we were worried about her. She said again she was okay. It wasn't much fun after that, Dad. They wanted me to go ahead and come home so I could tell you as soon as you got here. So, I called Neil about midnight, and he came and got me. The rest of the girls stayed. What are you going to do, Dad?" she demanded. "You've got to do something." Finally she took a breath, and waited for David's reply.

"Yes, I do, Alyssa. Let me think about it and pray about it. I'll talk to you about it again tomorrow. I need to go to bed now. Are you sure you're okay?"

"Yeah, Dad. It was just soooo scary. I feel better since I told you. Are you going to fire him?"

"Is that what you want?"

"I don't think so. But I don't know what to do. I sure as heck don't want any guy beating up on me and I don't want Tim beating up on Cindy."

"Me, either, Alyssa. May we go to bed now?"

"Yeah." She yawned. "I'm sleepy now that I've told you. 'Nite, Dad. Thanks for listening." She hugged him.

"Morning, Alyssa," David said as he hugged her, reminding her how late it was.

CHAPTER SEVEN

As always, morning came much too soon for David. He was overwhelmed with what he had to deal with today. It wasn't enough that he had to attend family therapy with Ann's parents, Jack and Anita Grimes, at the psychiatric hospital! Now, he had to figure out what to do about Tim. He hoped Carl wasn't too busy to talk with him about Tim. Carl was his only hope today.

The psychiatric hospital was beautiful inside. Cool colors, green plants, indirect lighting, soothing music, and waterfalls and flowers outside *Were all therapists' offices alike—always cool colors and dim lights?* Everyone spoke softly. Felt like a funeral home, he thought. He met Carl and Jack and Anita Grimes at the front desk. These people should look like monsters, he thought. But Jack looked like he always did—a businessman in a suit and tie. But his charming exterior belied the obvious pain in his grayish-blue eyes. *No wonder he looks older than I do.* And Anita? An engaging, lovely lady. The best way he could describe her would be tall and regal. Every move seemed planned without appearing stilted. She was the epitome of a gracious hostess. And these folks were supposed to have sexually abused their daughter? It was incomprehensible to David. It must take professionals to analyze people like this.

"Is everyone ready? Let's go back," Carl said, taking his hospital keys and opening the door to the locked unit. They followed Carl into a small room marked, "Conference Room." Jack and Anita seemed nervous. For that matter, David thought, so did he. He was always uncomfortable at the psych hospital even though he was only visiting. He guessed he was afraid they would decide he also needed to be locked up! Ann came in right after them. Carl asked all of them to be seated and they sat in the various soft chairs and sofas. Carl switched off the overhead light and turned on the lamps. *Of course. Dim lighting.*

Jack and Anita, although they tried not to show their feelings, gasped when they looked up and saw Ann. They had not been allowed to see her for the twenty-five days she had been on the unit. Their young daughter, who always took such good care of herself, looked as if she were a war refugee. Disheveled hair, bags under her eyes, no make-up, unkempt hair and clothes—they didn't know what to make of what they saw. They came out of their chairs and started toward her, desperate to give her a hug and make it all okay. Ann looked at them with knives in her eyes. What was going on?

Carl asked them to be seated again and to give Ann her space and not to touch her without her permission. Continuing to speak softly and tenderly, Carl opened the meeting by suggesting they pray together. "God, You desire truth in our inward parts, and that is what we are after today. Your truth. Please guide us in that journey and help us to be honest before you and before each other. Encourage Ann to be brave and to be totally honest and encourage her parents to be willing to listen and hear her so that she can heal. In Jesus' name, Amen," Carl finished.

Ann kept her head bowed, Jack, Anita, and David looked at each other, not sure what the prayer meant. David had not had the opportunity to talk with Jack since Carl had disclosed the sexual abuse accusations. Even though he had his own doubts, David knew Carl believed Ann totally.

Reaching out and touching Ann's hand gently, Carl said, "Ann, would you look at me, please? You know the memories you've discovered in hypnosis. Now you need to let your parents in on those memories. Okay?" he asked encouragingly.

She shook her head slightly. Then looking at her parents, Carl said, "Jack and Anita, are you willing to hear from Ann the things she has remembered? They are not pleasant. But if you truly want to help her heal, she needs to confront you with the truth."

Jack and Anita looked at each other, their eyes wide. They weren't sure what to expect. They were somewhat familiar with therapy since Jack had recently been released after a month of hospitalization at this very institution. His insurance had run out after that. However, his depression had improved drastically after he began taking an antidepressant; still, Anita was afraid to upset him. More than anything, though, they wanted their little girl to be well. They had always been at their wits' end to know how to help her. From a child, she'd seemed so perfect and never caused them any trouble. Then they noticed she wasn't eating, and they learned from Carl that she had an out-of-control eating disorder. They were terrified she'd starve to death. Then, they'd observed a cut on her arm, but when they inquired, she had covered it up quickly, relating that it had been a silly accident. Now they noticed she had stitches in her arm!

"Anything!" Jack exclaimed. "We'll do anything to help our little girl get well." Anita shook her head in agreement.

"Ann? Did you hear that your parents are willing to hear what you have to say? Go ahead. It's okay. You're in a safe place, remember. I'm here. And Pastor David is here, too, in case your parents need him. You don't have to take care of them any longer. It's not your job, and you can give it up," Carl said soothingly.

"Jack. Anita." Ann looked at her parents. They looked back questioningly. Why was she calling them by their first names?

"First of all, I am not your 'little girl!'" At first sounding strong, when Ann saw her parents' faces, her lip started quivering. She looked at Carl.

"Do you need Barry to do this for you, Ann?" he asked.

The Grimes were speechless. So was David. Who in the world was Barry, and what did he have to do with any of this?

"No, I can do it." She started again. "Jack. Anita. I finally know the truth about you. I finally know why I've been in such pain all my life. Why I'm anorexic. Well, Melinda is bulimic, actually, but, me—Ann—is anorexic." Again the quick, what's-going-on-here look between David and the Grimes.

"You're doing well, Ann. Keep up your courage," Carl said gently, keeping his eyes focused on her.

"My first memories are from the time I was two. And you, dad—Jack, that is! You're not my dad, because a real dad would never do what you did. You sexually molested me while I was in my crib."

Jack gasped; his face turned ashen. Anita's also. She looked incredulously at Jack and then back at Ann. "That's impossible, Ann," she exclaimed. "Your dad would never do anything like that."

"Oh, yes, he did. And so did you. When I got older, you sexually molested me, too. You helped hold me down while Grandma and Grandpa abused me as well. And you made me watch while you cut up my little white rabbit while it was still alive so I would be too scared to tell what was going on, what you were all doing to me!" Ann became more agitated and angrier by the moment.

"Me? Me?" Anita could barely get a word out. "Ann. You have been my pride and joy my whole life. You think I molested you? Ann, what's wrong with you! What have they done to you in this snake pit?" She shook her head and looked pleadingly at Carl. "This can't be happening. It's a horrible nightmare, right?"

"I'm sorry, but I'm afraid not, Anita. And if you guys aren't willing to hear Ann, and quit denying what you did, we are going to have to call this session to a close. Ann really needs you to believe her," he said firmly and smiled at Ann.

"She needs to be believed? What about us?" Jack was raising his voice. "I think you must be the one who abused her—you've raped her mind! She knows these things aren't so!" He looked at Ann. "Ann, tell him the truth. You know this isn't so."

Ann's eyes looked strange. She rubbed her forehead as she bowed her head, holding it with her hands. Suddenly, she looked up with rage-filled eyes, a strange voice spewing out hatred. "Are you people stupid? You think we don't know what happened to us? Ever since we read about having the courage to heal we started remembering our past. You can't fool us any longer. And we hate you. Our dreams and our journals are full of your atrocities." Venom seemed to spew from—whose?—mouth.

David and the Grimes were totally taken aback. Carl seemed to understand what was happening. This—this—person was Ann? What did she mean, "our" and "we"?

As Ann glared at them, Carl informed them that Ann was a victim of Dissociative Identity Disorder, "but you probably know it as Multiple Personality Disorder," he said. "When the body has experienced so much trauma that it can no longer endure it, a part of the person dissociates and another comes to take its place. These 'parts' are called 'alters.' The person, or alter, you have just met is Barry. He's the part that holds all Ann's hatred and rage toward her abusers—you, as well as her grandparents," Carl explained.

Ann—or whoever—jumped in. "You thought we'd never remember, did you? You didn't think we'd remember all the electric shocks you gave me, the drugs, the horrible utensils you used to punish me. Well, here's the surprise. We do remember. And you are going to pay for what you did to us!" Barry was livid.

"The pain Ann has experienced has been devastating to her," Carl explained. "She has begun to understand why her past has made her the way she is." Turning to Ann, he asked, "Is someone there who is willing to talk about the Ritual Abuse? Barry?"

"No." His eyes blinked and he seemed to shrink before their eyes. A small, childish voice said, "I will. My name is Anna. I'm five years old."

"Are you sure, Anna, that you want to do this?" Carl asked. "You don't have to—wouldn't it be better if someone older does this?"

"No. I can." Looking at Jack and Anita, the small voice continued. "You made me kill the little baby. The one that Melinda had. I had to stick a knife in it and it was all bloody. I was scared. So was Melinda. That's why Melinda is bu-bu-"

"Bulimic," Carl finished for Anna.

Anna started crying. She curled up in a ball and started sucking her thumb. "I want to go now," she said. Then she straightened up, blinked, stood up, and another voice said, commandingly, "You will not meet any more of us today. We want to leave now."

Carl took Ann's hand. "It's okay, Ann. Come back. It's safe here for you." Ann's eyes blinked. She looked dazed. "Some others came, didn't they," she asked Carl.

"Yes, but they helped your parents understand what your problem is," he said. "You owe your alters your thanks for helping you, just as they always have. They must want you to get well since they were willing to show themselves to your parents this first session with them."

David did not know what to do or say. He'd never seen anything like this before. Jack and Anita appeared to be in shock themselves.

"We need to meet again," Carl said, "and you need to be open to continue to hear Ann's pain. Ann is the core personality. The rest of the personalities, or alters, need to integrate with her. But she has been tremendously hurt, and the sooner you acknowledge it, the better off we'll all be. It took an enormous amount of courage for her to do what she did today. I know God gave her the strength to tell the truth because He wants this family to be healed." He smiled at Jack and Anita.

They didn't smile back. They were devastated and unsure what to do next. Carl continued. "If you aren't willing to hear Ann's pain and you continue to stay in denial, she will not meet with you again. Sometimes people like Ann, who have endured the worse abuse imaginable, choose not to talk with their parents ever again. I hope that won't be the case with this family. I hope that you will pray and ask God to reveal your own possible repressed memories to you so that you can ask Ann's forgiveness for what you have done to her."

"I guess I might need to have some hypnosis myself, Carl, to see if I do have any of those repressed memories, but it's beyond me how that possibly could be true," Jack said slowly.

"Very good, Jack. Your willingness to do that will help Ann. It is possible you have repressed some memories. Perhaps that's what is at the bottom of your own depression. You may have abuse in your background from your own parents, Ann's grandparents, who abused her. Abuse is usually intergenerational." Carl got up and told Ann they needed to go and debrief what had just happened. He told Jack and Anita he had asked David to come so that they could process with him.

"I'm not a therapist, Carl!" David finally found his voice. "I don't know what to do."

"Right now, they just need you to be with them. Explain to them what I told you about DID. Pray for them, David, and for Ann, that this family may be healed."

He and Ann started out of the room. Ann didn't look at her parents. As they went through the door, Anita said softly, "Ann, Ann, please come back. I love you, honey. I want to give you a hug. Please," she pleaded.

Ann turned her head and glared at her mother. "I will let you know when I want to see you again. Until then, you may not contact me. If you try—although the hospital will protect me from you—it will be even longer before I will talk to you again." She followed Carl out of the room.

Anita gasped in pain. She felt as though she'd been knifed in the back. "How can I bear this?" she said. "What will her brother Steve and sister Carol think? What will the church think—how can I continue to teach my Bible study?" How could she ever face her Bible study group again? Anita had always done her utmost to live her life before God in a way that would please Him. Right now, God seemed very distant. "Dear God!" she agonized silently. "Dear God, I cannot bear this. I'm supposed to be there for Ann? While she accuses me of..." Anita seemed to wither. She thought she would faint.

"Pastor, what are we going to do? What are we going to do? Please, tell us, what are we going to do?" Jack said the words over and over as if saying them one more time would give him some insight. David was glad Jack kept talking because he sure didn't know what to say. *God, give me words to help these people. I'm at a total loss as to what to do.*

"Jack," he said, "I have to ask you. Could there be any truth at all to what Ann said? I mean, have you ever, in any way, been inappropriate with her?"

"Pastor, I swear on a stack of Bibles. I'm willing to take a polygraph test—whatever. Even hypnosis like I said. But I swear I never touched Ann in an inappropriate way. Not that I remember. Never. How could I forget doing something like that?"

"Anita, what about you? What do you think about what Ann said about you and Jack's parents?" David asked.

Anita just looked at him. She seemed like a statue. She didn't say anything as tears flowed silently from her eyes. Finally, she found her voice. "If one word of this is true," she said, "I deserve to die."

"Honey, don't talk like that," Jack replied. "We know it's not true. Ann is hurting and we need to care, but it's not our fault. I'm sure we'll get to the bottom of this and find out it's all some kind of terrible, terrible mistake."

David knew that If Carl heard these statements he would say the Grimes were in denial. He was sure—at least he thought he was sure—that none of it was true. But, like Carl said, why in God's name would anyone make up such horrible things and go though such agony to be well? He'd known Ann since she was a little girl, and she didn't seem to be someone who lied or spread rumors. But Carl obviously knew more than he did about this. He wasn't trained to deal with this kind of problem. Thank God he didn't have to! He was happy to leave these kinds of problems to the professionals.

"Why don't we pray and then you guys go home and get some rest," David suggested, "and I'll call you later to see how you are doing."

Jack and Anita slowly shook their heads in agreement. After David prayed, they looked for someone on staff who had a key and could let them out. He was afraid he was going to have to carry Anita, but slowly, she made it to their car.

Breathing a sigh of relief that the ordeal was over, at least for now, David suddenly remembered he had to deal with Tim. He had to decide what to tell the elders about Jack, also. There was no end, it seemed, to what he needed to do. He wanted to talk to Shelby. A professional would help, he thought. And Carl was so wrapped up with Ann he thought it would be helpful to talk with Shelby.

Instead, he thought maybe he should go by home for a few minutes and see if he could talk with Nikki. *Or maybe by Shelby's office? For a professional's opinion?* He was totally shaken by the morning's events and could only imagine how Jack and Anita must feel.

CHAPTER EIGHT

Jack's and Anita's hearts were breaking. As they walked into their spacious, two-story white-columned Colonial (Ann's home for all her life; Jack's and Anita's for over 30 years), the delightful memories of Ann and the other children spilled from every square inch, attesting to the fact that their recent experience must be a bad dream that would surely go away!

Like most men, Anita thought, Jack will make a beeline for the TV to escape his feelings. Sure enough, he went straight to the sofa and grabbed the remote. He was surfing the channels as if he had no other concern in the world—as if their world hadn't just fallen apart. Anita stared at him, realizing he was gone into that never-never land where, in her opinion, men go so they don't have to deal with reality. She walked over and stood in front of the TV and said, "Jack, we really need to continue to discuss this. It's not going away."

"Anita, not now!" Jack emphatically. "Maybe later." She walked to the doorway and turned and faced him. "Jack..." she started to say, but abruptly thought better of trying to continue the conversation. She wanted desperately to talk, to be held while she cried on his shoulder; she knew he wanted desperately to avoid talking right now. If she continued trying to dialogue, she knew they would fight, and that was the last thing she wanted right now. Slowly, she walked upstairs to Ann's room.

The room looked as if Ann had just walked out since Anita had chosen not to clean it after Ann left for the hospital. Ann usually kept her room neatly, but in the last few months, she had started leaving clothes strewn all over her room. Anita hadn't wanted to be on Ann's case while she seemed to be having such a difficult time, so she hadn't said anything to her about her room. When Ann had gone into the hospital, Anita still hadn't straightened the room because she didn't want Ann to feel she was treating her as a child or that she was invading her boundaries. An involuntary, audible gasp that was almost a moan escaped from Anita's mouth. How ironic. She was afraid she would violate Ann's boundaries by making her bed! And now she was accused of vile, unthinkable boundary-crossing!!! It just didn't make sense.

Ann's white four-poster bed reminded Anita of the many times she'd prayed with her before bedtime and then come in to wake her up in the mornings with a cheery, "Wake up, sleepyhead." Ann was notorious for wanting "just a few more minutes, pleeeeease, Mom?" The bed also reminded Anita of all the late-night talks they'd had when Ann came in from her dates. Ann would knock softly on her mom's door asking, "Mom, are you awake?" knowing Anita would be waiting up for her. Nearly always, Ann would ask her to come to her room and they'd pile on her bed while Ann told her about the evening. Anita had never asked many questions, but then she didn't need to. Ann had always been open about her life and was quick to ask her mom's advice on dating.

Anita thought Ann had respected her as a Mom and as a Bible teacher because she seemed to value her input. For as long as she could remember, Anita had taught Sunday School classes that matched the age of at least one of her children. Now that all seemed so unreal. Which scenario was true? Had Ann been faking all those years? Had some "good little girl personality" been covering up for who Ann really was? *I*

In Whose Steps?

just can't believe that. There's no way she could have been faking all those years. Then what happened?.

It had been about a year ago that Ann had told her mom she wanted to see a therapist. Anita had been shocked. She thought she and Ann were very close and this seemed to come out of the blue. Ann—seemingly so stable, well-adjusted, responsible, and independent, but never in a rebellious way—was now saying she had a bad emotional problem—that inside she was in turmoil. When Anita questioned her, all she could say was, "I don't know what's wrong with me, Mom. I'm really scared to find out. Something's not right with me."

Since several of Ann's friends were in therapy, Anita thought it was a passing fancy for Ann. Anita had felt comfortable in suggesting Ann see Carl James at their church, knowing she'd get Christian counseling. Although Ann was in college majoring in drama, by her own choice she lived at home. That enabled her to stay under her parents' insurance coverage. Anita was thankful for the coverage but in her worst dream, she would never have thought it could turn out like this.

Continuing down the hall to the kids' playroom, she thought of the hundreds of times she and the kids had romped and played games together. Even Jack was often part of the family times. They'd had a great time. Anita's mind (although she was beginning to wonder if she still had one) drifted off, and she heard the kids giggling and shrieking with pleasure as they "sledded" down the stairs in a box! She didn't think they had been too strict—or too lenient—as parents. She and Jack had committed to being different parents than their own parents had been. Neither of them blamed their parents for not being better parents; they both acknowledged that their own parents had done the best they knew how.

Nevertheless, Anita had bought and studied all the latest Christian child-rearing books and had attempted, by the grace of God, to implement everything she read.

One Man's Search for Answers

She turned and went back down the hall. Even more good memories were evoked as she looked into Carol's and Steve's rooms. They were both grown and married, but she kept their rooms as they were for the grandchildren she was sure would eventually come. She and Jack were looking forward to having good times with the grandchildren and creating the same fun-filled happy memories with them that they had shared with their own children. With that thought, Anita felt as if she had been struck in the face. Were all these happy memories just a farce? She refused to believe that they were. What could have happened to Ann, a young lady who was known for telling the truth?

Doubt crept into Anita's mind. Where could that monster voice from Ann have come from? What she'd heard sounded like to her the way a demon must sound. Her first thought was that Ann would never make up something like that. Was it a product of hypnosis and Ann's drama background? Was it from Satan? Was it based on any facts—dear God, no!—there was no way she and Jack had done even one of those atrocities Ann had accused them of doing. It was impossible that Ann could have repressed those things she said she now remembered. That would mean she and Jack would have had to repress them, also. Absolutely impossible! God, who could she possibly talk to about this? No one. She didn't want even her best friend to know about this horror. It was bad enough that Carl and the pastor knew.

Her head was killing her. She went downstairs and into her and Jack's bedroom. This lovely room, with its soft pastels and bright accents, had always been such a sanctuary. Knowing it would be impossible to sleep, she thought she'd try and read God's Word. She was afraid to sleep, anyway, for fear of nightmares. It occurred to her, however, that no nightmare could be worse than the one she was experiencing. With her Bible, she sat down on the bed. Instead of reading, she leaned down to put her face on her pillow. It's cool softness felt so good to her burning cheeks. As the sun came brightly through the window and reflected the room's soft colors, they appeared to dance across the walls. Anita slowly closed her eyes but was immediately greeted by shameful images. What little peace there was in the room immediately disappeared. No matter which way she turned her head, the images continued to haunt her mind. *Get thee behind me, Satan,* she commanded silently, knowing that such evil could not be from God.

During Jack's depression, he'd mentioned suicide more than once. She'd never been able to understand how Jack—or anyone—could feel so desperate and hopeless that he would want to take his own life. It had scared her for Jack to talk that way—it just didn't make sense to her how anyone who knew Christ could ever feel badly enough to want to die. But, she was beginning to understand.

Sometime after Ann had started seeing Carl, Jack had mentioned that he thought he'd like to talk with him, too. Said things were just catching up to him "in his old age." She doubted that. He was a very active man. Once she'd opened the door to his study and seen him with his head in his hands over the books for his business. He'd owned his own businesses since before she'd met him. The most recent one he'd purchased in the last couple of years. He'd mentioned that it was somewhat risky, but he believed he could turn it around and make it profitable in a short time.

Noticing how worn and distracted Jack had seemed recently, Anita had asked him if there was a problem with the business. He'd said an abrupt no and asked her to leave him alone. Well, on a husband scale from 1 to 10, she supposed he was as open with her as most husbands were with their wives. He was quite factual and analytical; he had a wonderful business mind. Sometimes he would spout facts about his life and business for several minutes, as if he'd been saving them all up for a while. Then it was silent again for a long time.

But Anita still wished that he would be more open about his thoughts and feelings. Although, from her interactions with other women in her life and church, she knew he was no more closed than most men. She also wished desperately he were more of a spiritual leader. It was somewhat ironic, she thought, that he was an elder—a spiritual leader in the church—but not much of one at home. Wouldn't it be great, she'd thought, if the church asked the wives and children of the elder whether they thought their husbands and fathers should be elders? Just because they were good businessmen didn't mean they were spiritually qualified to be elders.

So she often felt spiritually adrift when it came to leadership at home. She loved teaching Sunday School and the women's Bible Study; she had loved teaching her own children about God. For years, she had continued to pray for Jack to be the spiritual leader for her and for Ann who was still living at home. Then, with a sobbing return to reality, she realized that Ann might never again live at home—or even speak to them again, for that matter! As tears ran unchecked down her face, she asked God to lead Jack to pray with her, to comfort her with his arms and a reliance on God and His Word, and to reassure her that He was in control of even this horrible mess.

Dear God, I cannot handle this alone. Please help me. Please intervene in our lives. Please bring Ann to her senses. If there really is something we need to know and deal with, please God, bring it to our attention. Nose running and tears streaming down her face, she went into the bathroom for some Kleenex and Jack's sleeping pills. She'd had all the reality she could stand for one day and she did something contrary to her normal way of dealing with life: she swallowed a handful of pills and prayed for relief from her pain.

CHAPTER NINE

After he left Ann, Carl went to staff meeting. It was composed of everyone who worked with the patients on the unit. They met each week to process what was happening with the patients to see if they needed to make any treatment changes—and to satisfy the insurance companies' questions about the patients' need to be there. Today they started with Ann. Carl reported to the staff what had happened in Family Therapy with Ann and her parents. He also reported that he had asked his and the family's pastor, Dr. David Cunningham, to be there during therapy.

Dr. Billings, Ann's psychiatrist, and also a Christian, asked Carl, "Why did you include the pastor? What was your thinking?" In his estimation, most pastors and church leaders, as well as so-called "Biblical counselors" were sadly in need of therapy themselves. They tended to live in denial of their own issues or in the belief that the Bible alone gave the answers to mental illness—although, in his estimation, they knew nothing about mental illness! In fact, they were probably the sickest bunch of people he knew. Ignoring their own deep pain, they taught their parishioners to do the same: "If people are mentally ill, just give them some Bible verses and they'll get over it" seemed to be the magical thinking that kept them going. Why couldn't they understand that people, pastors also, were only as sick as their secrets!

No wonder the Body of Christ was in such emotional pain. Certainly the pastors did not possess the necessary skills to counsel others when they wouldn't deal with their own issues. And regardless of their good intentions to help others, they usually did more harm than good. Thankfully, many of them were finally learning to recognize their inadequacies and refer to the experts.

While Carl was contemplating an answer, Dr. Billings threw in another question: "Has your pastor had any psychological training—or at least some counseling himself so that he has dealt with his own issues?" Billings was irritated as he continued to think about the harm well-meaning but ignorant pastors and counselors could do.

Carl laughed. "I know what you mean, Ted. Isn't it unbelievable that pastors often try and do our jobs? But here's where I'm coming from: I thought that if I could expose my pastor David to some serious emotional illnesses, he would be faced with his inability to counsel—except for strictly spiritual issues, of course. Sure enough, once he saw what happened, he didn't want any part of the therapy! I thought he could help comfort Ann's family, though, since that is in his area of expertise."

"But we don't want them comforted, do we? Don't we want them to be in enough pain that they will have to own their responsibility for what they did?" Dr. Billings was still skeptical about David's attendance during family therapy. The rest of the staff listened to the interchange, concerned about the outcome. They, too, wanted to see Ann get better, and they knew that meant the parents needed to believe Ann and admit their culpability.

"I don't think David could give them enough comfort to change their feelings," Carl said. "They were obviously in great pain. The other point is that David has just begun therapy himself and is learning the value of it. He's begun to recognize what denial is and what it means to look at himself—so I think he can help them in this process. Since the Grimes do trust him, and since he's learning how valuable therapy is—actually, he's even going to a 12-step group!—I believe he can be an ally in the Grimes' family therapy by helping them to come out of denial.

"Alright, I'm willing to chance it," Dr. Billings relented. "I'll include the pastor in her orders for FT with you. Then let's discuss it again after you have the next meeting with them. Do you also want me to write orders for him to see her individually for her spiritual issues? Do you think he will help or hinder her therapy?"

Carl thought about it. "I think it would be good for her to see him individually. I don't think he'll do anything that would take away from her therapy, and she does want to look at spiritual issues. His time is pretty limited, though. I know he wants to see her, but I don't think he can make visiting hours."

"Okay, I'll write orders for him to visit her anytime, even if it's interrupting other therapies, other than IT or FT, of course." Looking at the nurses, he added, "And if you see that his visit is upsetting to her, let me know. Okay. Now, does she need to be on one-on-one suicidal watch?"

"I don't think so," Carl replied. "Ann seems to have more ego strength since she confronted her parents. What do you think?" he asked the nurses.

The nurses agreed that Ann had seemed stronger when she came back on the unit after meeting with her parents. Usually, when parents disagreed with their adult child's accusations, the patient was worse, but Ann seemed to be handling it well. She knew that the staff believed her; they had validated her story and encouraged her many times to stay strong and "speak the truth in love" to her parents. But, they were also aware that they might not be dealing with Ann. Their interactions were conceivably with Melinda, the alter who handled most of the tough issues. If that were true, then

Ann might come out later and be self-destructive. They had lots of experience with patients who wanted to hurt themselves. Invariably the patients found a way to do it, even in the hospital.

"Okay, continue to keep close watch on her for the evening," Dr. Billings said. "We'll leave her meds as is for now. Contact me if you notice any change."

Since Carl didn't have any other patients on the unit at this time, he left as the staff began discussing other cases. He realized he had a whole thirty minutes to himself before he had to see another client, so he walked out onto the patio. Since no one else was outside, he sat down on the bench to enjoy the solitude as he listened to the waterfall splash into the small pool. Although sessions like the one he had this morning with Ann and her family were frequent, they were still emotionally draining. He knew the Grimes were being defensive, and he needn't take what they said personally, but still, it did hurt to be called a "mind raper" when you were only trying to help.

A thought flashed through his head. Once, one of his psychology professors had shown them on the board that the word "therapist" could be separated into two words: "the rapist." From there, he went on to talk about the power therapists could weld over their clients. Funny. He found out later that the same professor had been involved in sexual relations with at least one of his clients and several of his students. "Well, at least I don't have to worry about being "the rapist," Carl thought. Nevertheless, it was draining to hear that accusation.

More than once, his wife, Susan, told him that he didn't have any energy left for her or the children when he got home in the evenings. While he understood that was true—it was often after 10:00 when he got home—he knew God had called him to minister to these hurting people. Usually his family supported him, but sometimes they said they felt cheated and got mad at him for giving all his energy to his patients rather than his family.

But for as long as he could remember (way before he had a degree and was licensed) people in his life had talked to him about very personal issues. He knew God had spiritually gifted him in counseling, and that he was a patient listener who genuinely cared for others. That came across to the people who poured out their troubles to him. When it had first started happening, he had enthusiastically proclaimed God's Word to those who came to him. After discovering psychological literature, however, he became aware that those psychological insights greatly enhanced his ability to help others. It wasn't enough to depend naively upon God's Word when God in his common grace allowed man to make scientific discoveries that revealed man's motivation and his behavior.

It had been a hard decision whether or not to go back to school. He had talked to Susan for her help in discerning what he should do. They had prayed about the decision and both believed that if he was going to counsel others, he should "study to show himself approved" to counsel—and that meant going back to college for a graduate degree in psychology. He was grateful to Susan for continuing to work and helping him to get through school as quickly as possible.

Carl knew his education would expose him to many worldly and ungodly psychological theories. It was his fervent prayer that God would allow him to glean only the truth from those theories. He was determined he would not deny God's sovereignty in the healing process. Ultimately, he knew, it was God, and God only, who did the healing.

God had allowed him to be a good gleaner, he thought, a careful integrator of psychology and Scripture, and he was grateful. Countless "ah ha, so that's why I/they did that!" occurred as he listened to explanations of behavior in his various psych classes. Insightful theories and almost-magical techniques showed him the value of what he was learning—and there were Bible verses to confirm the truth of what he learned. When taking "Abnormal Psychology," it was difficult for him not to diagnose everyone with whom he came into contact (only in his mind, of course!) with the illnesses he was learning about in the *Diagnostic and Statistical Manual of Mental Disorders,* or as it's usually known, the *DSM* for short (Edition III at the time he was in school).

The manual had gone through several revisions, adding numerous illnesses and their symptoms in each revision. Carl was able to apply these scientific DSM diagnoses to the people he saw at the church, as well as in his private practice. He could do more than just call their problems or illnesses "sin." Thanks to David's support, his church was willing to recognize that "all truth is God's truth" whether it was from God's Word or the psychological (scientific) world.

Truthfully, he sometimes admitted to himself that parts of the psychological world seemed far-fetched (like what he had experienced today). But he knew there was nothing in God's Word to deal with a problem as complex as MPD--besides, it hadn't been written to do that. Yet, due to general revelation, God had allowed man to discover so many wonderful insights into the complexities of self.

Something else bothered him, though, about the psychological world. He was glad he was on salary at a church so that he didn't have to charge his patients individually. Somehow it didn't seem quite right to charge people for giving them God's truths so he had to remember he was giving them more than that. What he wondered about, though, were people in the Christian mental health field—like Dr. Billings (funny name, he thought to himself—or maybe appropriate?)—who seemed to rake in the money. While it was one thing to make a lot of money, even if it was on other people's misery, and to be able to drive a Mercedes and live in an incredible home, it was another to do it dishonestly. He couldn't prove it, but he'd heard snippets of conversation among students that made him suspect that Dr. Billings' unpaid practicum students' clients' insurance companies were charged as if it were Dr. Billings himself who saw them, at his $200.00 an hour rate. He knew the students were unaware because if that turned out to be true, it was insurance fraud. Carl had attempted to talk with Dr. Billings about it, but with no proof, he had done it in a roundabout way. And Dr. Billings had responded in a roundabout way.

Carl was praying about what to do next. If he was responsible to be ethical in his profession, how much more was he ethically and morally responsible as a Christian! The sad thing was, he didn't think Dr. Billings was the only Christian practitioner who was scamming the insurance companies. But that wasn't the reason, he thought, why some of those in the church—people like die-hard Paul in his own church!—didn't accept psychological training as necessary to help people because they didn't even know about the money part.

Then Carl found himself getting irritated again as he thought about some of the preachers he'd tried to educate over the years. Often they were incredibly stubborn and refused to be educated (*like Paul,* he said again to himself). Praise God that Paul was not his pastor! Carl was sure he'd find himself in another office and another church and far away if Paul were the pastor. The guy was a burr under his saddle. Sometimes he thought perhaps Paul irritated David the same way.

Why did Paul have to cause such disunity? It wasn't only irritating; it was distressing to Carl that both of them had the same stated goal of helping others to be more like Christ, but their ideas about how to get there were so different. Paul's was so simplistic. He was always saying good discipleship was the answer. Carl knew that wasn't enough, however, because it didn't get to the root of man's problem. *God,* he prayed silently as he sat in the sunlight, *I know You love unity; I know you love both Paul and me. Please help me not to cause any disunity. Give me the grace to be kind and loving as I teach people how psychology's insights into their lives can help them to love You and their neighbor more.* Just then, a bell rang inside the hospital, reminding him he needed to jump and run. *Uh, oh, I was to call Susan if I had a break. I'll just try later. Maybe she'll forget.*

Susan hadn't forgotten, however. When Carl came dragging in at 10:30 later that night, she was fuming. Immediately Carl started explaining why he was later than he had thought he would be. It had been a matter of life and death!

"It's always a matter of life and death with you. Somebody's always suicidal; somebody's always about to hurt themselves. When is it my turn? When is it the kids' turn? They're in bed, of course," she said, as she continued to fume, "just waiting for you to come in and kiss them goodnight. If you have time, that is, before you have to return calls to your other clients," she added sarcastically.

Not fair! What she's saying isn't fair! God, you know it isn't fair. I'm giving my life to help your children and my wife stays furious at me for not giving her time. Help! His silent prayer didn't seem to go any further than the ceiling. Susan stood there with her hands on her hips just daring him to try and give a satisfactory answer.

"One of my clients..." he began.

"I DON'T WANT TO HEAR IT!" Susan yelled, her brown eyes radiating hostility. "I just don't want to hear it. It's always 'one of your clients' needed you and you had to make an emergency stop or an emergency phone call. I guess the only way you'll call me is if I attempt suicide?" she demanded.

"Don't be ridiculous, Susan. That's childish."

"Don't tell me, 'don't.' Why is it you listen to everyone but me? You're so patient with everyone else; you listen to every word; you validate their feelings. But me you just want to shut up. You sure don't want to listen to my feelings, do you?" Susan was on a tirade.

"Of course I do..." Carl started saying.

"Well, then, you can start right now. I'm mad and hurt and angry and sick and tired of being second or third—no, more like tenth on your list of priorities! I know you're thinking you shouldn't have to listen to this after listening to all your sickies all day, and that if I were a good wife, I'd just support you in your work. But I need some support from you, too!"

While he wanted to be defensive, instead Carl started toward her to touch her short, shiny brown hair, to pull her close, and to give her a warm hug. "I'd like to give you some support, honey," he said, making every effort to stay calm.

"Don't even think you can just give me a hug and everything is okay," Susan retorted, pushing him away. She might be short, but she was strong. "That's not enough. I need some time with you, a long time. I don't mean our usual ten minutes at the end of the day where you collapse onto the sofa and tell me how tired and drained you are and then you watch the news and go to bed. I'd love a hug from you, but right now it feels like a panacea just to shut me up. It wouldn't be real. Without some talking first, well, it just is not going to work, Carl."

Carl was too tired to think. Even though he tried not to be defensive, it was the only feeling he had. All he wanted to do was to return phone calls so he could go to bed, even though he knew Susan was irate. He knew their argument would probably be an all-nighter if they continued.

"Susan, please believe me," Carl said. "I'll call my secretary in the morning and ask her to cancel my appointments for the day, and you and I will talk. We'll do something fun. I promise I'll spend the whole day with you, and then I'll do something with you and the kids when they get out of school tomorrow." He attempted a smile.

Skeptical didn't even touch how Susan felt. "I don't believe you," she said. "I just flat don't believe you. You'll get a call in the middle of the night and stay up talking someone out of suicide, and then you'll think you have to see them tomorrow. Or something. Something will happen, and you won't keep your word."

"I promise, Susan. I can't do any more than that. Please forgive me for hurting you and give me a chance to make it up to you tomorrow."

"You're just doing your psychological games on me so I'll shut up, be nice, and leave you alone, aren't you!" Now she was cool, rigid, and fearful of softening and believing him.

It was hard to get anything by Susan. He wasn't sure of his own motivations, but she picked up on every nuance of them. He asked the Lord to help him be honest so that Susan wouldn't think he was just being psychological.

"Susan," he said softly, "I truly want to hear you. You're right that I have a difficult time saying 'no' to people who are in lots of pain, and I often put them before you. But that doesn't mean that it's right for me to disregard your pain, just because it doesn't look as bad. I am sorry and ask your forgiveness." He hoped he meant it; he wanted to mean it, but he knew it was difficult to change, especially when his beeper went off and a suicidal client needed help.

She softened some. "Alright," she relented, "we'll see what happens tomorrow."

Thank you, Lord. Carl slowly let out his breath and said, "thank you, Susan." Then he risked her rage again. "Do you have anything left from supper?" he asked.

At first, Susan's look said she was going to throw it at

him. Then, "Sure," she said, and walked into the kitchen to reheat his meal. He walked behind her and sat down at the table.

"This has been a really bad day," he told Susan.

Briefly, her eyes told him "frankly, my dear, I don't give a darn," but she said, "Would you like to tell me about what you can?" She understood the necessity of his confidentiality with his patients and wasn't asking for things she knew she shouldn't hear. But so often she felt he was more bonded with his patients than with her because they shared on such an intimate level—especially the women. She'd tried to explain that to Carl, but he didn't seem to understand—as always, he was "only helping others," he would say. He also seemed to understand everyone else but her.

Well, I'm not going to go there again. If I do, I'll just get angrier and angrier. Busy with supper, she didn't say anything else and waited for his reply. When the silence continued, she turned and looked at him. He was asleep at the kitchen table, his head resting in his hand. She sighed, waked him up and helped him to bed.

"I need to return my phone calls," he said, as he crawled under the covers.

"Would you just give it up?" Susan asked. *Well, another lovely day at the Jamison's.*

CHAPTER TEN

David sighed as he thought about the day's happenings. Now that he was home with peace and quiet, he needed to try and make sense of what he'd seen and heard. He knew Nikki wanted to ask questions, but he told her he needed some time by himself.

Earlier that day, instead of going home after leaving the hospital, he had driven by the lake. It was just past Shelby's office. It had occurred to him he could drive by her office and see if her car was there, but it looked as if others were there, also. He'd needed to clear his mind, to pray, and to think what to do, and it would have been great if he could have bounced some ideas off Shelby.

The main thing on his mind had been what he was going to say to the elders—not only about Jack, but about Tim, too. He knew he would have to talk to Tim before he said anything to the elders. And it was getting close to Easter Sunday. *So many things need resurrecting, God, that You better start now.* His life, as well as several others—Jack's, Anita's, Ann's, Tim's, Nikki's—all seemed dead or at least dying, especially in comparison to the vibrant colors of the azaleas all around the lake. They were bursting into life. *God, You bring new life into them every spring. But what do You do about people!* He knew he was demanding that God answer him!

In Whose Steps?

He knew Carl would say he was asking the wrong questions; God certainly cared, and He was there, but people had to learn how to get rid of the junk in their lives before they could truly learn to love God and love others. At least all of them were—and now he was, too—working on their junk! God would surely be pleased about that. When he looked down at his watch, he realized he'd been sitting there daydreaming almost two hours. Okay. He knew he had to go to the elders' meeting and face the music. Well, more of the music, that is.

Once he got to the church, all of the elders, except Jack, of course, were there. David told them about the accusations and they were totally shocked. What else could you be in the face of such news? They had discussed what might be the best course of action. Certainly Jack needed to step down. David had given them the letter of resignation Jack had already written. Some of the elders thought it would be best for Jack to leave the church. David had told them that was not the biblical way to handle it, although he could understand their feelings. Since he was repentant, they were to restore him, not ostracize him.

David had wanted Carl to be there but (of all days!!) he'd said he was too busy to make the meeting. Though Carl was not an elder, he usually tried to attend even though it cost him the profit from a couple of therapy sessions. Since David wanted Carl there, he'd thought of postponing the meeting until he was free. But David knew he had no choice but to deal swiftly with the news about Jack before the rumors about him started in the church. Of course, that didn't even count discussing Tim, but David knew Alyssa and the others would keep quiet about him—and obviously Cindy had kept quiet a long time about him.

David had been surprised at the help Paul had been during the meeting. He thought Paul would come down hard on Jack, but he actually was very compassionate. Tears were in his eyes as he asked how Jack and Anita were doing. Go figure. When David said they needed to restore Jack, Paul was the first to agree. He even took an active part in helping David formulate a plan for restoration. After a time of prayer, all the elders were unanimous in their approval. David thought Jack would feel loved and cared for by their plan. Although it occurred to him that he wasn't sure how he, David, would feel if he'd been accused of molesting Alyssa and people just assumed he was guilty! Nevertheless, they had to act on the accusation.

Paul had asked David to stay after the meeting. He was very tired, but then, he supposed Paul was also. He'd consistently put Paul off every time he'd tried to talk to him in recent months—maybe even years. Although Paul hadn't complained, David knew he must feel badly that he no longer listened to him. When David first came to the church, he had leaned heavily on Paul's wisdom.

However, David wanted to process the meeting with Carl and to go over the plan they'd formulated. Knowing Carl wouldn't be home until late, he told Paul he would talk with him. Actually, it reminded him of when he'd started reading <u>In His Steps</u>, since Paul's concern and what he wanted to discuss was what Jesus would do in any given situation, especially the one regarding the Grimes. Certainly David was interested in what Jesus would do, also, but he didn't think Paul had the whole picture, or that they could agree on what Jesus would do. Then Paul had suggested maybe David didn't have the whole picture and had asked his permission to share some insights he'd received from his biblical counseling friend. Wearily, David had agreed, surprised at what Paul wanted to talk about.

Later, sitting on his bed, still thinking about the day as Nikki slept, David recalled his conversation with Paul:

"Okay, Paul, what is it? Will it take long?"

"No, Pastor, I don't think it will. I won't waste your time; I'll get right into it. What I want to talk about is something called 'false memories' or 'repressed memories.' Do you know what those are?"

"Seems I may have seen something about them on the news or one of those news stories. I guess you'll have to refresh my memory—or it'll probably be false," he added facetiously.

"It's not a laughing matter;" Paul said, "it's as serious as a heart attack. Maybe worse because I think you have a better chance of surviving a heart attack."

David responded defensively. "Whoa, that's a pretty serious statement. I guess you better start at the beginning and explain what you mean and where you got your information."

"The information came from my biblical counseling friend, as well as TV programs and tapes I've listened to, and books I've read."

"So, you're quite a scholar yourself. But why do you keep saying your 'biblical' counseling friend like there's a difference between a 'biblical' counselor and a 'Christian' counselor?"

"People who call themselves 'biblical' counselors see things differently than 'Christian' counselors. They don't believe in integrating psychology with theology, whereas Christian counselors do. Their worldviews are different as to whether psychology is a necessity to counsel well."

"Okay, I see—I guess. Sounds like semantics to me. But, I'm thinking that's another discussion, right?" David was afraid he'd get sidetracked onto another issue, and he'd have to be there all night. "So go ahead about the false memories. And what this has to do with me?"

"What it has to do with you is the fact that you are Jack's, Anita's, and Ann's pastor, and Ann claims she has 'repressed memories.' I don't think Jack and Anita know anything about 'false memories.'"

"I don't either. So what's your point?"

"My point is that Ann's memories may not be actual memories at all. They may be false."

"That's quite an accusation, Paul."

"Not nearly as strong an accusation as the one she has made against her parents, I don't think."

"Looking at it like that, I do see your point. If there's any chance she isn't telling the truth..."

"I didn't say she was lying," Paul interrupted. "Not purposely lying, anyway. I'm saying that many therapists believe that memories recovered during the process of therapy, whether it's through hypnosis, guided imagery, or suggestion, are suspect."

"Suspected of what?"

"Suspected of being false. What I've read is that real memories are memories that have never been forgotten or ones that can be brought up with a minimum of effort. And remember that no one has perfect and total recall of any memory, abused or not."

"What makes you say that?"

"Just take the elders' meeting tonight. Do you think each of us remember it the same way, or that we'd all relate it just the same?"

"Hmm." David thought a moment. "Probably not. So?"

"So people who have been abused and have never forgotten seem hesitant to dwell on their past. They are more likely to want to get on with their lives—like the Holocaust survivors."

"Again, I see your point."

"And the Salem witch trials, also. You know, how those young women accused random people of being witches? And a lot of those accused were hanged just on the girls' testimony? The more attention the girls got, the more symptoms they had, and the more people they accused of abusing them. Their descriptions became more graphic. Likewise, the ones today who recover their memories—or who are still trying to recover them—seem to want to spend time talking about them over and over again—in detail. You see or hear about the agony they are in or have experienced, and it seems obvious it must be true. Those who saw the agony the girls in Salem were in were sure the girls wouldn't just make…"

"Wouldn't just make it up. Right. I've heard that before. So you think Ann may belong to the latter group?"

"Well, sir, I'm not sure. I don't claim to know someone else's heart. I just wanted you to be aware of the possibility that there are some therapists who would question Ann's recovery of her repressed memories."

"Which would mean—well, I guess you're saying then, is that Jack and Anita might be innocent?"

"Yes, sir, I am," Paul said. "You wouldn't want to hang innocent people, would you? You know in our country we're supposed to be innocent till proven guilty, not the other way around. And we're all acting like Jack and Anita are guilty."

"Isn't there any way to prove it one way or the other?"

"I don't think so, unless there is corroborating evidence, like maybe Ann's brother or sister also remember some abuse by their parents, or some of her teachers from grade school remember something odd about Ann's behavior, medical records…"

"That would be hard to do, wouldn't it? I mean, unless the brother and sister remember something?"

"Yes, obviously it would."

"But what about helpless people who are abused and no one is around? No one else was there?"

"I'm not sure what to do about that. I sure don't think that's right, either. And I think we should listen to their stories. But when both people have two totally different stories, how do you know which one to believe? It's one word against another. What would God have us do, Pastor? Scripture does say that we're not to entertain an accusation against an elder without two or three witnesses."

There he goes again, Keeps on bringing Scripture into what I thought was a professional situation. But what David said was, "So what are you suggesting? I have a problem with not believing either one of them, frankly."

"I don't have the answer, Pastor. I just wanted you to know about the controversy so you wouldn't do anything hastily."

"You were in agreement with removing Jack from being an elder..."

"One of the qualifications of an elder is that he must have a good reputation with outsiders. Right now, his reputation is suffering. And, he has resigned anyway. Makes me think more of the man. Eventually, we may need to reinstate him with a public apology."

"You're saying, then, that this may not be true, that Jack has helped us out by giving us his resignation, and that we may eventually owe *Jack* an apology if this proves untrue?"

"We may never really know whether it's true or not, Pastor."

"The plot thickens, doesn't it, Paul?"

"Yes, it does. Okay, well, that's all I wanted to say, except that if you want to talk about this some more, I'll be available, or I can introduce you to my friend who knows a lot more about this than I do."

"I guess you mean your friend the biblical counselor?" David asked.

"Right. I'm headed home now. Thank you for listening to me," Paul said humbly.

"Thank you—I think—for telling me. We'll talk some more."

Paul had left then, and David had come home shortly after that. Now here he sat wondering what to do. He wondered about calling Carl this late but decided against it. Although he was curious about the point Paul made, it wasn't as if it were a burning issue to him. But, he could see that it could make a great deal of difference in what he did about Jack if he took that information into consideration. *Actually, if I were Jack or Anita, it would be a burning issue to me.*

Well, maybe he could call Shelby? Was it too late? Almost in reply to his silent question, the clock chimed 11:00. He did have her home number...and Nikki was asleep...just a quick call, he thought, as he went downstairs to use the phone.

Shelby picked up on the first ring. "Dr. Wilkerson," she said. Evidently she answered the phone the same at home as she did at work—or maybe she just thought that anyone calling at 11:00 at night was a crazy so she'd better identify herself as a doctor! He almost hung up wondering what she'd think about his call.

"Hello, Dr. Wilkerson. This is David Cunningham. I know it's awfully late..."

"It's okay, David. I'm glad to hear from you. And please, call me Shelby."

"Thanks. May I ask you a question? I have an idea you could give an extended answer, but I don't want it to be a long, drawn-out process. I'd like just your initial comments, if you would, and you can give me more information later."

"No problem. Shoot."

"One of my elders is a friend of someone who calls himself a biblical counselor, and he said he got some information from him. Plus the man reads a lot. Okay. You know, I told you about the nineteen-year-old young lady who accused her mom and dad of sexual and ritual abuse? That she'd just recently remembered it in therapy?"

"Right. What does that have to do with your elder-who's-a-friend-of-a-biblical-counselor?"

"He kept me after our meeting tonight to talk about differences between repressed and recovered memories—at least I think that's what he called them—and actual memories. Said people could have false memories. What do you think? Is that possible?"

David detected a note of anger in Shelby's voice as she answered. "This is why child abuse is so rampant, David! People either don't believe or don't want to believe the children who finally get the courage to tell! They don't want to be involved with this tragic issue."

"You'd say there is no such thing, then, as a false memory?"

"I suppose it could possibly happen in rare cases. Just think about it, though. Why would someone make up such horrible stories?"

"That's what Carl said when I first told him I could hardly believe that these folks were involved in abuse. I guess they wouldn't make it up, would they? Ex-except..." he stammered. He was embarrassed to continue.

"Except what?"

"Well, this elder also talked about the Salem Witch Trials and how everyone believed the girls, and how innocent people were hanged because they believed the girls without any concrete evidence..."

"And you're buying the comparison?" she asked, rather icily.

"No, I didn't say that. I just don't know for sure. And I'm thinking I'd rather err on the side of..."

"Err on the side of what, David?" Once more, David could feel an angry edge in her voice. He knew she would want him to err on the side of the accuser if he had to err.

"Uh, on the side of justice." He was pleased with his

answer. Yeah, it was probably a little political, but hey, it wasn't his turf anyway. He was tired of the whole issue.

Evidently she was, too. She changed the subject. "How are you doing since our therapy session? Have you changed your mind about our discussion?"

"No, I think you were right on, well, except for thinking I'm angry, that is."

Her contagious laugh went to his heart. "You'll see that I'm right, David, just wait and see. So did you want to talk about anything else? Are you ready to say good night?"

That caught him off guard. "Well, yeah, I guess so."

"You guess so?"

"No, I know so. It's late and I've kept you too long. Thank you for taking the time to talk with me. I'll see you again in a couple of days, right?"

"I'm not sure when you're scheduled next, but I'll be looking forward to it whenever it is. So now we'll say good night?"

Not sure why he was so reluctant to let her go, David slowly said, "Yes, I guess so."

"You're 'guessing so' again."

"You analyze everything, don't you," David shot back, enjoying the repartee.

"That's what I do best."

"Pretty obvious. You are great at it, too. Okay, this is good night. Next time we get together you can try and convince me that I'm an angry person," he conceded.

"I want you to see it for yourself," she replied. "I don't have any doubt that you will, though. So, it's good night for now. Oh, wait, David!" she exclaimed. "I almost forgot. I want you to know that I'll be at a counseling conference in Pendleton from tomorrow through the weekend."

"Why are you telling me?" David asked, puzzled.

"Well, I just told you that you could call me anytime.

But I won't be readily available the next several days. Just wanted you to know. My receptionist or my service can find me in an emergency, though," Shelby replied. He could hear the smile in her voice.

"Thanks," he said, feeling a slight sinking sensation. He didn't want her to leave town. He liked knowing she was available. "I'm glad you told me," he said to her.

Just then David heard Nikki call faintly from upstairs, "David, is that you? Are you talking with someone?"

"I need to say good night, Shelby, this time for real. I'm being paged. Thanks again for the information." David hung up and went upstairs. "It's me, Nikki. I was on the phone and didn't want to wake you," he said.

"Who were you talking to?" she asked sleepily.

"No one important. Just go back to sleep." Now why didn't he tell her who it was, he wondered. He didn't have anything to cover up. At least not in real life. But he was glad Nikki couldn't know his dreams—or his thoughts.

CHAPTER ELEVEN

David woke with a start. Was it late? It was already light outside. He noticed Nikki was up. It must be late! Jumping out of bed, he called, "Nikki." but there was no answer. She was already dressed and downstairs? And why hadn't she reset the alarm if she got up? He threw on a robe and went downstairs. Sure enough, Nikki was in the kitchen making breakfast.

"Morning, Dad," Alyssa said. "You're usually long gone by now. What's keeping you?"

"I just woke up. I didn't hear the alarm. Nikki, why didn't you wake me up?"

"Figured you were a big boy, and you would get up whenever you wanted to. You go to bed whenever you want to without my telling you it's time for bed," Nikki retorted.

He looked closely at her. Was she kidding? Was she mad?

"Whoa, Dad," Neil said. "I think you're in a bunch of trouble. Mom's mad."

"How can you tell?" David asked.

"Dad, how can you be so dumb? Just look at her. Besides, you can hear it in her voice. Aren't you supposed to be the adult and the expert on relationships?" Neil asked.

"Yeah, Dad. Can't you tell by now when Mom is mad?" Alyssa piped in her two cents' worth.

"I knew she was mad," David said. "I wanted to see if you guys knew it."

"Puh-leez, Dad, what do you take us for? A couple of dorks? Neil and I know when either one of you is mad. It sticks out all over you."

"Alyssa, are you ready to go to school?" Neil asked. Taking Alyssa to school every day was Neil's responsibility. It had been one reason they had allowed him to have a car. It wasn't what he wanted by any means, but at least it was better than nothing. Unless he was going on a date, that is—then he wanted his dad's Volvo. "I think we better get out of here and let Dad and Mom go at it because I don't want to hear it."

"You guys, it's not that bad. We don't fight that much," David said, noticing that Nikki hadn't said another word.

"You may not fight with words—but hey, you're fighting. Why don't you get some counseling or something? Just leave us out of it if you do," Neil added.

"I'm supposed to be the one picking up on attitudes," David retorted. "That's my job, not yours."

"Well then, don't have an attitude and we won't notice it," Alyssa laughed but got suddenly serious as she looked at David to see if she was in trouble for her statement.

"I don't have an attitude."

"Dad, will you stop it? That's like when you tell us we have a bad attitude and we say we don't, and you know we do. Come on, Neil, I'm ready. Let's go—I want out of this deep freeze."

"Alyssa, this is not a deep freeze. Your mom and I are going to have a polite discussion. That is, if she'll talk to me."

"Duh. Now you're getting the picture."

"I think I'm getting the picture that you have a smart mouth. I want you to speak respectfully to me and to your mother."

In Whose Steps?

"Yes, sir, Dad," both Neil and Alyssa said together, as they walked down the hall, picked up their books, and slammed the door behind them.

"Neil, do you think Mom and Dad might ever get a divorce?" Alyssa asked, as she got into his car.

"No way. What makes you say that? All parents fight just like all kids fight," Neil said as he got in the driver's side. He loved driving, even if it meant he had to take Alyssa to school.

"I don't know. This morning it seemed different—worse, colder, somehow—like they really don't like each other very much. I'm scared they'll split up. Most of my friends' parents are divorced."

"Dad would never do that. Just think what the church would say. And he'd never want his precious reputation at church messed up. Nah. They'll stick together if it kills them." Neil was confident of that. He backed out of the driveway and headed for Alyssa's school.

"I sure hope you're right. I don't like how they act together, but I don't want them divorced. Do you?"

"No, of course not. I wish they seemed happier together though. Although I can't imagine what'd it'd be like if they were lovey-dovey."

"Those two?! Smooching and hugging and holding hands?" Alyssa responded. "Fat chance that will ever happen! When I get married, things will be different. Michael loves me a lot, and I know we'll have a different kind of marriage than Mom and Dad do!"

"You're not going to marry Michael."

"And what makes you such an expert? We happen to be in love. Just like you and Christina. I saw you guys making out the other night."

"Shut up!" Neil demanded. "It's none of your business. We're here. Get out of the car."

"I think I made you maaad," Alyssa chanted. "Neil loves Christina and..."

"Get out, Alyssa. Now!"

"I'm going, I'm going. Don't forget to pick me up. And be on time."

Neil sped off without answering. *Sisters. Who needs one?* That was how Dad acted, too, about Mom. Wives. Who needs one? Maybe he wouldn't get married. Seemed like too much hassle.

Which was just what David was thinking. *Wives. Who needs one? Why did life with a woman have to be so exasperating and frustrating? They drive you to drink. I wonder what happened to Shelby's husband. Carl told me she's been married before. I'm sure the divorce wasn't her fault. She's so...*

"What, Nikki?" he said, realizing she'd been talking, but he hadn't been listening.

"Where are you this time? Seems like you've been daydreaming a lot, lately."

"I was thinking about our marriage."

"Revelation. About time. I've been thinking about it a long time. What are you thinking?"

"That neither of us is very happy. That somehow something is missing."

"'Duh', as Alyssa would say. Yeah, David, something is missing—YOU!" Nikki retorted

"You think it's all my fault?"

"Pretty much. It's hard to have a marriage all by yourself. You're hardly ever here and when you are, your head seems somewhere else. I guess you're always thinking about church, or something besides me—us."

"I don't think I'm willing to take all the blame, Nikki," David was getting angry.

"Didn't ask you to. You just asked me if I thought it was all your fault. You asked my opinion. I gave it. Don't ask me for it if you don't want it. I'll be glad to give you more if you want it—although I don't think it will do any good," Nikki said resignedly.

"Please. By all means." Coldly polite. But not angry, he was sure.

"Okay. I've been trying to tell you for quite a while—years, probably—that you aren't emotionally here. I don't know how to say it any better, plainer, or any more often. David, I want you, the you who used to love me." She looked at him pleadingly, her eyes beginning to tear.

Why did he feel she was demanding something of him? Why did he feel he wanted to run? But he said, "Tell me what that looks like, Nikki."

"Mostly, it looks like how you were with me when we were dating—when I felt I was special, number one, with you. I haven't felt that way for years and years."

"I send you flowers; I send you cards on Valentine's Day, your birth..."

"David, you're not getting it. I want you, not your cards and flowers. Those are nice, but I want you. And I want you to want me. Why can't you understand what I'm saying? Does it not compute in a male brain?"

"Nikki, I've gone to a therapy session. I'm trying to understand."

"*You*? You have? Why? Who? Carl? Why didn't you tell me? This is so typical. The wife is the last to know, I guess."

He wished she'd shut up and let him explain. He couldn't understand why she seemed upset. He thought she'd be glad. So *why didn't I tell her I was going?*

"I'm trying to explain if you'll let me. I've been feeling lousy, numb-like, and was wondering if it was some kind of mid-life crisis. I talked to Carl about it and he referred me to a lady therapist, Dr. Wilkerson. I've been once and I have another appointment set up."

"So when were you going to tell me? What did she say? Am I supposed to go with you?"

"There you go peppering me with questions again."

"David, I just want to know. It seems like you keep everything about what you're feeling from me."

He thought about how easily he had been able to talk to Shelby about his feelings. Trying to talk to Nikki about his feelings seemed useless. Even though she said that was what she wanted, she wouldn't listen.

"David, you're gone again, aren't you? Why won't you talk to me?" Nikki pleaded.

"I just realized it's time for me to dress, so I can get to thera...I mean, work on time." He wasn't ready for her to know he had another appointment today. But I want you to know that we'd like you to come to therapy, too, at a later date."

"We?"

"Yes, Dr. Wilkerson and I."

"So you've discussed me."

"Not really. I just said I'd like to have you come, too, so we could talk about our relationship."

"So you told this strange lady you were having problems with me, but you won't talk about it with me."

"Nikki, that's not the way it was. Honest. I want to work on us. That's one of the reasons I'm willing to go to therapy."

She looked at him, scared to death to hope that he was willing to work on their being close again. She wanted to be vulnerable, but it was so hard when he seemed so distant.

"Then thank you for going. And I'll be glad to go whenever you want me to go." Nikki swallowed her pride because inside, she desperately wanted the relationship to be different. Sometimes she felt she'd die from loneliness.

In Whose Steps?

"Would you please tell me what you talk about next time you go?"

"Sure," he said, relieved that she seemed to be backing down. He reached for her to give her a hug. Nikki's heart broke when he reached out to her. When David held her close, she cried as if her heart would break. Gently, he pushed her away. "I've got to go, now, okay?"

"Okay," she replied, reaching for a napkin off the kitchen table so she could blow her nose.

David dressed in a hurry, noticing that he selected his favorite sport coat and tie to wear to therapy. He didn't even realize he'd skipped breakfast. Going back downstairs, he gave Nikki a quick kiss before he left.

"David?"

"Yes?"

"Please just hold me for a minute," Nikki requested.

"Okay." He hugged her as he looked over her shoulder at his watch. He was going to be late. "I really have to go now, Nikki." He gave her a small smile as he left.

She stood in the doorway watching him drive off as tears trickled down her cheeks.

Speeding to his appointment, David thought about the interaction with Nikki. For a long time, he'd thought Nikki didn't care, but evidently she did. He just wasn't sure he cared anymore; he didn't feel like he loved her any longer. He caught his breath. He hadn't allowed himself even to think that! But what good did it do to think about it anyway? You're stuck in a relationship "till death do you part." Certainly he'd never get a divorce; his congregation loved Nikki and would never understand. He knew he'd likely lose his pastorate if he were divorced—especially since Nikki's dad headed up the convention. *Well, it's not that bad, David, you've made it this long...*

One Man's Search for Answers

"*What would Jesus do, David?*" he heard, quite distinctly. *Where in the world did that come from?* As if he didn't know. He was sure the Holy Spirit was reminding him of his marriage vows, and he knew, in no uncertain terms, what was biblical. No way out. *Funny, until I met Shelby—only a few days ago!—I was content just to get by with Nikki. But I feel so alive when I'm with Shelby. So complete. And she doesn't expect or demand anything from me!*

Arriving at her office, he quickly walked into the building. The receptionist told him Dr. Wilkerson was waiting and to go right in. He caught his breath as he went around the corner to her office. Would she be the same? Would he feel the same? She was. He did. Peaceful, relaxing, things he hadn't felt for a long time. It was wonderful. Shelby looked up at him.

"Good morning, David—and didn't we just say 'good night?'"

He seemed flustered when she reminded him of their late night phone call. Somehow it seemed intimate.

"I'm just teasing you. Please, sit down. I've been waiting for you."

"Sorry I'm late..."

"No, no, I wasn't meaning to chastise you. I just mean I'm glad to see you."

Already he was comparing Shelby and Nikki. Nikki would have been mad at him for being late and Shelby was just glad to see him. Maybe that was an unfair comparison, he thought, especially since he was paying Shelby to talk to him. Regardless, he was glad to see her, too.

"Listen, I didn't ask last night when you were leaving for your conference. I wondered if you'd even be here today."

"Right. I should have thought of that last night, just it was late and I forgot I had an appointment with you this morning. I could have told you then—now—that I have a conference. I'm actually not leaving till after lunch."

"I'm glad you were still able to see me this morning," he said, as he sat down on the sofa with a sigh.

"There you go sighing again. I think we have to see what that's about. Would you think I was making it up if I said sighing often relates to anger?"

"No, I guess I'd believe you. It just feels so good, so peaceful, to be here. I enjoy our time together."

"Just you wait until we get going. I hope you'll continue to feel the same. I'm probably going to provoke you to anger at times, David, as you look at your family and come out of denial."

"Shoot," he said, "I'm ready. Provoke me. You said you were going to show me that I was an angry person."

"So you're willing to start talking about your parents? I'm glad. That's a courageous first step, David."

She seemed to affirm everything he did. It was hard to do or say anything wrong. It seemed that with Nikki everything he did or said was wrong. No wonder he enjoyed being here.

"It's nothing," he said modestly. "What do you want to ask me?"

Shelby proceeded to delve into his family history. In less than an hour, she helped him see the patterns of behavior he had picked up from both his mom and his dad—one pattern being anger. Now he was beginning to understand Shelby's reasoning. She helped him make sense of his anger toward Nikki.

"This is what I think happens when you and Nikki are fighting, David," she explained. "You learned from your dad that the way to deal with women is to intimidate them with anger or to withdraw in silence. Silence may not seem like anger, but it often is. If you had been in another profession, you might have hit your wife as your dad did hit your mom. But, since you're a Christian, a pastor, what you do is withdraw emotionally when you're angry, leaving her very alone. I think that you're doing the best you can, though, considering the abusive background you've experienced. You must be pleased with yourself for not acting like your dad and beating up on your wife."

This is great, no matter what I say, Shelby puts a positive spin on it and recognizes I'm really doing the very best I can. Also, he couldn't help but notice she had incredible eye contact! He could see that her big brown eyes were full of compassion for what he'd experienced as a kid. Here he was revealing things about himself that he'd never told *anyone,* but he'd never felt safer or more intimate with anyone. Not even with Carl—or Nikki, for that matter. This woman was incredible! She could see right to his heart, his good points and his bad, but make the most of his good. *I wonder what it'd be like to be with her 24/7!*

Coming back to reality, David responded, "I'm beginning to get it, I think. You're really good at showing me the things I need to see in order to change."

She laughed.

I'm falling in love with that laugh. What am I saying! I just met her! I don't mean that. Do I?

"I told you I'm very good at what I do, didn't I?"

"You did. And I must agree with you. What's next?" he asked. *What is next,* he wondered—or hoped.

"Since your parents live too far away to come in, if you think you're ready, we can ask Nikki to come in next time. Would that be okay?"

He really didn't want to give up his one-on-one time with Shelby but he knew he should work on his and Nikki's relationship.

"Okay. I'll ask her. She's already said she'd be willing to come with me."

"What is she like, David?"

He thought long and hard. "Well, she's pretty; she's excellent at entertaining; she's a good mom, and she's a good wife. When she's not critical, demanding, nagging, and full of expectations, that is," he added angrily.

"I think I detect a note of anger," Shelby ventured.

"I think you do, too," David confessed. "I guess I hadn't realized I'm so angry with her for her unreasonable demands. I can't please her. She's always wanting something from me."

"If she's like most women, whenever they feel abandoned by their spouses, whether physically or emotionally, they do everything they can to pull them back in, or they push them further away so they won't hurt so much because of the distance in the relationship."

"Nikki told me she felt lonely."

"She probably does. When we meet together, I'll try and help you both to verbalize your feelings toward each other—her feeling of abandonment from you and your feelings of anger toward her."

"I'd rather talk about my feelings toward..." David stopped abruptly, realizing he was going to say "toward you."

"Feelings toward..." Shelby waited, typical therapist fashion.

Only she didn't seem like a therapist. She seemed... "Uh, I forgot what I was going to say," he said, realizing she was waiting for an answer.

"Likely story," Shelby countered. "But our time's up today, anyway. So I guess you'll have to tell me next time."

Not likely at all, that I'll tell you in front of Nikki. Not that I should tell you at all. David knew he was starting to sin in his mind because his loyalty was shifting to another woman. *And I was supposed to see her only once! What happened to my resolve?* At the moment, he didn't really care. He was looking forward to seeing Shelby again. At least here was one place he felt good. He had an idea.

"Shelby, can you do me a professional favor? As a pastor, I'd like some more information from you. I would appreciate it if you would expand on the issue we were talking about last night—you know, the thing about false or repressed memories. Is there any chance I could take you to lunch and pick your brain?" *Will she say yes? I'm as nervous as a teenager asking a girl for a date!*

"I think I could do that. Why don't you coordinate it with my receptionist? If she finds me a spot, I'll be glad to do it."

"Would that be a..." he remembered Carl's saying something about 'dual relationship' or something like that, that a therapist couldn't what—fraternize?—with a client. Oh, well, if she said okay, it must be okay. Not his worry.

"I'm beginning to think you don't finish sentences, so I'll have to hang around to see what you say," Shelby laughed.

If you only knew, if you only knew how much I want you to hang around.

Pushing her hair back from her eyes, Shelby reached out to shake his hand. Their touch was electric. He looked into her eyes. *She knows.*

CHAPTER TWELVE

David drove slowly back to his office. Therapy wasn't painful; it was intoxicating. How bad could it feel to talk about anything you thought or felt and have someone who would always accept you unconditionally—always look on the positive side, and then reach out and comfort you? And he even had a personal lunch appointment with Shelby! *Even though I told Shelby and Carl I'd go see my doctor, I'm canceling my appointment with him. Why do I need an antidepressant when I'm feeling on top of the world?* A stop sign reminded his heart that he needed to stop what he was thinking and doing. But David didn't want to think about what was happening in his heart. He would need an antidepressant if he started dwelling on that! Surely it wouldn't hurt if he enjoyed some good feelings for a while.

Linda caught him as he walked into his office. "Dr. Cunningham, you have lots of messages to return. I put them on your desk. Seems half the church has called this morning. Something must be going on?" Usually she knew when things were happening and didn't like to be left out of the loop. The information about the Grimes hadn't been made public, but he was sure Linda and most of the church already knew about it. She waited for him to answer, but he didn't want to talk to her right now.

"We'll catch up later, Linda. Thanks for your help," he said as he dismissed her. The only person he wanted to talk with was Shelby. *Not possible right now. I've got to get my head into catching up.* He had to talk to Jack and decide whether they wanted the church to know formally what was going on or whether they just wanted to tell the church that Jack's resignation was for personal reasons.

David knew he also had to talk with Tim today; that couldn't wait any longer. As he sat down at his desk, he noticed <u>In His Steps</u> was now under his chair. He picked it up and walked over to the bookcase. Well, as Carl had said, it just wasn't practical for today's world. At least not in the same old-fashioned way those people had done it. David thanked God for the psychological insights He had so graciously provided him through Shelby and both him and his church through Carl. At first, he had to admit, Carl's telling him that when the Bible said you must "love your neighbor as yourself" meant that you have to love yourself before you can love your neighbor seemed like heresy. Now it was making more sense all the time.

It takes a heart full of love for yourself since who you are before God overflows into love for others! Then and only then can you walk in His steps. David forcefully replaced the book in his bookshelves. Going back to his desk, he called Tim and asked him to come down to his office. Within minutes, Tim was knocking on his door, even though the door was open.

"Come on in," David said, "and shut the door behind you."

Tim glanced at David, wondering what this was about, and if it maybe had something to do with the 12-step group they'd attended a few nights previously.

David didn't hesitate in questioning Tim. "I've heard some distressing news about you since I saw you earlier in the week. I won't beat around the bush. It seems that some people think you might have hit Cindy."

It was obvious Tim was trying not to show any defensiveness. "Pastor, that's preposterous! I'd never hurt Cindy on purpose. You know I wouldn't. Who would say such a thing?"

David sighed. If it had been someone other than Alyssa, he might have dropped the matter. But he knew she'd be on his case about it, and even though she acted weird sometimes, he didn't think she'd lie about something like this. Besides, all the other girls also heard what sounded like a slap.

"I have it from a good source. I know this is uncomfortable for you and it is for me, too. But someone said they heard you hit Cindy."

"I'll bet it was the night of the slumber party. Am I right?"

"Why do you think that?" David didn't want him to know that it was Alyssa who told him.

"The girls were watching a video in the living room, and Cindy and I had gone to the bedroom to talk for a few minutes before I left for group where I saw you. We were just standing there talking, and she moved and slipped and fell and hurt her face." Tim wasn't making eye contact.

"I haven't been at the group very long," David ventured, "but isn't there a step about taking a 'fearless moral inventory' or something like that?" As soon as the words were out of David's mouth, he had a twinge of conscience thinking about what would happen if he took a 'fearless moral inventory' himself. "Not a pretty picture," Alyssa would say, he thought guiltily.

Tim then looked him in the eye. "Yes, sir, there is. And I'm not doing it," he admitted. I did kind of accidentally hit Cindy, and I'm sorry, and I told her I'm sorry, and that it wouldn't happen again. But I didn't think the girls heard it over the TV. I guess they did, though, right? They have to be the ones who told?"

"Does it matter? If you did it, you did it. I want to know what you're going to do about it, now."

"It matters to me what the youth think of me and what I need to do for them."

"That is definitely something we have to think about. You've done a wonderful job with our youth and I want you to stay. But we are going to have to do something about your relationship with Cindy. You just can't hit her, Tim."

"I know. It's just she just makes me so mad, sometimes, and provokes me so much, and I lose my temper. Most of the time I can control it, but at times, Cindy can be so obnoxious. I hate that I ever hit her, though—definitely not the Christian thing to do."

"Right. So how long has this been going on?"

"Uh, ever since we were married, I'm afraid," Tim acknowledged sheepishly. "This group's been great for me. I can't imagine what I would have done if I hadn't been a part of it. It gives me support and encouragement to do what's right. When I'm under a lot of stress, though, it doesn't take much to provoke me. Cindy should have known I was under a lot of stress and left me alone."

"I think you might need to get some counseling, Tim. I know Carl would see you. How about making an appointment with him for you and Cindy?"

Tim could see that it wasn't really an option. That if he wanted to keep his job, he better do the counseling. *Oh, well, it won't hurt.* "Ok, Pastor, I'll go by his office right now and see if I can make an appointment. Are you going to tell anyone else?"

"Not right now. But if you don't keep your counseling appointments—and I'll ask Carl if you do—I may change my mind." David knew he needed to require Tim to have some accountability with him.

"Would you meet with me, you know, disciple me?" Tim asked.

In Whose Steps?

"Me? Oh, no, no, I'm too busy. Thanks for asking, though. This is the kind of thing best left to the experts, I'm afraid. I'm not qualified to deal with spousal abuse." *I can't even deal with a spouse, much less spousal abuse.*

"So you'll get counseling?" David asked again.

"Yes, sir, like I said, I'll check with Carl now. Thank you, sir." Tim was obviously scared about his job.

David was sure he'd follow through on the counseling. He wondered if he should call Cindy and see how she was. Well, if they got counseling, they should be okay. One down, he thought as Tim left. Now for the Grimes—although he sure didn't want to deal with them again today. He was committed, however, with getting through his calls. He dialed and heard the phone ring; a man's voice answered.

"Jack, is that you? This is Pastor David. How are you this morning?"

"Okay, I guess, all things considered." Jack sounded terrible, as if he'd been up all night. *Probably had.*

"I wanted to check on you to see if there is anything I can do for you," David said, "anything at all."

"Carl's going to talk to you about it, but he said you're supposed to go see Ann at the hospital. Pastor, please talk to her. Please tell her we love her but that what she says just isn't true," Jack pleaded. "Tell her I don't know how much longer her mother and I can make it if she keeps this up. It's killing us." He sounded pathetic. David knew it would be agonizing to be in their dilemma.

"I don't know anything about seeing Ann," David answered.

"Like I said, Carl's supposed to talk to you about it. After he tells you about it, will you call us back?"

David could hear the desperation in his voice. "I don't know what we're going to do. Anita's taking this really hard, Pastor. Really hard."

"Sorry to hear that. I'll be glad to get back with you later, Jack. Take care of yourself, man. God bless."

"Thanks. Be talking to you later." Jack hung up.

Two down. Except now he had to talk to Carl. As usual, he wondered where the heck he was this morning.

"David."

On cue, as usual. "Good morning, Carl. What's going on?"

"I might ask you the same question. I heard what happened last night in the elders' meeting—that Jack resigned and you guys accepted his resignation, and that you suggested a plan to restore him."

"Don't you think that's a good idea? That it's biblical?"

"Probably is. But I'm not sure how Ann is going to respond to that action," Carl said warily.

"Why? What do you mean? Don't you think she'll be glad to have her dad resign?"

"Yes, that part I do. But she'll think you shouldn't offer him restitution if he hasn't repented and asked her forgiveness."

"That makes sense. Well, from her standpoint. From Jack's, however, that means the only way he can get restored to fellowship is for him to admit he hurt Ann and to ask her forgiveness."

"Exactly."

"But what if he didn't do it, Carl?"

"What do you mean, 'what if he didn't do it!'" Carl demanded.

"Just that. I've gotten some information recently on 'false memory syndrome'..."

"Aren't we the researcher and expert, all of a sudden."

"Look, I'm not saying I found the truth. I'm saying that I've heard that sometimes either or both the person abused and the abuser can be deceived. I don't know which person is telling the truth. But I don't want to condemn an innocent man—and woman."

"What about an innocent girl who has been beaten, scarred, mutilated, and molested," Carl said quietly, almost ominously. "What about her? Who's going to protect the innocent if we don't believe them? Proverbs 31 says we are to 'speak up for those who cannot speak for themselves.'"

"I'm not trying to have an argument with you or dispute your word..."

"Oh, really?" Carl was feeling more and more defensive for Ann's sake. She'd been in his support group for a couple of years, and he believed he knew her well.

"Really, Carl. We're friends, remember? I only wanted to ask you what you thought about it—your opinion as to whether or not there could be such a thing as 'false memory syndrome.' I asked Shelby already."

"I think I know what she said. And I agree. Why would anyone make up..."

"That's what you guys keep saying—why would anyone make up such horrible stories; why would anyone go through all this trauma and pain just to accuse someone unjustly?"

"And your answer is..." Carl asked impatiently.

"My answer is I just don't know. And even though you therapists have all the training, I guess I don't see how you can know for sure, either. Did I hear you say something about truth serum?"

"Yes. We do Sodium Amytal interviews with patients to try and get at the truth."

"And that's 100% correct? That the person isn't lying, I mean?"

"No, it's not 100% correct," Carl said. "But it's a useful tool."

"Again, you're saying you can't know for sure," David summarized.

"For sure?" Carl said sarcastically. "Well, why don't you come and visit my therapy group, David? Why don't you come listen to these girls and women who have recovered their memories of the horrific abuse they endured for years? The terror they lived in never knowing when their perpetrator was going to do it again. The silence they were forced into for fear they would be killed. The constant panic and alarm as they vigilantly scanned every person they came into contact with, wondering if it was someone else who would abuse them. The upheaval it caused in their young lives and continues to cause as those memories permeate their very existence—how many of their relationships with men have been ruined. Why some of them have had to divorce their impatient, unkind, and rigid husbands who didn't believe them. These men were cruel and unfeeling," Carl continued, looking at David as if he, too, were a perpetrator, "and unwilling to say 'no' to their own selfish demands for sex while their wives were trying their dead-level best to work through the heartless, savage, and inhuman— sometimes literally—details of their abuse. Why don't you come listen just once to these heartrending stories and then let's hear what you say about knowing for sure!"

David was taken aback by Carl's passionate defense. "Okay, okay," he said, holding up his hands in surrender. "I think you can calm down now. I hear you. I vote 'guilty' for the perpetrators. And maybe I will come visit a group. Maybe that will help me decide."

"I'll have to get permission from the women, first."

"Even though the group meets in our church, and I'm the pastor?"

"Right. That is immaterial, really. I can't betray any confidences. And you will also have to keep everything you hear confidential. Even if you heard something about an adulterous affair, you'd have to keep quiet. Are you willing to go by those rules?"

In Whose Steps?

"I guess so." David thought about Shelby telling him he "guessed so" a lot. He was beginning to wonder if he was wishy-washy.

"No guessing so. You must."

"Even if I found out a woman in the church was having an affair with a man in the church? I couldn't talk to her about it? Or him?" David asked.

"Nope. You have to keep the confidence, just like I do. The only time I can break a confidence—which I tell my clients up front—is if they are in danger of harming themselves or others—you know, if it's life threatening."

"Kinda does away with the Matthew 18 process of church discipline, doesn't it?"

"What do you mean?"

"That if you are offended with your brother you go to him but if he doesn't hear you—never mind." He wondered why he'd brought that up, anyway. It's not like they had ever done church discipline based on Matthew 18. "Obviously it doesn't matter anyway when it comes to keeping a confidence. Yes, I'll keep their confidences, and I would like to visit their group." He thought it would be good to see what was actually going on in the church support and self-help groups. *Maybe I should have done it a long time ago.*

"Will you be available tonight?" Carl asked.

"Probably so." He didn't really want to go home and argue with Nikki. His sermon preparation wasn't going too well, and he knew he should spend some time on it, but at this point he was at a loss what to teach, anyway.

"I can ask them at the beginning of group how they feel about your participation—well, observation, actually, I don't see any reason for you to participate—and if they are okay with it, and you're still here, I can invite you in."

"Sounds good to me. You can call me on my cell phone, and I'll come right down. Thanks."

"Thank you. It will feel good to me for you to understand on a deeper level the amount of pain these women are in. I think it will help you be more understanding and more confident of Ann's story, too."

David wasn't sure he wanted to be more confident of Ann's story, but he knew he needed to be more confident one way or the other, but he didn't say anything else.

"Well, I'll see you later, then, because I've got a client coming in five minutes," Carl said as he got up to leave David's office. "Oh, I almost forgot. I'd like you to go by and see Ann. Dr. Billings wrote orders that you could go at your convenience."

"Yeah, the Grimes told me you wanted me to do that. I'll try and get by to see her this afternoon, and I'll go see her parents as well."

"Thanks. See you later."

David picked up his Bible and left for the hospital. He told Linda he'd be at the psych hospital visiting a patient. She was dying to know who he was seeing. He didn't tell her.

CHAPTER THIRTEEN

"Mrs. Cunningham?" Nikki heard as she answered the phone. "Yes, this is she," she replied, wondering what would be the quickest way possible to get rid of this salesperson.

"This is Dr. Wilkerson's office. We'd like to confirm an appointment with you and Dr. Cunningham for next Tuesday at 10:00 a.m. Will that work for you?"

"Dr. Wilkerson? What doctor is this?" Nikki asked but suddenly realized who it was. This was the shrink that David said he was going to and that he was going to make an appointment for the two of them to see.

"Never mind. I remember. Sure, that will be fine," she confirmed as she hung up. She had mixed feelings about going. One, she was scared to hope that things could change and be different, and she tried to act as if it didn't matter. Secondly, there was a stirring deep down in her heart that God might be beginning to work on her and David and their marriage. *Thank you, Lord,* she breathed. Her step was a little lighter as she went about her day's chores. Once she even started humming.

When the phone rang later, she was surprised to hear from Susan. "I thought you were gone to a seminar and wouldn't be home until the end of the week," Nikki said, happy to hear from one of her best friends.

"I decided the kids needed me worse than the seminar did," Susan responded, "so I stayed home. They had a school program I needed to go to this week."

"I'll bet Carl's glad. I know he doesn't like cooking for himself and having to take care of the kids," Nikki laughed. "Besides, it takes away from his busy schedule when he has to take care of the kids." Nikki and Susan knew each other well and had talked many times about their relationships with their husbands.

"Easy for you to joke about, Nikki. I do like to be gone every once in a while. Then Carl misses me a little bit. Notice I said a 'little' bit. Most of the time he doesn't even notice whether I'm here or not as long as he has a clean house, clean clothes, and food to eat—and sex occasionally," she added.

"Guess that's the story of our lives, isn't it? Our guys are always out ministering to others and just don't have much left to give us—or the kids. Been going on for years and we just keep having these same old conversations. Well, not quite," she added. "Would you believe David and I are actually going to see a shrink—I mean, a ther..."

"It's okay," Susan laughed. "I'm used to Carl's being called a shrink. He's been called a lot worse. Some of it by me! But, anyway, you were saying..."

"David made an appointment for us to see a marriage counselor. Someone named Dr. Wilkerson. Do you know who she is?"

"Not personally. But I've heard Carl talk about her. He thinks very highly of her. Says she's one of the best. Very godly, too. I think she's divorced, though. Does that bother you?"

"Hmmm. I hadn't thought about it. It does seem rather strange to go to someone who's divorced to work on marital issues, doesn't it? But, we don't know the reason. Maybe her husband was unfaithful to her, or beat her up. I imagine she must have had a biblical reason to get a divorce."

"Probably, or Carl wouldn't have referred you and David to her. Nikki, that's great, really. I wish Carl would take us to see someone! But he's a therapist, of course, so he already has all the answers," she said, part-facetiously and part-sarcastically.

"Are you still mad at Carl?"

"Only because he's never here. Same old story. I hardly know him well enough to get mad at him! It's hard to argue with him, though, when he thinks he's doing God's work and that he's responsible for all his clients. I think he feels more responsible for them than for his family!"

"Same with David. It's hard to imagine us ever being close again. Maybe this is just part of marriage—always looking back to the days when we were dating and when we felt really special, like we were number one in their lives."

"Actually, I think we were—then! But those are just faint memories now. I have no hope I'll ever be number one again. I sometimes wonder if it's just a dream that I ever was." She heard a deep sigh from Nikki. "Nikki, are you about to cry?"

"I feel like it. I'd like to. But I know it won't do any good. Anyway, I'll let you know how things turn out tomorrow. Want me to suggest to David that he suggest to Carl that you guys need to talk with someone too?"

"Please. Although I've said it enough myself. But, maybe he'll hear it coming from David. Actually I think he'll be rather mad if he knows I'm talking about him. I suggested to him that he was a workaholic, and he got pretty irritated, so I shut up. It's hard to win an argument with him. Oh, well. On that hopeful note, I guess I'll let you go."

"Okay. I need to get busy, too. I will talk to David, though, I promise."

"I know you will. Talk with you later." Nikki and Susan hung up. Both went to their respective bedrooms and cried over lost dreams—over what they thought marriage would be. Their Price Charmings hadn't turned out to be too charming, at least not after they said "I do."

Meanwhile, totally oblivious to Nikki's heartache, David was thinking of his own. He kept dwelling on his feelings about how wonderful he felt when he was around Shelby. Once again, he tried to push aside those thoughts about her so he could concentrate on being a pastor. He was dreading the hospital visit to Ann and had no idea what he'd say to her. As he drove into the parking lot, he wondered how long he'd have to stay before he could leave gracefully. Not very long at all, it turned out. Checking at the front desk, the receptionist told him someone from the unit would be up to get him shortly.

He paced the floor, realizing again how uncomfortable he felt in this place. The mental health tech unlocked the door and escorted him back to the unit. At the nurses' station, he was told to go into the same room he'd been in before for family therapy with Ann and that Ann would join him shortly. It felt very strange to be here without Carl. He'd visited Jack in the hospital, but they'd always gone out onto the patio. That didn't feel so confining—so locked up, which is what he was. But even more worrisome at the moment was what about this MPD/DID—or whatever acronym it was—stuff with Ann? Would Ann be Ann?

"Hello, Dr. Cunningham," Ann said as she walked into the room.

David breathed a sigh of relief. If he could just talk with Ann a few minutes and leave before she got weird...

"Uh, how are you, Ann?" he asked tentatively.

"Just great," she responded with sarcasm. "Isn't that pretty obvious? That's why I'm on a locked unit for crazies."

In Whose Steps?

"You look as though you feel better than you did earlier in the week," he ventured, trying to make harmless conversation.

"No, I don't," she contradicted. "This looks better?" She thrust her arm in his face.

He saw several black stitches around an angry red cut. *What on earth had happened to her?*

"And why don't you quit beating around the bush. You want to know how I'm doing with God, don't you?"

"Well, uh, I guess so," he responded. He hadn't intended to get into anything deep.

"Not good. I don't have much of a relationship with Him right now. I'm just now coming to grips with what He allowed me to go through when I was a child. If He was a loving, caring God like He says He is, He wouldn't have allowed me to experience the abuse my dad and mom heaped on me!" she said angrily. "I'm actually angry at God for not protecting me!"

"Do you think it's okay to be angry at God?" David ventured another question. As he realized what he'd asked, David was aware that he was angry with Him too. Be interesting to see what Ann would say.

"I know good and well you'll say it's not okay. You'll say we should never be angry at God. Carl says it's natural to feel that way, though, when someone has been through as much as I have."

"I can imagine that's true," David said. He didn't want to get into the theology or psychology of anger at God. Looking for safer ground, he asked Ann, "Could you tell me how you know your memories are true? That they aren't false?" Maybe she could give him some help on this troubling issue!

Instantly Ann blinked and turned on him. "Who do you think you are? What makes you think you can question our memories, you imbecile," a throaty voice growled at him. "You don't even know what you're talking about. Our memories are real, alright. And you can go to you-know-where if you don't believe it!" she said as she lunged at him. Catching him off guard, they both fell into the floor.

Hearing the racket, the mental health tech who was just outside the door came running in. He grabbed Ann by the wrists and started talking calmly to her. Helping her up, he continued to call Ann's name. She looked blankly at him for several minutes. Finally, she made eye contact with the tech and said, "We're here. Quit saying 'Ann,' will you? We hear you."

"I think that's all for today, Dr. Cunningham," he said, as he led Ann from the room.

"I want to talk to my pastor some more," Ann—or someone—screamed. "You can't keep me from it!"

"You can check with the nurses to see if you can stay longer if you want," the tech said in an aside to David.

"He'll have to talk with the nurses to get permission," he told Ann, in a pacifying voice. She glared at the nurses behind the desk. "You better let him stay, or I'll cut myself again," she threatened. "Or maybe I'll hang myself."

"Now, Ann, you know you don't want to do that. You just got stitches last night. Let's sit down and talk about it," the tech continued trying to pacify Ann.

"Shut up! You don't know who Ann is." At that, she curled up on the sofa in the day room and started sucking her finger. "I want my mommy," she cried.

David's heart was racing. Some safe ground he'd picked. No one ever talked to him like that! No one ever attacked him like that! What kind of place was this? What kind of person was this? Just let me out of this crazy place, he thought. Now! One of the nurses walked him to the door and unlocked it. David felt better just knowing it was unlocked. She smiled at him.

"A little tough on you, Pastor?" she asked.

"I'm just not used to abusive language or being attacked physically," he said. He was still feeling anxious. Even though Ann—or whoever she was—was a small lady, he hated to admit he'd been scared to death of her.

"You get used to it. All in a day's work for us. I know Ann enjoyed your visit and would like you to come back. See you again?"

"Sure," David said as he walked quickly down the hall toward the reception area. *Over my dead body.* No wonder mental health experts need to deal with these kinds of cases! Even though it had been a short visit, he felt he'd been there for hours. He hated to visit the Grimes but knew they were next on his list. The sooner he got the visit over with, the sooner he could go back to church. Not that he had the faintest idea why he wanted to go back to the church other than not to have to deal with such severe trauma. *Just give me a plain old death and funeral any day.*

When he pulled into the driveway, he noticed there were several cars in front of the Grimes. Quickly he walked toward front door. Jack met him before he got to the porch.

"What's going on?" David asked, noticing Jack's face was ashen. Seemed to stay that way recently.

"It's Anita," he said.

"What's wrong with Anita?"

"Ever since family therapy with Ann the other day, she's been feeling bad physically. Her heart was feeling funny so we asked a friend who's a nurse to come over and look at her. She said Anita was having heart palpitations. She said it's probably just stress but that we should take her to the ER and get it checked out. So we're just about to leave." Anita came to the door. The nurse friend was holding her arm.

"I'm okay," Anita insisted. "I can walk to the car myself!" She was afraid her physical symptoms would make others think she wasn't depending on God. When she saw David, she straightened up even more. "Oh, hi, Pastor. Isn't this silly?" she asked. "They're making too big a fuss over me."

"Best you get yourself checked out, Anita," David responded. "I'll come with you guys to the hospital." He dreaded going to another hospital, even if it wasn't a psych hospital.

"No, we're fine. And Ruth's going with us. She works in the ER, anyway. Please. You can check with us later."

"Well, okay," David said. "I'll be sure and call back. By the way, I just saw Ann."

Jack and Anita stopped cold in their tracks and looked at David, waiting. He didn't know what to say and wished he hadn't told them he'd seen her since he didn't have anything positive to say about the visit. They didn't need that news right now. "She was feeling better and hopes things work out with the family," he lied. He didn't want to make Anita's heart worse!

They looked relieved. "Thanks for going by, Pastor. We really appreciate your care and interest," Jack said. "We'll talk to you later."

David helped them to the car and watched them drive off. He prayed that both Anita and Ann would get well. And, knowing what was in his heart, he wondered if God was even listening to his prayers. Slowly, he got in his car and headed back to the church. *What would—what could—the rest of the day bring?*

CHAPTER FOURTEEN

Once again, Carl was waiting for him at his office.

"Don't you have therapy sessions or something else to do other than bother me?" David asked half-jokingly. They went into his office out of Linda's earshot.

Carl wasn't in a joking mood. "I heard you saw Ann. That it didn't turn out too well."

"Boy, does word get around quickly."

"One of the nurses left me a message. Said Ann reported that you'd asked if her memories were false!"

"I thought maybe she could help me. Could shed some light on the problem," David said, beginning to feel defensive.

"I thought we ended that discussion this morning—at least for the time being. I can't believe you did that to Ann! That you questioned her beliefs!"

"Carl, I didn't. I just asked her how she knew they were real, that's all."

"That's enough! To her, that's the same as telling her they aren't. That's the same as being another perpetrator to her!"

"I'm sorry. Believe me, you have no idea how sorry I am. Do you know that she actually attacked me?"

"In her condition, I can't say as I blame her."

"Carl!"

"You just don't understand how fragile these victims are, David. I was hoping—praying—you were beginning to understand!"

"I thought I was. But I concede. You are the expert. I'm sorry I meddled into your business. I'm a believer."

Carl seemed somewhat mollified. "I've had phone calls from two of the ladies in tonight's group," he said, "and I asked both of them how they'd feel about your being there. They said it would be fine. I think the rest of them will be okay with it too. So, you'll probably understand—believe—a lot more after group tonight. They are being very vulnerable to allow you to come. Don't do the false memory thing. I'm not kidding."

"I'm chastised, okay? I know I'll learn a lot tonight, and I appreciate your willingness to educate me."

"Sure. You stick to theology—to spiritual issues—with my clients, and let me do the therapy."

"No problem. I never meant to do therapy in the first place."

"I'll concede one point. You must have done something right, for her to trust you like that. It's the second time you've been around her, and she allowed you to see several of her alters. Maybe you're good for her in some spiritual ways, but not in therapy ways, David. Thanks for seeing her," Carl added as he started out of the office.

"Sure. Anytime," David lied. Again.

After Carl left, David sat down at his desk to begin working on his sermon notes. The Bible seemed awfully dry as he attempted to work it into his message. Strange how at one time it had seemed so alive and vibrant. *It seems to be going downhill with me.*

Linda buzzed him. "Nikki's on line three," she said on the intercom.

David picked up. "Hey, Nick, what's going on?" he asked her.

"What's going on is that we have a therapy appointment with your doctor on Tuesday at 10:00. Did you know?"

"I wasn't sure of the time. I told the receptionist to set it up with you and that I'd come whatever time was okay with you and Dr. Wilkerson's schedule."

"You've very accommodating with her schedule. When I ask you to do something, you say you have to check your schedule first."

"Nikki, please. I said to check your schedule, too. And that I'd accommodate *both* your schedules." *Again, no pleasing her. Couldn't win, no matter what.* "So that's the time we're going?" he asked.

"Yes." She was hesitant, but plunged on into her fears. "David, I don't know what to expect. I want things to be better for us, but I don't know where to start."

"Just let Dr. Wilkerson guide our time, Nikki. She's very good at what she does."

"And I'm not."

Sigh. "That's not what I said." *Why did she have to take everything negatively!*

"Do you think I do anything well?"

"You know that I do."

"Like what?"

"I think it would be good to talk about it in session with Shel—Dr. Wilkerson, Nikki. Seems we can't talk about anything without getting into an argument. She can help us say things in a more positive way."

"I think telling me what I do well would be pretty positive."

"I'd just rather wait, Nikki, okay?"

"I get the message. Okay, I'll wait. Put the time down on your schedule. Do you want to tell Linda to put it down or should I?"

"I'll take care of it." He had no intention of allowing Linda to know where he was going. He had no intention of the church's knowing he was in therapy. Even though he'd been the biggest advocate of Carl's coming to the church and of self-help and support groups starting in the church, it seemed different when he was the one in counseling.

"Alright. One other thing. I talked with Susan today. She said she doesn't see much of Carl and that she misses him because he's never home. She wondered if you might be willing to say something to him about their going to therapy too, or that you might even talk to him about spending more time at home. You know, the way you do," she added sarcastically.

David had thought Susan was on Carl's case just like Nikki was on his. Even if she weren't, the way things were going with him and Carl right now, he didn't think he wanted to risk any more of Carl's displeasure. "I'll think about it and see if I get the opportunity."

"Is that a yes?"

"That's an 'I'll think about it and see if I get the opportunity,'" he repeated slowly. He was not going to be pressured or manipulated into doing something he didn't want to do. Evidently Nikki heard his displeasure at her insistence.

"I guess I'll see you at supper, then."

"No, I don't think so. I'm going to one of Carl's groups tonight around 7:00, and there wouldn't be time enough for me to go home and come back, so I'll just pick something up around here. If you've fixed something, I know the kids will love it. Thanks anyway."

"Would you like me to come meet you for supper?" Nikki asked, fearful of more rejection, but hoping he'd want to spend some time with her.

"No, it's too much trouble for you and too far for you to come. I know you want to be there to fix the kids' supper. Thanks anyway," he said again.

"No problem," Nikki said, thinking to herself it was useless to even go to counseling. David wasn't interested in her. She hung up without a goodbye.

In Whose Steps?

Still holding the phone in his hand, David considered calling Shelby. He thought he could give her some information—but no, he was honest enough with himself to admit, he just wanted to talk with her. It had nothing to do with more information. He put the phone down. But he couldn't seem to put down the vision he had of her in his imagination: contagious laugh, sparkling, compassionate eyes, leaning forward to catch his every word, reaching out to touch his hand. *Don't go there, David.* He made himself concentrate on his sermon.

Surprisingly, he made it through the rest of the afternoon with no interruptions. Linda left at 5:30, and David ordered a pizza. He had a TV in his office, and he watched the evening news as he munched on the pizza. *This is so peaceful, much more so than if I went home to eat.* Around 6:30, he made sure his cellular phone was turned on so Carl could call him about group. Sure enough, around 7:15, the phone rang.

"David. The group said they would be willing for you to come," Carl said without preamble, "so come on downstairs."

"I'll be right there," David said, already headed out the door with the phone in his hand. He was at the bottom of the stairs before he had his phone turned off. He put it in his pocket as he knocked on the door where Carl's group met.

"Come on in," Carl said.

David didn't know what to expect. He walked into a roomful of ladies, and without actually counting he guessed there were about eight in all. Probably ages around seventeen to fifty or so—and they all seemed so intense. Actually, they all seemed to be intensely staring at him. A couple of them he recognized as members of his church. He didn't know if he should act like he knew them or to act like he'd never seen them before in his life—that confidentiality thing.

Carl pointed to an empty chair in the circle of ladies. "Please sit down."

David wondered why he felt he was going to his execution as he sat down. *Hey, this doesn't have to do with me. These ladies are just scared to death of men—and I am one.* "I appreciate your letting me be here tonight so I can learn more about abuse victims," David started.

They all continued to stare at him. He shut up. He was afraid to say anything more without Carl's permission. Group started.

As David thought about the group later, he could barely process what he'd seen. It'd been like something from the twilight zone. It was like the time with Ann a hundred times over because some of them were multiples too. Some of them Carl had called "borderline," whatever that was. Seemed like they were all over the border, alright, David thought, but he wasn't trying to be funny. Carl had started the meeting with prayer and asked Jesus to be with everyone there. He said that if any participants went back to childhood tonight and re-experienced their trauma, that Jesus would go with them this time and keep them safe. He then asked that the 'little ones' (whatever that meant) would see Jesus crying as He watched what happened and know that He was sorry because He loved and cared about them. They were to remember they did not go through the abuse alone because even though they may have thought Jesus wasn't with them, he was. *What is that about? I'm not about to ask now; I'll check with Carl later.*

Later in the evening, a lady started writhing in the floor while the others gathered around her and encouraged her to let go. *Let go of what?* They'd said for her to be honest and allow the evil to speak. *Evil's being spoken alright! This afternoon with Ann showed me that!* Yet the visit with Ann paled in comparison to what he continued to hear. The ladies' vocabulary had been incredibly obscene! Carl had explained during the group that they took on their perpetrators' language, and that they experienced *(was the word he'd used "introjected"?)* the same amount of rage, hatred, and hostility as their perpetrators had when they were abusing them. The stories they were re-living were vile, foul, and loathsome—David couldn't think of enough bad words to describe what he heard.

And Carl heard this kind of thing every day—several times a day? *Incredible, it's absolutely incredible to think things like this exist.* He was beginning to understand what the ladies must feel like since he felt dirty just from listening—how dirty they must feel from actually experiencing the abuse! When group was almost over, the ladies had gotten more vulnerable, deciding that they'd risk David's trustworthiness. Then he'd found out that one of the ladies in the group, a member of his church, was having an affair—but it was with another lady in the group who was "safe," unlike her "unsafe" husband. Then he found out another young lady was having an affair with a man in his choir—someone he'd thought he knew well!

Thinking back, he wished they hadn't trusted him so much, because many of the things he'd learned he knew he needed to individually confront as a pastor. Of course, he was unable to do so because of confidentiality. He thought about their need for confession. He wondered about their own reactions to the abuse. Was there any responsibility for them to be godly, or were they justified in not forgiving such abominable and revolting behaviors? Did forgiveness apply in their situations? Was there no place for Scripture? He guessed not; Carl told him assuredly not at this time, but that it would happen in due time as God dealt with each of them where they were. *Besides, you don't have any right to confront any of them when you consider what you're thinking about!*

It was impossible to experience what he'd just witnessed and think that it was from false memories. As the ladies' repressed memories had continued to surface, they screamed, cried, yelled, or withdrew in stony silence. It was obvious they were suffering profoundly, and like Carl had said, no one would do something like that on purpose. David wondered if he'd have bad dreams. No wonder all those poor ladies had such a hard time sleeping. Their waking hours were nightmares—much less their sleeping hours. He wondered how Carl was able to sleep every night after observing all the trauma. It was obvious he cared and that it hurt him for his clients to be in such deep pain.

David had had a new respect for Carl when the evening was over. Never again would he think he was competent to find out about true versus false memories; he was exceedingly happy to allow Carl to handle all of those kinds of problems! David sure didn't know what to do with them—just like he didn't know what to do with his own problems, especially the ones with Nikki. Actually, he had mixed feelings about their marriage therapy meeting with Shelby. Maybe she'd work some magic so he would be in love with Nikki again. After all, that was what he wanted, wasn't it?

CHAPTER FIFTEEN

He decided to go by Jack's and Anita's house on the way to work the next day. It was early, but he knew they were early risers. Anita actually answered the door on the first knock. David realized he should have called before he came.

But Anita was thrilled to see him. "Pastor, it's wonderful to see you," she said. She looked much better than the last time he'd seen her! "Thank you for coming by. As you can see, I'm feeling a lot better."

"Well, you are certainly looking better. I know it's been an extremely painful time for you. I'm glad to see you up and around. Did you get a good report from the hospital?"

"They said it was anxiety and that I needed to unstress my life. If they only knew. Anyway, they gave me a prescription for Xanax. It sure helps too. I never thought I'd take any kind of medication for something like that, but it's like a miracle! Helps me feel better and cope better too. I can handle Ann's tirades without falling apart now. The doctor said it wouldn't be any problem to take it as I need it."

David thought her eyes looked a little glazed, but he thought it was from grief. Maybe it was the drug. At least she felt better. "That's good," he said, "I'm glad to hear that. So where's Jack this morning?"

"Would you believe he's still in bed? He's usually up with the sun, but he stayed up late last night. I didn't wake him when I got up."

David felt uneasy alone with Anita, especially with her still wearing her robe. He hadn't thought about Jack's not being up. *It's just with all the accusations flying around, I sure don't want to do anything that might be considered impure.* Then it hit him again that he was being a hypocrite.

"Would you like a cup of coffee? Got some fresh."

"No, thank you, I just wanted to stop by and check on you. I need to get on up to the church. Please call me if I can do anything."

"Your going to see Ann means the world to us. If you can go again, we'd be eternally grateful."

"I'll try. Give Jack my best. Tell him I'm praying for all of you," David said. He was still holding the door so all he had to do was turn and walk out. He waved at her as he left. *Thank you, God, that Anita's better and that she didn't experience a heart attack.*

I keep telling people I'll go see Ann again, too, but that's the last thing I want to do. Thinking of the day ahead, he realized he didn't know his schedule for the day. Then he got a brilliant idea. Of course Linda was already there, and the coffee was made. As he fixed himself a cup, casually he asked Linda what his schedule was for the day.

"You've actually left yourself a couple of days free so that you could work on your Easter sermon," she said. "So, unless something unexpected happens, you've got two whole days to do just that."

"Seems like something unexpected always happens, doesn't it?" Without waiting for an answer, he said, "With everything that's been happening around here, I think I'll drive to Pendleton for a couple of days of peace. I can take my laptop and get some serious study done without having to worry about interruptions. It's only a few hours away and I can think and pray while I drive. Would you call and see if you can get me reservations?"

In Whose Steps?

"Yes, sir, I'll try." Linda thought that was odd; it was certainly out-of-character for the pastor, but, like he said, with all that was happening lately—she wasn't sure what it was, but she knew something strange was going on, what with Jack Grimes resigning from the elders!—she could understand his wanting to go away. Couldn't say as she blamed him.

"Carl mentioned that there was a Christian Counseling Conference going on in one of the hotels there, but he wasn't going to get to go. Would you see if you can find the brochure he received and book me there if the hotel isn't full?"

"Actually, it's right here on top of his stuff. He was saying yesterday he wished he could go. I'll call right now."

David went into his study. He started gathering his sermon materials. He guessed he needed to take his Bible although knowing what he had in mind, it seemed hypocritical to him. Nevertheless, it would look strange if he didn't take it. He was getting more excited by the moment. Wouldn't Shelby be surprised to see him! He could just see the look on her face, wondering what he was doing there!

"Okay, you're booked," Linda called out. I've written down all the information including your confirmation number. You lucked out. They said they had a couple of cancellations."

"I guess I did!" David was smiling. "This will be a good time to get away. Too bad Nikki is subbing at school the rest of the week. It would have been a good time for us to get away," he said.

"But you'll probably get a lot more done without her, Doctor. It's a sacrifice that's probably good for you to make. Anything you need me to do while you're gone?"

"No, just your usually fine job. I'll call you and—well, you already have my number, don't you? You know where to reach me if you need me. I won't be back in the office this week."

"I'll pray you have a refreshing time with God, then, and get lots of good sermon ideas. Have a good time. You deserve it."

"Shall I bring you back a Pendleton tee shirt?" he teased, big town that it was.

"I'd rather have a ticket for a cruise," she teased back. "That can be part of my vacation package."

"See what I can do. Okay, I think I have everything from here. I'm going home to pack. See you Sunday."

David could hardly believe he was going to go! He wondered if Nikki would buy the same line. Actually, he couldn't believe he was going off without telling her. She would already be at school and wouldn't know until he got home. But, she knew he'd been having a hard time on his sermon, and once before he'd gone off to work on his sermon—once in seven years. Oh, well, he'd leave her a note. *She'll understand I'm sure—right, I'm lying to myself. Of course she won't understand.* Arriving home, he ran in and packed quickly. As he came out of the house with his overnight bag, Neil was walking up the steps.

"Dad, what are you doing here? Or, rather, where are you going?" he asked, looked at the overnight bag. "Is something wrong?"

"I was wondering what you were doing here," David said to Neil.

"I had a free period and I needed to come home to think. I wanted to talk to you, actually, and was thinking of coming up to the church. So where are you headed?" he asked as he continued to eye David's bag.

"Couldn't seem to get my sermon together and I thought I'd go stay in a motel for a couple of days and get my thoughts together. You know a lot has been happening around here."

"Mom didn't tell us this morning that you were going."

"Actually, Mom doesn't know."

"Dad! You're kidding!"

"She won't mind, I don't think. I got this opportunity to use someone's room so it won't cost much. It was now or never. It's only for two days and I was going to leave her a note."

"I hope I'm not here when she gets it. She's going to be so mad. And you know it, too, Dad."

"Oh, well. If it's not about that, it's about something else. So what's on your mind?"

"I didn't say I was going to tell you. I said I was thinking of talking to you. I hadn't made up my mind yet."

"Here I am. Do you want to talk? We can go into my study," David offered.

"I guess so. But it's really embarrassing, Dad. I'm not sure how to talk about it."

"Sounds like girl trouble, Son. Is that it?" David sat down on the sofa in the study. Neil sat down beside him on the other end. He put his head down and didn't make eye contact with his dad.

"It is." Silence.

"Are you going to tell me what the problem is?"

More silence from Neil. His head hung lower.

"Son, it's okay. You can talk about whatever it is." David decided it must be about sex. *Oh, no, could Christina be pregnant?* Although he thought Neil and Christina were sexually abstinent, he asked quickly, "Is she pregnant?"

"No, sir."

"Oh. That's good." Sigh of relief.

"Not this time." Ashamed, Neil looked at his dad, wondering what his reaction would be.

"You're telling me you're sexually active. Is that right?" David tried to stay calm.

"Yes, sir, I guess I am. What I wanted to talk to you about though, is that we don't want to be. Well, that's not exactly true. What I mean is we want to be, but we know it's not right before God. When you're in love, it's hard not to be involved, and Christina and I love each other. You know what I mean, Dad?"

"I can imagine."

"We can't get married just so we can have sex. We're too young even though we both graduate from high school this year. We still have to go to college and all that stuff. And we sure don't want a baby. Dad, we want to please God in our sexual lives, but it seems almost like mission impossible." Although Neil was embarrassed by the discussion, he continued to be honest with his dad. David was embarrassed also—for more reasons than Neil knew about. It was convicting to hear Neil talk about being sexually pure when David knew what he was thinking about.

"We had the birds-and-bees talk quite a few years ago. Do you remember?" David asked him.

"How could I forget? I thought you were going to pass out, Dad," Neil actually laughed, then was immediately serious again. "And you said that if I ever wanted to talk about it again, you'd be there. Well, I really need help, Dad. Christina and I have promised God and ourselves time and time again we'd stay pure, but we continue to fall every time we're together. And, we don't want to break up. We really love each other and want to get married, but not now."

"I'm impressed with your maturity, Neil, and I'd like to help," David replied, "but I've got to get going soon, or I'll lose my reservation. Why don't we talk about this when I get back on Saturday? Will that be okay? And for goodness sake, in the meantime, use protection!"

Neil was shocked. For a moment, he just stared at his dad. "That's like saying it's okay, as long as we plan for it.

We plan to let it not happen, Dad! That's the last advice I expected from you! I expected hollering, maybe, or a lecture or a sermon—I expected you to tell me what I was doing wasn't right, not for you to help me and Christina not to get pregnant."

"Of course I'm saying it's not right. And we will talk about it later. I promise."

Dejectedly, Neil looked at his dad. He'd never felt so vulnerable and unimportant—and exposed!—in his life. Here he'd opened up with his innermost secrets, and his dad didn't have time to talk to him. And, gave him the same advice he got at school—use protection. "I just wish I'd never brought it up," he said.

"Neil, I promise. We'll talk when I get back," David said again. "I won't forget. And I was serious about your maturity. It means a lot to me that you want to follow God. I'll be praying for you while I'm gone." David got up. He was being a heel and he knew it. He was also being a hypocrite and he knew it.

"Let me give you a hug," he offered.

Neil stood up beside his dad. He was almost as tall and could look his dad in the eyes. David averted his eyes when Neil looked at him. He knew what a traitor he was being to his son—and God—but his mind was set on his own plans. And nothing was going to come in their way. He reached out and put his arms around Neil.

Neil stiffened and jerked away. "Don't worry, I'll work it out on my own. You don't have to talk to me about it," Neil said. "Or maybe I'll talk to Tim. Sorry I bothered you when you're so busy," he said sarcastically. "When I first drove up and saw your car, I thought God brought you home just for me to talk to. I thought it was an answer to prayer, so I made up my mind I'd go ahead and tell you. Obviously, I was wrong."

One Man's Search for Answers

David knew he was letting God down and that he was unfeeling to Neil while his heart was breaking. But, hey, it wasn't the end of the world. Neil had his whole life ahead of him and he'd get over it. "I have to go, Neil. We'll talk Saturday afternoon."

As David walked out, he heard Neil muttering, "No way. Over my dead body will I try and talk to you again—about anything."

"He's young, he'll get over it," David thought again, driving fast and furious to make up for the time he'd spent with Neil. About an hour down the road, he realized he hadn't written Nikki a note. No doubt Neil would tell her where he was. He thought he'd better call and leave a message for her—but it could wait until he got to the hotel and unpacked. She wouldn't be home from school before then anyway.

He made Pendleton in record time. When he checked in, he saw the "Christian Counseling Conference" sign as well as quite a number of people standing around talking. He wondered how he'd find Shelby with all those people there but then decided he could just ask at the desk. Even if they wouldn't give him her room number, he could leave her a message to call him. As the room clerk gave him his room number and key, he asked casually for Dr. Wilkerson's room number. "I'm sorry, sir, but we can't give out that information," he was told.

"Okay, thanks. I was to meet her here, but she forgot to give me her room number."

The clerk looked at him. He turned his head. "Well, sir, you could call the desk and ask for her room by her name and we'll connect you. Then she can give you her room number if she wants to."

She continued to stare at him. *Do I look guilty? I'm not used to doing things like this.*

In Whose Steps?

"Thank you. That will work out fine. I appreciate your help," he said, taking his bag and going to the elevator. The doors to the elevator opened. David started to get on and there she was! Shelby! She looked at him in obvious surprise.

"David?" she asked. Obviously it was him, but she couldn't imagine how she could be seeing him in Pendleton. "What on earth are you doing here?" They let the elevator go and stood talking in front of the doors.

"When I got to my office this morning, after I left you, Linda—my secretary—asked me if I'd forgotten about the pastor's conference in Pendleton this week. I told her yes, and she quickly got everything together for me and sent me on my way. Imagine my surprise when I got here and found out she had the days right but the dates wrong! It's Wednesday through Friday of next month! She doesn't usually make mistakes like that. I didn't want her to feel bad, so I told her that since I had a room, it would give me a chance to work on my Easter sermon in peace and quiet."

Shelby looked at him, not sure what to make of what he said. Was he telling the truth? Why wouldn't he be? It just seemed to be too much of a coincidence. Well, what now? "I see," was all she could muster, for once rather speechless.

David didn't think she looked very happy to see him. He knew he was a lousy liar. Somehow he didn't think she'd respond to "I think I'm falling in love with you and I can't stand to be without you and I want to be where you are every minute." And he couldn't think of any middle ground between the two. He looked at her. What would the verdict be? Was she going to buy it? "So, since I'm here, how about letting me buy you dinner?" he asked.

Shelby said, "David, look at me please." As much as he'd wanted to stare at her, to drink her in, he'd kept his eyes away from hers. He was afraid to look at her. Could shrinks read your mind? Would she know he was lying if she looked at him? Somehow it felt like looking at your mother when she knew you'd been in the cookie jar, and you told her you hadn't, and you didn't know you had crumbs all over your mouth. He knew he couldn't hide the lie. But what he could do was allow his feelings for her to show, and they weren't a lie. Slowly he looked into her eyes, allowing his overwhelming desire for her to be evident in his eyes. She actually blushed and seemed flustered and unsure of herself. *Well, it's nice for her to be out of control instead of me! She's usually cool as a cucumber and now the shoe's on the other foot. Good choice, David! Now what is she going to do?*

"I'm flattered by what I see, David, but it's not right. I'm busy tonight, anyway."

"Got a date?" he asked, trying not to allow the fact that he was jealous to show.

"No. Not that it's any of your business; I have a therapy session with my psychiatrist."

"You mean you go to therapy?"

"Of course. Many therapists do. It helps us be better clinicians. We do have some issues too, you know." She laughed her silvery laugh.

"How late will you be?"

"Not tonight, David. If you're still here tomorrow, I'll talk to you again. Maybe breakfast, if you'd like." That seemed much safer to her than a late night dinner.

David was desperately disappointed not to be with her but it was wonderful to see her and know he was sleeping in the same hotel that she was. He didn't want to push her away, though, so he said, "That's fine. I'd love breakfast. Just let me know. I'm in Room—"he looked down at his key—307." And you're in..." he ventured.

"I'm in 414. Call me about the time for breakfast. The first workshop is at 9:30 tomorrow morning. I need to be through before then."

"How about 6:00 a.m.?" David asked, looking straight into her eyes. "That should be enough time."

"Enough time for what?" she asked, flirting a little herself. She couldn't deny that she was attracted to the man.

"For me to buy you the best breakfast ever, of course." He didn't want to go too far. "Date?"

"Date. But let's make it 7:00. I hope you were kidding about 6:00. Why don't you call me about ten till 7:00 in the morning?"

"Will do. See you then, Shelby." He loved to say her name.

"Okay. I really need to go now, though. There's a workshop coming up I'm dying to go to."

"On repressed memories?" David asked.

She shot him a warning look. "Don't start that with me," she threatened.

"Just kidding. Have fun."

"You, too," she said in parting, as she walked off to greet her colleagues.

Yeah. Some fun without Shelby, he thought. But at least he was here. What had he expected? He'd walk up to her and she'd fall in his arms? At least she was going to spend some time with him. Maybe they could do dinner tomorrow night. *Dinner!* he thought, looking at his watch. He hadn't called Nikki yet. He'd better do that quickly.

CHAPTER SIXTEEN

As soon as the workshop was over, Shelby hurried to her room. As she changed her clothes, she thought about her relationship with David. Since she and Dr. Billings were both going to be at the conference, they had decided to have their regular weekly session at the hotel over dinner. She'd been seeing him for a couple of years—since her divorce—and she had found him immensely helpful for both her private and professional life. Sometimes they talked about her issues, and sometimes they talked about her clients—she often joked with him that she got supervision and therapy for the price of one!

She glanced in the hall mirror before she left her room. There was a sparkle in her eyes that she didn't think had been there earlier. Brushing her hair back, it occurred to her that she looked like a woman falling in love. "That would be bad," she thought, "very bad." Going down the elevator she hoped she didn't run into David again and was glad that she didn't. Dr. Billings—Ted—was waiting for her at the entrance to the hotel restaurant, and she waved at him as she walked across the lobby. He was nice-looking in a fatherly sort of way, she thought. She seldom saw him outside the hospital setting, and it seemed a little strange to be meeting him at a restaurant. She knew his wife, too, and liked her as well. But Mary Ann hadn't been able to come this trip. Shelby knew Mary Ann trusted Ted implicitly. Wonder what that would feel like, Shelby thought, to trust a man implicitly?

In Whose Steps?

Ted was smiling at her. "Good evening, Shelby. How are you enjoying the conference?" he asked.

"It's been super," she said. "I've already gotten some good information that I can put to use. How'd your presentation on 'The Christian and Anti-depressants' go?"

"Really well, actually. But of course, most of my audience were mental health professionals who agree with me, rather than an audience of those who really need the information—pastors and lay people. However, it may be that the professionals can use some of the information I gave them to educate their pastors. But that's neither here nor there at the moment because right now I need to get our table, don't I? I made reservations earlier." Shelby thought that was thoughtful of him.

He walked over to the hostess, gave his name, and they were seated immediately. "I hear the food here is wonderful," he said. "But let's get the ordering done so that we can discuss you."

Quickly, they both looked at the menu, made choices, and ordered. That finished, Ted turned his attention back to Shelby. "So, young lady, how are things with you this week? Anything new going on?"

She always felt like laughing when he called her "young lady." But it was relative, she supposed, as she looked at his gray hair.

"I do have a problem," she said.

"Well, there's no time like the present. Let's hear what's going on. Is it a client or is it personal?"

"Actually, it's both," she said.

"Looks like we have a problem already," he said, anticipating a dual relationship between therapist and client.

"He's a pastor and I started seeing him last week—my gosh, was it only last week? Seems like I've known him forever. Anyway, I met him at another conference where I was speaking before I knew he was going to be my client. Ted, I'm attracted to him. And he is to me, too—big time."

"I can imagine that any man would be attracted to you, Shelby. You're a lovely woman. But you know the answer to your problem: terminate therapy."

"I'm not sure it's that simple."

"You mean, you don't want it to be that simple, don't you?"

"I can never get anything by you, can I? You're right. I don't really want to terminate. Here's where I'd like help from you, though. As you know, my ex was a pastor. Well, he called himself a pastor. There are many more words to describe him, and none of them nice. What a jerk! And that's putting it nicely. There are several four-letter words that fit him a lot better. Anyway, in some ways, David reminds me of him. And, boy, is that scary. Here I hate my ex for committing adultery—among other things—and then I'm attracted to a man, a pastor no less, who wants to commit adultery with me? Can you explain that?"

Ted started to answer, but Shelby interrupted him. "Ted, that's not all. He's here!"

Ted looked at her as if he didn't understand. "He's here? What do you mean, 'he's here'? You mean at this hotel?"

"Yes. And he gave me some weird story about why he's here, but I think he came because I'm here. I think he's pursuing me. I'm used to guys being attracted to me in therapy, but this is different."

"This sounds serious. Fatal attraction?"

"No, I don't think it's anything like that. More like fatal lust," she laughed.

"And you're wondering why you would even be interested in someone who's messing around on his wife the way your husband—sorry, ex-husband, did on you. Good question. Have you come up with an answer?"

"I was hoping you could."

"Why don't we look at what it is about him that attracts you. Is it the parts that are more like your ex or something different?"

"Hmmm. Hadn't thought of that. Well, he's very handsome and charismatic..." The waitress arrived with their food. Shelby waited until she left but before she continued the conversation, Ted offered to pray over their meal. Shelby found it hard to concentrate on the prayer. The questions Ted was asking her were much more intriguing than either prayer or her dinner.

As soon as Ted finished, she continued as if there had been no break in her conversation, "articulate, sensitive—nope, my ex wasn't sensitive, although he did appear that way at first, so I guess I can't rule that out. What I was thinking was that I like it that he's so attracted to me, but men are often attracted to me in therapy—just as women are to you too, I know. There's no way we can discuss such intimate things and be on such intimate levels with our clients without attraction occurring occasionally. So it must not be just the attraction I feel from him. Maybe it's that I'm attracted back. But then that's what you asked me..." Catching a whiff of her steak, she said, "I can't let this spoil my appetite. This smells delicious."

Even though she picked up her fork, it didn't get to her mouth as her thoughts continued to race. "Maybe I've got it. Don, my super handsome ex put down my femininity all the time. He made me feel ugly and undesirable as a woman. Now here comes a man who is like Don, very handsome, and who is almost drooling at my feet. So..." She continued excitedly, as if she had an "ah hah," "even though other men have been attracted to me, none of them have been of Don's caliber, if you will. Well, caliber is tongue-in-cheek, when you consider his track record. I mean caliber strictly on an external level. It's like he's—David, I mean—validating my femininity, making me feel desirable again! Ted, you figured it out!"

"Uh, would he be tall, dark—with a little gray—and handsome?" Ted asked.

"That's a pretty good description. Are you being facetious?"

"Take a look behind you. There's a man of that description looking at us—you, I think—as if he's mesmerized."

Shelby turned and looked. Across the room, staring at them, sat David. He waved. "Ohmigosh," she said. "Yes, that's him. Does he have no shame?"

"Looks like he's infatuated with you, Shelby. What are you going to do? You are a professional and that comes first, whether your femininity needs to be validated or not. And of course, you're also a Christian."

"You're right. I need to terminate therapy with him. I'm supposed to have breakfast with him in the morning. I guess I could tell him then. I also have a therapy session scheduled with him and his wife next Tuesday. But, I think it would be okay to follow through with couple therapy."

"I think you need to consider terminating the marital therapy too because I think you'll have serious transference issues if you don't, due to your attraction to him. By the way, Shelby," he interrupted himself, noticing she still wasn't eating, "this steak is incredible. It's as good as they said it was. You have no idea what you're missing. I suggest you try it!"

"Anyway, back to your thoughts. Are you truly attracted to him or is it you're just attracted to the fact that a handsome man is pursuing you? Is there something about him that truly interests you?"

"I guess I wonder if he's genuine. Don wasn't. I keep answering my own question, don't I? If he's genuine, why is he after me instead of being faithful to his wife?"

"And as much as you say you hate Don and everything he stood for, why are you interested in this supposed man of God"?

"Do you think I have some vindictiveness toward him? Displacement? Or, that maybe I'm projecting? Reaction formation? I want to hurt him since I can't hurt Don? Maybe I'm just the stupid female Don said I was?"

"Shelby! I don't like it when you put yourself down like that. You know that isn't Christian. My guess is just what you said: his undeniable attraction to you validates your desirability as a female. That feels really good to you and you hate to give it up. I think it's as simple as that. I think you're over the fear-of-abandonment-so-I'll-take-anything problem you had with Don. The physical and sexual abuse you endured as a child taught you that love was related to destructive behavior—usually toward you. It taught you that everything bad that happened to you was your fault, both as a child and as Don's wife. We've done a lot of work in that area, but maybe it hasn't been tested yet. What do you think?"

"Basically you're saying I'm still attracted to narcissists?"

"Yes. As you know, many pastors would fit the description of narcissistic personality disorder. Your dad did—I know, he was a deacon, not a pastor. And Don did, no doubt still does. Do you think your admirer does?"

"You gave me great therapy for that. It was a super idea for me to watch our old home movies of Don. Helped me spot narcissism a mile away! Quite honestly, Ted—present company excepted, of course—most men are narcissists at heart, anyway. Just look: they're grandiose, require inordinate admiration and get bent out of shape if their spouse asks for anything in return;, they usually don't have empathy for anyone except themselves—you get the idea—oh, present company excepted, of course! Anyway, I don't think David would meet the clinical definition, just my men definition. Maybe he's just having a plain old mid-life crisis, or maybe mid-life lust would be a better description."

"I think you sell yourself short. What you're saying is he only wants you sexually and couldn't possibly fall in love with you as a whole woman, a person with a great mind. So, I'll say again that I think you have much to offer, but I think you are a little stereotypical about men and narcissism."

"No doubt you're right. I probably have residual back up—how's that for a clinical term!" she laughed. "So, all men in my life get caught in it. I hope that's not true, though. Then I would be a poor therapist."

"There you go again, putting yourself down. My guess is that those feelings only come into play when you're involved in a personal relationship, not a therapeutic one."

"I hope you're right, Ted. Looks like you've finished eating."

"I have. And you've barely touched yours."

"I'm still not hungry. I have lots to consider."

"Are you going to terminate?"

"No doubt I will. I'm going to my room now. You can ask me in our time next week what I decided, okay? And thanks for your time and input."

"No problem. I'll send you my bill," he laughed. Not that it was a joke. She paid him every week.

Without even looking to see if David was still there, she left the restaurant and went straight to bed. He called early the next morning to remind her about breakfast, and she assured him she'd be there on time. When she got downstairs, David was already waiting. He took her breath away when she saw how he looked at her. It was becoming more and more obvious that she was walking on dangerous ground.

169

"Good morning," he said, his face wreathed in a smile. "Did you sleep well?"

"I suppose. Seems like I just got to bed and it's already time to get up. Did you?"

David looked at her until she turned her head to look at him. "Yes. I had great dreams," he said pointedly.

She blushed again. He wasn't being very subtle. "I do dream analysis, too," she said. "You'll have to tell them to me and let me analyze them." She was trying to keep it clinical.

"I don't think they were very symbolic. Pretty straight forward. Shall I tell you?"

"I don't think so, David. Listen, let's just sit down here in the lobby. I don't want to eat. I need to talk to you for a few minutes." Seeing her seriousness, David was fearful of what she might say. His fears were confirmed. She told him she couldn't see him any longer because she was getting emotionally involved with him. The part about being "emotionally involved" told him what he wanted to know—he had been sure she was attracted to him, also; the part about not seeing him anymore upset him greatly.

"Don't I get any say in this? You're making a unilateral decision?" His eyes were pleading with her to change her mind.

"No, you don't get any say. I'm willing to hear your feelings and have closure with you, but that's it. And I'll still see you and Nikki once if you like. Then I can refer you and/or the both of you to someone else. This—you and me— isn't going to work."

"You mean because you are attracted to me, too."

"That's not what I said," Shelby said, but she was blushing. "You're putting words in my mouth."

"That's what therapists do all the time, isn't it? Why can't I? Besides, you know it's true. I can see it in your eyes, Shelby."

Shelby was afraid she was fast losing control. She was finding it difficult to keep her emotions in check. A part of her wanted to say forget ethics, forget God, and just continue to show me that you love me. She was in a great internal struggle. But she'd been on the other side and knew how it felt to be the wife of an unfaithful husband.

"David," she said firmly, "this is good-bye for now. I'm going to the rest of my seminar. Whether you stay here the rest of the week or not, I will not spend any time with you. I am honored and flattered by your attention, but it is wrong. Unless you cancel your appointment next week, I'll see you and your wife then."

"Shelby, please... please..." She interrupted him by standing up and walking off. Watching her leave, he was determined that this was not going to be the end. She had no idea how persistent he could be. He had a professional lunch appointment with her next week and he wasn't going to let her out of it.

CHAPTER SEVENTEEN

David somehow got through the next few days, even preaching a Sunday sermon, although he wasn't sure how. Monday dragged by; finally it was Tuesday and the day for his and Nikki's appointment with Shelby. They hadn't talked much about his leaving abruptly the week before even though Nikki had been very angry when he got home, and an angry silence continued to hang in the air all weekend. He'd tried to talk to Neil as he promised, but Neil made himself scarce every time he saw David. David couldn't really blame him and hoped he'd come back around. He had mixed feelings, however, about talking to Neil because he knew the advice he'd give him would be hypocritical.

Tuesday morning he left early for work. Nikki had directions to Dr. Wilkerson's; David told her he'd meet her there. The morning had gone badly. Not that they were fighting, exactly. They both just seemed irritated that the other even existed. But, he was terribly nervous about meeting with both Nikki and Shelby because he couldn't control how it would turn out. Nikki was so impossible to get along with—always wanting her way, especially when he compared her to Shelby. He didn't get how ironic that was—he was angry because he couldn't control Nikki, but he hadn't been able to control Shelby, either. Lust—he called it love—is blind.

David arrived at Shelby's office before Nikki did and the receptionist allowed him to go on back to the therapy room. It didn't exactly feel like a breath of fresh air today, though—Nikki's being there was going to ruin it, he thought. He looked at Shelby as he walked into her office. Same wonderful smile; same wonderful composure. She didn't seem nervous at all. No mention of last week's encounter at the hotel. It was obvious she wanted to act as if it had never happened. Well, he intended to remedy that!

"Why don't you sit down, David? I'm sure Nikki will be along in a moment. I'm looking forward to meeting her," Shelby said coolly, dispassionately, as if he were just any other client and not someone special to her.

David hadn't been sitting down thirty seconds before he was up pacing again. Okay, he was ready for Nikki to get here and to get it over with! Then he heard her in the hall. The receptionist ushered Nikki in.

"I see you're already here, David," she said. Looking at Shelby, she held out her hand. "I'm Nikki, Dr. Wilkerson, as you already know—along with other things about me too, I'm sure." David could tell that Nikki was uncomfortable but trying hard not to show it.

"Please call me Shelby. If you'd like to have a seat over there by David, we'll get started." Nikki sat on the opposite end of the sofa from David. She desperately wanted to sit next to him, but she could feel his desire for distance. *Oh, God, what if he's gotten someone to help him ask for a divorce? I don't think I can stand it!*

Now that Nikki was here, David became rigid. He decided he didn't want to be here at all. It showed. Nikki didn't know when she'd seem him so cold. What was going on? She was terrified. David knew he wasn't making it any easier for Nikki, but at this point, he didn't really care. After all, how often did she make things easy for him?

Shelby suggested they start the session in prayer. Without waiting for their answer, she bowed her head and asked God to guide their time together. She prayed for David and Nikki to have the courage to "speak the truth in love" to each other. Nikki caught her breath when Shelby said that. What truth did David want to tell her? Her anxiety level was rising even though she was trying to pray.

Shelby started by asking each of them to talk about what had attracted them to each other in the beginning. Nikki felt more comfortable then; it was easier to talk about "back then." Shelby asked her to start.

"I distinctly remember the first time I saw David. I thought he was incredibly handsome." Shelby did, too, and she tried not to react to Nikki's words. "I was watching him play flag football on campus, and I loved his obvious athletic ability. My best friend saw me watching him. She told me I looked like I was falling in love—love at first sight, she said." Nikki giggled, remembering, and then looked at David.

He was staring straight ahead; his face was hard. It was difficult to continue being vulnerable, but Nikki was desperate for a renewed relationship. "When he finished playing, he came over to the sidelines and saw me. He grinned at me and—isn't this silly?—I thought he had the most beautiful teeth! I thought, if we had children, they'd never need braces—and they haven't, I might add. He ran off with his buddies, and I didn't know if I'd ever see him again. But, he knew my friend, and he got my number from her. Later that day he called me. Remember, David?" Nikki's eyes began to puddle as she looked to him to confirm their attraction to each other.

David turned to look at her. He had been stricken with Nikki's good looks, it was true. And as he had recently acknowledged to himself, she still had them. But it wasn't the looks ...it was her stinking attitude.

"Okay, your turn, David. Can you top that?" Shelby asked. He took a deep breath. This was hard. Because what happened so long ago didn't match what he was feeling now. But he knew what Shelby wanted. To recapture some of those old feelings he and Nikki had for each other. The same feelings he was feeling now for Shelby. And she knew it, no matter how she acted. He'd play along, he thought.

"Nikki didn't know it, but I'd seen her before. I'd asked her friend—who was my friend, too—to bring her out to watch the game. I hoped to catch her eye."

"David, I never knew that! You never told me that!" Nikki gasped with pleasure. "You saw me first."

"Yes, I did. And I wanted you to see me. I was showing off, shamelessly. When I came over to get a drink, I made sure it was by you, so that I could talk to you and honestly, flirt with you. Do you remember my winking at you?"

"Now that you say that, yes, I do. When you winked, you took my breath away," Nikki said, thinking that he still took her breath away. She loved this man so much. But he was so distant and uncaring, and she didn't know how to reach him.

"So, you winked, and made plans to get with Nikki later if she responded to your winking and flirting," Shelby laughed.

If she just wouldn't laugh! It gets me every time. And it sounds as if she wants me and Nikki to be okay together. Not going to happen.

Shelby asked him to continue. "Then what happened, David?"

Nikki thought Shelby said "David" in an intimate way, as if Shelby knew him better than she did, but then decided that was paranoid thinking. At this point, she was jealous of anybody and anything.

David continued. "Well, I called and talked to her that afternoon. We talked for hours. We had so many things in common: same subjects at school, all kinds of sports, books, movies, zeal for God, and a desire to minister. Seemed like everything was going for us. So I decided that day that she was the one I was going to marry. And I usually got what I wanted. I had to fight for everything I got when I was growing up, and I learned to be persistent and keep on until I was successful."

With that comment, he glanced at Shelby, wondering if she was hearing that same determination to get what he wanted in his voice. And that it was directed toward her. "So I did and here we are," he ended.

Nikki was feeling a warm glow as she remembered David's pursuit of her. He never took no for an answer; he was persistent, like he said. And she had loved his intense devotion to her. *Which was there until he got me. Okay, doctor, where do you go from here? Please fix us.* Nikki tried not to cry.

"Yes, here we are today. And now what I'd like to know is what it would take for each of you to recapture those same feelings. What would need to happen for you to feel close to one another again?"

David was silent. Who cared? Nikki started first again.

"All I need is for David to let me in, and to know what's going on with him. He used to share everything he was thinking and feeling, but he hasn't for years. That's all I need." She looked longingly at David. "Can't you give me that, David? Please?"

He felt angry. Why couldn't she understand that she demanded more of him than he could give? He wondered to himself what he should say. Should he be honest? That was what she said she wanted, wasn't it? But he had just begun to be honest with himself. He wasn't sure he was ready to say anything to Nikki yet. He didn't want to burn any bridges. He couldn't stand the thought of the wrath of her dad, or of his church. Maybe he should try a little, he thought, since he didn't know for sure what was going to happen with Shelby. Not that he'd thought it through, anyway. What would he do if he and Shelby did get together?

"I'll try, Nikki, honest, I'll try," he said with a bit of softness.

Shelby looked at him with surprise. It was obvious that after his cold behavior toward Nikki that she hadn't been expecting him to allow her into any part of him any longer. "Excellent, David," she replied. "What are some concrete ways that you can allow Nikki in?"

He wished she wouldn't push; he didn't want to be accountable to her or to Nikki. And besides, he'd rather know ways he could let *Shelby* in. But, he was beginning to feel like he was between the proverbial rock and a hard spot. Maybe it hadn't been such a good idea to have this session just so he could see Shelby again. He thought that if Shelby could see how impossible the relationship between him and Nikki had become, she would understand his attraction to her. But, the best thing for now, it seemed, would be to at least act as if he were trying to make the relationship okay. He took a deep breath. "How about if I set aside thirty minutes every day, no matter what, to talk about what's happening in my life and in yours, Nikki? Will that help?" he asked.

"It would be heaven to have thirty minutes of uninterrupted time with you, David. I'd love it!"

He had a hard time looking at Nikki because he knew he wasn't being honest. She was thrilled at his response, but he just felt more angry at her. Why didn't he just tell her he was angry with her? One, he wasn't usually that honest about negative feelings. His dad's anger had never resolved anything. Two, he wanted to stay angry at her, although he was unaware how much he was using that anger—and intensifying it—toward her to justify his feelings about Shelby. Vaguely, he knew his anger at Nikki had been much more intense since he'd met Shelby. He was surprised that Shelby hadn't asked about his anger. He figured she'd get to it, though. And even as he thought it, she did give him the opportunity to be more honest.

"Are you being totally truthful, David? Is there something else going on you'd like to talk with Nikki about?"

Nikki looked at David with fear in her eyes. *All this was just been a set-up to tell me he wanted a divorce! I just knew it!* Then she felt ashamed of herself for thinking that David would be so deceitful. She tried to look at him without her fear showing. It was extremely difficult. "It's okay, David. You can tell me anything, and I'll try and listen. I'll do anything to work out the problems in our marriage," she promised, silently asking God to help her to be courageous in spite of her fear.

The longer David sat there looking at Nikki, the more he decided he did not want to work out the problems in the marriage. He wanted it over. He wanted to pursue Shelby. But he couldn't lose his church! He covered his eyes with his hands, afraid that either Shelby or Nikki could see his thoughts in his eyes. After a moment, he looked at Nikki, avoiding Shelby's eyes.

"Nikki, I told you. I'm going to try," he said, angry at himself for being a wimp and not telling the truth. God didn't even cross his mind at this point. Shelby tried to make eye contact with him, but he wasn't about to let her. Obviously she already knew how deceitful he was, and he wasn't going to let her corner him. *I'll explain it all to her at lunch, then she'll understand.*

"Okay, David, what do you need from Nikki in order to feel close to her again?" He knew she wanted him to say that he needed to be honest about his anger and for Nikki to be willing to hear it. He wasn't going there.

"I guess I'm going to have to think about it awhile," he said, smiling wryly at Nikki. "I'll let you know soon. Will that be okay?"

"Yes. Whenever you're ready, I'll be willing to hear." Nikki was grasping at straws at this point, although she was disgusted with herself for wanting David so much. She wished she'd just stand up and tell him to get lost. Most of the time she could be strong. She hoped it was strong in the Lord, but was afraid it was just retaliation against his coldness. Knowing that David had set up therapy had given her hope; now it was hard to get back in her shell to protect herself from his coldness.

Shelby talked about communication skills and then gave them exercises to do with each other. She asked them to spend those thirty minutes a day practicing ways to effectively communicate. Then she handed them a list of questions and suggested that answering the questions would help them know each other better and to learn to know what their needs were, and to choose to meet some of them every day. She knew the questions would help them even if they didn't meet with her again to discuss them.

It's not David's communication skills that need help, Nikki thought. *He's a great communicator. It's his heart that needs help. He needs a heart transplant because his has disappeared.* She pleaded with God to let her know what David had done with his heart—then she wondered if God was hurting because he missed David's heart, also. *You have to do something, God, nothing else is going to work.* It was difficult not to feel despair over what seemed like a hopeless situation.

Shelby said, "Our time's almost up, and we need to discuss one other thing. It's not going to work out with my schedule for me to continue to see either or both of you, so I need to give you a referral if you want to continue therapy."

In Whose Steps?

    Nikki was both shocked and disappointed. Here they'd finally started working on their marriage and the therapist wanted to refer them! She looked at David to see what he wanted to do. He said, "We'll discuss it and let you know"—which sounded to her like he wasn't going to continue. Nikki walked out blindly, her head bowed so David or the doctor wouldn't see the tears in her eyes. David walked behind her. When she got to the front door, David opened it for her.

    "I'll talk with you later, Nikki, okay?" he asked.

    Without looking up, she said, "okay." As she walked out to her car, it occurred to her that David hadn't left the doctor's office. She guessed he stayed to pay the bill. She had no idea he'd stayed to take Shelby to lunch.

CHAPTER EIGHTEEN

"David, why are you still here?" Shelby asked as she came out of her office.

"Because you are going to lunch with me," he told her. "I made the appointment with your receptionist last week and it hasn't been cancelled."

"Not going to happen." She was adamant.

"You said that you'd have a time of closure with me if I wanted. And you said you'd get together with me to answer some questions for me about false memories. You're not going to keep your word? Please say you'll go," he pleaded. "I know you'd like to." Once again, he allowed his longing for her to show in his eyes.

"Okay. Just this once, David, for closure." She hoped she wasn't making a bad decision, knowing how she felt about him. It had been hard not to call him and tell him she'd continue to see him in therapy. She enjoyed her time with him and loved the way he treated her. But she knew it wasn't right. She couldn't be objective. Besides, she had to report to Ted later this week. It was good she'd set up that accountability, she told herself.

"I need to return a phone call right quick. Please sit down out in the reception area and make yourself comfortable," Shelby told him. She needed a minute to collect her thoughts—feelings, actually. She knew her face was flushed, and her heart was racing at the thought of spending time with him.

In Whose Steps?

David paced the floor. He couldn't sit down. He was too excited to think about sitting down. He was going to have Shelby all to himself. He was going to get to be alone with her again at some place other than her office! Impatiently, he jingled the keys in his pocket and tried to look at some colorful pictures on the wall.

"Are you ready?" Shelby called as she came down the hall.

"Never been more so," David said, pointedly, as he opened the door, this time for Shelby. She ignored his remark. "Would you like to go in my car?" he asked.

"You have a two o'clock," the receptionist called as they went out the door.

"Okay," Shelby said to the receptionist. "I'll be back on time. Sure, I'll ride with you," she said, looking at David. "I don't suppose we need to take two cars."

"Where would you like to go?" he asked.

"Doesn't matter. We just need to get this over with. What about you?"

"Actually, I have a favorite restaurant that has great food: seafood, Italian, Mexican—whatever you like. It's also quiet so we can talk. Does that sound okay?"

"Fine by me, as long as it's not too far, since I have to be back by two." She leaned back in David's leather seat and closed her eyes. "Hard morning—not the least of which was with you two!" she said, once again trying to keep the conversation clinical.

"I didn't make it easy on you, did I?"

"I should say you didn't. I was giving you an opening to be more honest with your wife. You both need to be more vulnerable with each other."

"It's easier to be vulnerable with you," David ventured.

"You really don't know me, David," Shelby laughed, "even though you think you do. You might not say that if you did!"

"Well, why don't we correct that? Tell me about you," David said as they drove up to the restaurant.

"The Breakers? Looks nice. I don't think I've been here before. Looks like it's part of the hotel; is it?"

"Yeah," David said offhandedly, as he pulled into a parking space and jumped out to open Shelby's door. She took his hand as he helped her from the car. Again, their eyes met and electricity flashed between them. *This may not be a good idea. I know it's not a good idea.* Nevertheless, she continued walking in with David.

They were able to be seated right away. David asked for a quiet corner and the hostess escorted them to a small table overlooking the terrace. Just like at the lake, spring color cascaded down the landscape.

"Isn't it a beautiful day?" David asked.

"Gorgeous," Shelby answered, as he held out her chair. *Wonder when I last did that for Nikki? Not that it matters; it wouldn't change anything.* Handing them the menus, the waitress went through the day's specials. David handed her back the menu. "I'll take the special," he said, "and coffee." He didn't want to waste a minute of their time reading the menu.

"That was quick," Shelby laughed. "I guess I'll take the same, except I'll take iced tea. Sounds good and the special is probably fast," she said, as she also returned her menu.

The waitress thanked them and left, to return shortly with their coffee, tea, and salads. Shelby placed the white linen napkin in her lap and sweetened her tea. David picked up his coffee cup and tasted his coffee. It was hot!

"You didn't answer me," he said, putting down his coffee to cool.

"What do you mean?"

"You said that if I knew you, I might not be vulnerable with you. So I said for you to tell me about you. I'm waiting."

She laughed again. "Who's in charge, here, me or you? I'm the therapist, remember? I ask the questions."

"So I'll be your pastor and you be my therapist. I can ask you questions, and you can ask me questions. Fair?" He winked at her.

She understood why Nikki said David still took her breath away when he winked at her. "Well, I'm not sure it is," she conceded, pretending not to notice his wink, "but I'll concede 'fair' for the moment. What do you want to know?"

"Why aren't you married?" David shot back.

"Whoa. I thought I was quick to the point. Why do you want to know?"

"Let's just say that I'm very interested in you because I care about you."

She put down her fork and looked straight at him. She knew she shouldn't even respond to what he said, but she had to know. "How can you say you care about me when you barely know me?"

David laughed. "What do you say when all your clients say that to you?"

He'd retreated back into joking, so she stayed surfacey, too. "Got me, didn't you? So let's leave it there and remember that our lunch was so we could discuss something theoretical—false memories or something like that?"

"You changed the subject, didn't you? Are you scared of me?"

She couldn't keep up with him. One minute she thought he was going to be serious and vulnerable, the next joking. But she responded honestly to his question.

"Actually, David, after seeing your interaction with your wife, I don't know why I wouldn't be; I don't know why I'd want to be vulnerable with you. You were very cold to her. And she wasn't asking for something unreasonable, you know—she just wants to be a part of you."

"I don't want Nikki. I want you to be a part of me," David said in a low voice. The intensity in his voice scared him as well as Shelby. This was what she'd feared, and on some level, hoped for.

"I'm not sure I heard you," Shelby said, continuing to look him in the eye. "And I'm not sure I should or want to hear you." She was afraid.

"Okay," he said, jumping back to the first subject. "Why aren't you married?"

"I'll tell you. I was married to a pastor for fifteen—count 'em, fifteen—lousy, miserable years. The guy paraded around like he had it all together, 'Mr. Super Spiritual,' but at home the only thing he used the Bible for was to beat me up," Shelby said angrily.

"Literally?"

"Well, he didn't literally use the Bible in a physical way. He used it against me spiritually and emotionally, and he was, at times, physically abusive, all the while living behind the facade of a supposed spiritual giant. It was disgusting. Thank God we had no kids!"

"So you're divorced? For how long?"

"Thanks for the caring," she said sarcastically, when he didn't mention any of the distressful things she'd just revealed to him. "Typical male, aren't you? For two painful years." Well, she'd figured as much. He was so narcissistic he couldn't hear her pain.

"Shelby, you don't understand. It's that I do care, too much—desperately, I'm just trying to stay on safe ground, since that's what you said you wanted." He looked up as the waitress brought their steaming plates of spaghetti. She set them down and asked if they needed anything else.

"No!" David said abruptly. He wanted her to leave.

"Let me know if you do," she said, making a beeline for another table.

"Do you understand me, Shelby?" It felt good to him to say her name out loud to her, with her. It was feeling more and more intimate, much more than it had at the conference. But he wasn't sure she felt that way, too. He knew it must be difficult for her to trust him.

"I'm not sure. I don't trust men very much. I don't trust you very much. Why on earth should I? Besides, I just observed how you treat your wife, 'Pastor.' Like mine treated me!" She jabbed at her spaghetti with her fork. "And, what about unfaithfulness?"

"Shelby, look at me, please," David said tenderly.

She caught the emotion in his voice and looked at him as she put down her fork and placed her hand on the table. He reached out and covered her hand with his own, curling his fingers around hers. She knew she should remove her hand, but she didn't. It felt good to her, even though she was terrified.

"Please listen to me," David entreated her. "I know it's only been a week! I know it's crazy—but you have changed my life. I was feeling depressed and miserable until I met you, and now I don't know when I've felt more complete or more alive. I don't know what I'm going to do if you won't continue to be a part of my life."

"And what is it I have done to supposedly create this miracle?" Shelby started to laugh to get things back on the surface, but she didn't. It was rather hard to do when she was allowing him to hold her hand. She knew she should probably nip this conversation in the bud. While it was true that David was a pastor, and was responsible to be godly to her, she knew she also had responsibilities to her profession.

"You have treated me like I'm special, important, number one. You have listened to me as if every word I say is important to you. You have looked into my eyes and shown me comfort and compassion when I told you about painful things. And, I hate it when you tell me about the painful things that have happened to you. If I saw your husband, I would want to hit him so I could protect you." His voice choked.

Shelby wasn't sure whether to believe what was happening. While it felt wonderful for him to say those things to her, she wondered how she could trust a man who was acting like her ex by flirting with other women. Of course he'd done a lot more than flirt. It was true she continued to feel a strong attraction to David that several days of absence hadn't abated. *I probably shouldn't have allowed this lunch to happen because I know David didn't really want to discuss closure and certainly not repressed memories.* But, she felt so special to him, and it felt so good to see him looking at her with such longing in his eyes. She didn't want to give him up either. She tried to make light of his comment.

"Even though you're tall, he's a lot bigger than you—I'm not sure you'd win."

"But I'd try. Whatever happened, it would be worth it to try and protect you." He continued to look at her as if she were dessert. Both of them left their spaghetti untouched.

"Then I'll give you 'E' for effort," she said, attempting to add some levity to the situation.

"The only effort I'd like an 'E' for," David risked saying, thinking it's now or never, sink or swim, "is escorting you upstairs." He picked up her hand and kissed her fingertips.

"David! Stop! Someone will see." Shelby gasped.

"Then why don't we get a room and go where no one will see?" David asked. He shut off everything, except desire for Shelby, in his mind. He'd reckon with God later. *After all,*

King David got by with adultery and murder and when he asked forgiveness, God forgave him.

Shelby knew David had crossed the line from fantasy in his mind to making his fantasy real. Why wasn't she upset, or angry? She faced the truth. She'd had a good idea of what was going to happen and she wanted it to happen, also. What was she going to do? She had a two o'clock and glanced at her watch.

"Can't you call your receptionist and ask her to cancel your next appointment?" David asked, reading her glance. "Tell her whatever you tell her when you want out of an appointment. I'm sure you've done it before. Please say yes. I want us to be together." Her fingertips were still in his hand and he started them to his lips again.

"No. I mean, no, not here. I mean, I'm not sure."

"If we get a room, we can talk about it more privately, can't we? Shelby, I think I'm falling in love with you. You're everything I've ever wanted. Don't you feel anything for me? I know you do."

Love. He used the word 'love.' Could it be possible? But what about his wife? What about his church? What about my ethics? What about God? Why do I think he's any different than Don?

She decided. "I'll call Judi and cancel my next appointment," she said, smiling at him, "while you get a room. Do you think anyone will see us at this place?"

"I've never run into anyone I've known here. It's off the beaten path for lunches. I'll meet you at the elevator, okay?"

"Okay," she said breathlessly. She was finding it hard to talk any longer. She wasn't sure whether it was from guilt or desire. She called and lied. He paid for lunch and got a room for "Mr. and Mrs. Smith." Then he called and lied. They walked toward the elevator together. As they got on the empty elevator, he grabbed her hand. "You won't be sorry, Shelby, I promise. I'll make everything okay for us," he said.

"I don't know how you could ever do that," she said, wondering what he meant by the statement, but not caring at the moment. When they reached the sixth floor, he held the door open while she exited. They walked down the hall, and he took the key from his pocket. All caution thrown to the wind, he quickly opened the door and ushered Shelby in.

"It's beautiful," she said, quite surprised at the luxuriousness of the room in this out-of-the-way hotel.

David took her shoulder and turned her around to face him. "Not nearly as beautiful as you, you know." He looked at her with defenseless longing, gently taking her face in his hands. She turned her face away. It had been a very long time since she had felt desirable. It was a wonderful feeling. But she didn't think she could go through with it.

"David, you said we'd *talk* about this in private," she reminded him. He pulled his hands away from her shoulders quickly. He didn't want to betray her trust, he thought, not even realizing the hypocrisy of his thought. She walked to the window; he followed her. Pulling aside the curtain she looked out, staring at nothing, no longer seeing the brilliant spring day.

Again, David gently touched her shoulders. Again, he turned her around to face him. "If you want to leave now, we will, before it's too late—before I completely and totally fall in love with you."

"David, you can't love me. You don't know..."

"I know all I need to know. If you'll look at me, so will you," he said, once again gently taking her face in his hands and turning it up to face him. "Look at me," he said insistently.

In Whose Steps?

She looked into his eyes. This time she didn't turn away. She said words that at one time she thought she'd never say again: "I love you, David."

David pulled her close in a tight embrace. Her head against his chest, she felt as if she'd come home. She'd been waiting so long for someone like this to sweep her off her feet. And almost as if he'd read her mind, David did just that.

CHAPTER NINETEEN

"Susan, it's Nikki. I told you I'd call as soon as the session was over."

"Are you already home or on your cell?" Susan asked.

"No, I'm home. I needed some time by myself to process what happened."

"Well? Are you going to keep me in suspense or what?"

"I'm not sure what to say. At first I felt a little hopeful. The therapist had David and me think back to what first attracted us to each other. I thought at the time that was good."

"But you don't think so now?"

"No, because when I did that, I let my guard down. I started thinking of when we first met and how I fell head over heels for him—all the fun times we used to have."

"So what's the problem with that?"

"David didn't respond."

"What do you mean?"

"He told me—us—facts about when he met me. He said nice things, even, about how much he was attracted to me; how he asked a friend to have me at one of his games so he could meet me—something I hadn't known before; how he was pursuing me. I was excited at first, but there was no emotion when he said it. It was like he was reporting facts that had nothing to do with him. He was so cold to me, even colder than usual. Recently I'd felt a kind of a numbness, but today it was more like a deep freeze. Susan, it was almost like he hated me for being there."

"Therapy didn't help, then? You're not going back?"

"We made plans to. I don't know if we'll follow through. I thought at first he was going to ask me for a divorce!"

"No way. David's not that crazy. Besides, Nikki, he does love you! You guys have just lost the spark—like Carl and I have, I'm sorry to say—too much time away from each other. No, David's not going to ask for a divorce. He has too much to lose."

"He didn't ask for a divorce, that's true, and he would have a lot to lose with the church and all. I hate to say it, but Daddy would probably make sure he never got another church in this denomination. Guess that's not too Christian, but he gets vindictive when his little girl is mistreated. He wouldn't be too fond of the fact that his son-in-law left his wife, or that he had to leave the church Daddy helped him get."

"Does your dad have any idea about the problems you and David are having?"

"I don't think so. Well, he's not stupid. He probably picks up vibes—like the anger I show to David most of the time—but he hasn't said anything."

"Have you told David you're angry with him?"

"About a million times, give or take a few."

"What does he say?"

"I have no right to be angry at him because he's doing the best he can. Actually, I think he's angry with me, too, but is too scared to tell me."

"Why? Has he yelled at you or something?"

"No, but today Dr. Wilkerson tried to get him to tell me something he'd told her but not me, and he wouldn't do it. Knowing David and his fear of conflict, I think she was trying to get him to say he was angry with me, and he didn't have the nerve—not even with her there."

"How'd you like her? Did you think she was any good?"

"I guess I don't have any way to compare. Seemed like a nice enough lady and seems to know what she's doing. David had already met with her a couple of times and they seemed to have a good bond. So I think he trusts her. I hope so. I hope he's been able to talk to her about his anger at his parents."

"You didn't discuss that today?"

"No, we stayed focused on us. She gave us communication homework to do. God only knows whether David will follow through with it. I'll be shocked if he does."

"You sound pretty discouraged, Nikki."

"I am. Susan, don't you dare mention this to Carl. I'm actually thinking of telling David I want a divorce."

"You are not."

"Yes, I am. When I allow myself to be vulnerable to him, like I was today, he walls me out even further. He thinks I'm demanding when I ask him to be vulnerable with me. Well, I'm sick and tired of it. And I like me better when I'm angry than when I'm wimpy. Staying angry to keep from being vulnerable with him gets old. I told you, I did a lot of thinking today. And I can't believe I'm saying this, but I think I just want out. I love David with all my heart—all my heart, Susan, but it just feels too hopeless. And I'm tired of trying."

"I hear you. It wouldn't take much for me to jump on the same bandwagon. Are you going to threaten him with a divorce so that he'll have to think about how much he's going to lose?"

"It won't be a threat. I think I'll talk to a lawyer first and see what my options are. Then I'll tell him."

"What if he says he's willing to work things out then?"

"Then hallelujah. I'll be happy to work on it. I'm just tired of doing it all myself."

"What about God, Nikki?"

"What about Him?"

"Well, it's not like you have Scriptural grounds for a divorce, do you?"

"Not that I know of," Nikki said, then wondered why she hadn't said, "No! Of course not" because it wasn't as if she suspected David of any unfaithfulness.

"You're just willing to do it anyway, God or no God?" Susan ventured.

"I only said I'm thinking about it. I'm feeling pretty desperate right now. How about praying for me?"

"You know I will. Thanks for telling me. I need to go. The kids are home from school and yelling for food. Talk to you later?"

"Probably. Thanks for listening. You're a good friend."

"You, too. Later."

"Bye," Nikki said, feeling very alone again. She knew Susan would support her emotionally even if she disagreed with her getting a divorce. *I can't believe I've said it out loud. But the more I think about it, the more it becomes an option. Why should I continue to try when Saint David, the Pastor, doesn't try? I wonder who has gotten a divorce lately and would know a good attorney. I'll ask Susan the next time I talk with her. Carl usually knows good divorce attorneys. One thing's for sure—the kids aren't going to like it. Like I do?* Nikki screamed silently at herself. She was exhausted from thinking about the whole situation and found herself lying down for a nap, something she never did. The next thing she knew, Alyssa was shaking her.

"Mom, Mom! What's wrong? Why are you lying down? Are you sick?"

Looking up and seeing the fear in Alyssa's eyes, Nikki quickly answered her to calm her fears. "I'm fine, honey. I was just tired."

"But I've never seen you sleep in the daytime, Mom," she said, relieved that Nikki was okay. "Or have you been doing it for years and I just now caught you?" she teased.

"You caught me. I've been doing it for years," she teased back. "How was school?"

"Okay. Mom, I want to get a tattoo."

"No way. You know your dad would freak out."

"Oh, and you wouldn't?"

"I wouldn't like it, that's true. But your dad would hit the ceiling. What kind of tattoo do you want and where do you want it?" Nikki asked.

"I'm not sure yet whether I want it on my ankle or my tummy."

"Your dad would prefer your tummy, I'm sure, if you do it, and preferably below your bikini line!"

"What's the use of that? What a waste of pain getting it when no one would even see it!"

"Hopefully not," Nikki laughed. Alyssa cheered her up. "You'll have to talk with your dad about it. I don't know when he'll be home today—tonight. Whatever. Tomorrow. You know your dad. Always busy."

"Are you mad at him for not ever being here, Mom?"

"I suppose so." That was the most truthful she'd ever been with Alyssa about her relationship with David. But if she were thinking of getting a divorce, she better start being honest at least a little at a time!

"I knew you were. I can tell, even if you're quiet, when you're mad at Dad."

"Sorry. I didn't mean for it to show."

"I know, Mom. It's okay. Don't sweat it. Why don't you tell him?"

"I have, many times. Enough of this conversation, though. Looks like you have some books to do homework and I'll bet you're starving, huh?"

"Right! Mom, listen, I just heard Dad drive up. I'm going to go talk to him and tell him I want a tattoo. I'll bet I can talk him into it. He doesn't want to damage my self-esteem, you know," she added smugly.

"Dad!" she yelled, loudly enough to wake the dead, and ran out to David's car almost before he opened the door.

"Hi, Alyssa, what's up?"

"What's wrong, Dad?" she asked, as soon as she saw his face.

"What do you mean what's wrong?"

"I can always tell if you or Mom are mad or upset. You seem upset."

"I am not upset in the least. Did you want something? I can't imagine your giving me such an overpowering welcome home unless you do."

"You know me pretty well, too, huh, Dad?"

"Sometimes, Alyssa. So what is it?"

"I want to get a tattoo."

"*What*? You will not get a tattoo."

"Daaaad. All the girls are getting one. Cute little butterflies or stuff like that. Come on, Dad, say yes."

"Can you imagine what all the people at church would think if the pastor's daughter has a tattoo?"

"I don't care. Do you?"

"Well, of course, I care. And so should you. It doesn't set a good example. It's a no, positively, unequivocally, no."

"Daaaad. Some of the girls *at church* already have tattoos. No one has said anything."

"But they've thought it."

"So are you gonna live your life by what people think?"

She hit the nail on the head for David. He knew he was a people-pleaser who lived in the fear of man more than the fear of God. "No, of course not," he replied.

"Besides, I'll get depressed if I can't do it. And I'll start spending lots of time in my room by myself. My self-esteem will go down. Then you'll have to send me to see a shrink to help build it back up again and it'll cost lots of money. And what if people knew the pastor's daughter was seeing a shrink? That's even worse than a tattoo!" she concluded.

"You do have a case," David said. "I'll think about it and let you know tomorrow."

"Thanks, Dad, you're the best," Alyssa said and ran for the phone to tell Whitney she was going to get a tattoo. She knew how to manipulate her dad and knew the answer would be yes! Dashing into the house, Nikki stopped her.

"You seem very pleased with yourself, young lady. You must have finagled a yes from your dad. Don't tell me he gave in."

"Not yet, Mom, but as good as. He's gonna let me know tomorrow. But he'll say okay. I know him." She was giggling as she ran upstairs.

Better than I do, evidently. Just then, David walked into the house. "You're home early," she said. "About five hours early. To what do I owe the pleasure of your company?"

"I got through sooner than usual. I thought maybe we could do something together tonight."

Nikki's heart leaped. Despite her best intentions to be cold, her wall melted. "Really? I'd love to," was out of her mouth before she realized it. Maybe he was really going to try? "Well, what did you have in mind?" she asked.

"I thought perhaps we could work on the exercises Dr. Wilkerson recommended."

"Are you okay?" she questioned. "You seem a little weird."

"I've just had some time to think, and I know I need to change some things with you."

"That's good, because the same happened with me."

"And what were your decisions?" David asked.

She drew her breath in before saying anything. Should she mention what she had been thinking, or should she let it go and see what happened? The words he was saying *were* positive, and she did want to try—but that same coldness was in his eyes. She had enough of the same old cycle: Nikki feels bad. Nikki tells David. David changes. David feels bad. David tells Nikki. Nikki changes. So, she decided to tell him.

"Actually it's only one decision."

"What is that?" he asked.

"I'm thinking of getting a divorce."

"What? You're thinking of getting a divorce? That's absurd!"

What a shock. She got a reaction. His eyes weren't cold any more, they were angry. That didn't take long.

"Let's face it, David, things aren't working between us. I love you, and you know I want a good relationship with you more than anything in the world—but I can't tell that you want one with me. I know you aren't happy with me. So why is it absurd to consider a divorce?"

"Nikki, I never thought you'd go back on our commitment. You're a Christian. You made a vow before God," he said angrily.

"I did, you're right. And so did you. To love and to cherish me till death us do part. And you aren't loving or cherishing me, are you?"

"Those are not Scriptural grounds for divorce. And you know it. How could you do this to me? You obviously have not thought of how it would affect my career, or the church, or our kids—or your dad, Nikki!" He realized how angry he was getting. How dare she mess up his life like this!

"I only said I was thinking of it, David. I never expected such a strong reaction."

"You thought I'd say sure, go ahead and ruin my life and my career? How selfish can you get!"

"Pretty selfish, I guess, according to you. But I think you're the one who is selfish because you won't share your life with me." Nikki was angry now, her eyes flashing. She'd given her adult life to this man doing all the little pastor's wife duties and now he was calling *her* selfish???

"I don't think we need to get into this at this time." David retreated back into his cold shell. "We'll talk about it with Dr. Wilkerson. You ruined my plans for the evening. I wanted to work on the marriage, and you ruined my desire to do so." He stalked upstairs.

Guess I blew that one! Here he wants to give me something and I get mad and mess it up. It is all my fault. God, I'm not very patient and kind, am I? No wonder David gets upset with me. Nikki was back in a cycle she hadn't recognized—that of blaming herself for all the problems in the relationship or getting angry and withdrawing. Except today she'd gone further in her withdrawal cycle than ever before—to actually consider divorce. Dejectedly, she went into the kitchen to finish supper.

CHAPTER TWENTY

As Nikki trudged upstairs for bed, David was coming downstairs.

"I left supper warming in the oven for you, since you never came down to eat," Nikki said. "The kids and I ate hours ago." Then she noticed he had bedding in his arms.

"What are you doing?" she asked.

"What does it look like?" he retorted. "I'm sleeping on the sofa."

"David, we've never slept apart. That's not necessary. Can't we talk about it?"

"You've already given me your position," he said coldly, as if to a stranger. "If you want a divorce, then you best proceed with it."

"What I want is for you to talk me out of it, to tell me you love me, and that you want things to work for us." She started crying. His sleeping on the sofa seemed so final.

"Stop your stupid crying. You're the one who wants to mess everything up," he said. "But I tell you what. I'll think some more about it tonight. I need some space right now. You've rejected me once too often."

"*I've rejected you?*"

"There you go again. It's impossible to tell you how I feel or what I think because you won't listen to me. Just give me some space."

"Alright," she said. "I do love you, David, and I don't *want* a divorce. I wasn't trying to threaten you but I wanted you to know how much I hurt."

"Okay. I know. Now you're happy. So leave me alone for now."

Nikki went upstairs, crying. No matter how mad they'd been, they always slept together. She felt so totally alone, even more than she had. *God, what should I do?* She cried until she finally fell asleep.

David lay awake the whole night. He was absolutely furious that Nikki would consider divorce. If she were to follow through, his whole life as he knew it would be over. He knew he had some serious decisions to make. Many options went through his head. Around dawn, he settled on one. He went upstairs to see if Nikki was awake yet. She was.

"Nikki?" he called softly. "Are you awake?"

Her eyes were red and swollen from crying. "Yes," she mumbled hoarsely.

"I've been thinking all night about what we should do. I think we need a new beginning. We need to forget the past and start from today."

Nikki didn't know what to think. It was too good to be true. She breathed a heartfelt thank you to God for answering her prayers. "That would be wonderful, David. What do you propose? That we do the exercises Dr. Wilkerson recommended?"

"No. I think we need to do some things on our own. I was thinking about what we talked about yesterday and how we were first attracted to each other. It was when we were doing things together! We enjoyed skating, swimming, hiking...remember?"

"Oh, yes. We laughed all the time. We haven't done anything like that forever. You've been too busy."

A flash of anger crossed David's eyes, but quickly went away. "You're right," he conceded, "I have. And I want to make it up to you."

"That's music to my ears," Nikki said. "That's what I've been longing to hear. So what are we going to do?"

"What are the kids doing today?"

"Both have plans. They'll be out all day. That is, Alyssa will be leaving as soon as you give her your answer about the tattoo. Which I guess is yes?"

David laughed. Nikki thought it was the most wonderful sound! She hadn't heard him laugh for ages. "Yes, she talked me into it."

"And that will be music to her ears. Why are you asking about the kids?"

"I thought that if they were going to be busy, and since it's supposed to be a pretty day today, up around 75 or so, you and I could go to Long Rock by ourselves for a hike and a picnic."

She looked at him. Could he be serious? He looked as if he were. And he was smiling at her. "David!" She laughed out loud. "I would adore going hiking with you. I'll get a lunch together in no time!"

"Not necessary. You are Queen for a Day. We'll stop and pick up some chicken--or whatever you want." *This is too good to be true. God must have transformed his heart during the night. Hallelujah!.* She bounced out of bed, headache and swollen eyes forgotten in the happiness of the moment. "I'll be ready in no time."

"It's still early. If you want to take a relaxing bath, that's okay with me. If you like, I'll even give you a massage afterwards." This was the David she'd fallen in love with. The man with the servant's heart. She thought her heart would burst with love.

"Thanks, but you don't have to do that."

"I'd like to. I know I have a lot of making up to do," David confessed again. "I need to ask your forgiveness for so many things. But I'd rather talk when we get there, if that's okay with you."

"Okay by me. I'm headed for the shower," she said. Jumping in the shower—she decided she was too excited for a relaxing bath—she doused her head, put on shampoo and actually started singing. She hoped she'd have time to call Susan to tell her the good news and to thank her for praying. Evidently the thought of divorce had turned David's heart around. Turning off the water, she stepped from the shower and wrapped a large towel around her hair. She thought she heard David talking softly to someone and decided Alyssa already must have cornered him this morning. Sticking her head out of the bathroom, she saw that David was on the phone.

"Who are you talking to this early?" she asked in a whisper.

He made a face. She knew the look. He was disgusted that someone had caught him on the phone. "I'll tell you in a minute."

Quickly, but carefully, she dried her hair and put on makeup while he finished his call. She hoped he didn't think her swollen eyes looked too badly. Scanning her closet, she picked a warm-up suit in David's favorite color: light blue. If it got too hot outside, she could always take off her jacket. She was looking for her good tennis shoes, but all she could find were her smooth-soled ones.

"David, have you seen my good tennis shoes?" she called. "The ones I use for hiking? These don't have any traction."

"Haven't worn them lately," he laughed. Nikki couldn't believe he was in such a good mood!

"Would you rather not go since you can't find your good hiking shoes?" David asked.

"Are you kidding me? We just won't hike up very far. Besides, we may not have enough time. When we stop to eat our lunch, who knows what may happen in that desolate place?" she said suggestively.

"I can only dream," David said.

"Well, handsome, maybe your dreams will come true!"

"Should I hold my breath?"

"Don't need to. Aren't you going to get ready?"

"Be ready in a jiff," he said. "I need to talk to Alyssa before we leave. Be right back."

Nikki sat down on the bed. Could this really be happening? It was like a miracle. She was so grateful. She picked up the phone to call Susan, hoping she wasn't too early and wouldn't wake her up.

"Susan! Did I wake you?" Nikki asked.

"No, I just got up. What's going on? It's pretty early," she said, and Nikki heard her yawn. "Good news. Great news, actually. I told David I was considering a divorce. He spent the night on the sofa—by choice—and this morning he's a changed man! I just wanted to thank you for praying. I am so grateful."

"Nikki, I can't tell you how happy that makes me for you. I'll tell Carl. He was praying, too."

"You didn't tell him what I said about the di... "

"No, I told you I wouldn't and I didn't. But David had told him that the two of you were seeing Dr. Wilkerson and he asked how it went. I told him not good and so we prayed for you guys last night."

"Thanks again. And guess what! We've going to Long Rock to go hiking this morning. And taking a picnic lunch!"

"No! That's incredible! David's taking the day off? With his Easter sermon coming up? To spend time with you? This is too good to be true."

"That's what I keep saying. Anyway, here he comes, so talk to you later. Pray for us. We're supposed to talk about things today while we're out."

"Who were you talking to, Nikki?" David asked as he came into the bedroom.

"Susan. She and Carl have been praying for us. And I just wanted to let her know that God was answering her prayers because we are going to start over on our relationship again today."

"Did you tell her where we are going and what we are going to do?"

"Sure. She was happy for us. Are you ready to go?"

"Yeah. Alyssa is thrilled I said yes although she didn't act very surprised. Neil was yelling at her to hurry up or they would be late for school. They both wanted to tell you 'bye but I said you weren't feeling too well."

"David—I don't understand. Why did you do that? I was going to tell..."

"Because your eyes are so swollen. I didn't think you'd want them to see you like that."

"You're right, I guess. I'd rather talk with them tonight when I look better. That was thoughtful of you."

"Thanks. I'm glad you appreciate my taking care of you. So let's go, hiker!"

The day was beautiful. Like a perfect picture postcard, the sun was shining brightly, the sky was blue, the flowers were blooming, the birds were singing . . . *it's like a picture of how my heart feels. All of this is like a wonderful dream. My heart feels like Easter, like it's been resurrected.* Once again, she thanked God for David's transformation.

One of their favorite spots to hike was at Long Rock Park. *Correction, one of our favorite spots to hike used to be Long Rock.* They hadn't been in years. As they got closer to the park, she got more excited. The chicken in the back seat smelled delicious. They could eat it for a late breakfast, she thought. As soon as they got there, sure enough they had a picnic breakfast at the base of the rock and under the trees. She hadn't seen David in a wonderful—not even a good—mood in months and months. Her heart stayed in continual thankfulness to God for what He had done in David's life to change him toward her. And the way he kept looking at her! *If this place were a little more private...*He looked at her as if he could read her mind.

"Nikki," he said softly.

"Yes?" she asked tentatively. Surely he wouldn't suggest . . .

"Are you ready to climb?"

She laughed. "I didn't think that was what you were going to say . . . "

David laughed. "I'm not quite that immodest—later, though?"

The longer he continued to be gentle, tender, and kind toward her, the more irresistible he became. Her wall toward him was quickly tumbling down. Right now she was just happy to be close to him and for him to touch her, to hug her, and hold her hand. She leaned on his chest, closed her eyes, totally content for the moment. *I'm not kidding myself. I know all our problems aren't over, but at least we can communicate about them now.*

"Nikki, let's climb! I can't wait."

"Okay, me too." She took his proffered hand and jumped up, and almost slid down due to her old tennis shoes.

"You're going to have to be careful. We need to stay on the path where it isn't slick," he cautioned her. "You better go first and I'll be behind in case I have to catch you," he teased.

"That will be the day! When you have to catch me! I've always been better at climbing than you," she teased him. She started jogging up the gentle base of the rock. But it wasn't long before she had slowed way down. "I'm really out of shape," she said. "It's been too long since I've gotten any real exercise."

"Maybe we can remedy that by doing some other sports together, like old times," David said.

"That would be great," she said, out of breath, but still climbing steadily. There was a lookout about halfway up that she knew would be spectacular. All of God's spring colors would be showing. She couldn't wait. "I want to go far as the lookout," Nikki panted.

"I think we can get that far. I'd like to see it, too. Besides, it's a romantic spot," he said, beginning to be out of breath also.

"I see it!" Nikki cried. "It's not that much further. I-think-I-can, I-think-I-can, I-think-I-can," she chanted to herself.

"I think you could if you'd save your breath for climbing instead of silly rhymes. But I'm going to beat you," he challenged, as they got to a narrow place in the trail. It was a little scary, because there was an extremely high drop off on the side.

"Oh, no, you're not. Just watch me." Somehow she found an extra burst of energy and charged ahead. David was right behind her. She was going to beat him, she just knew it. She wasn't going to let him pass, either. If she could just get to the narrow place right ahead, he couldn't get by, and she would win, because the lookout was right ahead. She could hear him right behind her breathing hard and she lengthened her stride, coming up to the "Caution, Steep Drop" sign. As she reached the narrow part of the trail, she crowed, "I've got you beat."

"Oh, no, you don't," David said, and came up almost right beside her on the inside, as if he were jockeying for position.

"David, stop, you're pushing me, I'm going to..." she screamed as she started sliding over toward the edge. It was no use. Between the gravel-like rocks and her slick tennis shoes, she had no traction. The little rocks were sliding, propelling her over.

"DAVID HELP" she screamed in panic, throwing out her arms but grabbing only air. At the last second, she grabbed a very small bush suspended precariously on the side of the cliff. Hanging on for dear life, she felt her legs dangle over the bottomless chasm below.

"David, where are you?" Nikki whispered, terrified that any movement would send her all the way over the edge.

"Oh, God, Nikki, I'm right here. Don't move," David said. "I'll get a branch to help you. I'll be right back."

Sweat was pouring off Nikki's face. "Oh, God," she begged, "help me."

David hurriedly grabbed the first strong stick he could find. "Here, Nikki, here's a long limb. Reach out and grab it," David said.

"I'm scared to turn loose," Nikki breathed.

"It won't hold you forever," David said. "You have to turn loose and grab this branch. One hand at a time, slowly now," David said, trying to talk her through the ordeal. She would have to turn back up toward the top of the cliff to take hold of the branch and she was too petrified to move.

"Just a minute." Small rocks fell with her every tiny movement. She could hear them going off into nowhere. She didn't look down. Her eyes were closed tightly. *Okay, you have to do this. You have no choice.* Slowly, she inched her head around so she could look up to where David was holding the branch toward her.

"Come on, Nikki, hurry, grab it," he said, sweat pouring from his face, too.

With all the courage she could muster, she let go of the bush with one hand and grabbed the branch. Rocks flew everywhere. But she had a secure hold with one hand. Now she just had to let go with the other hand and let David pull her up. *You can do this*, she continued to say to herself, *you can do this*. Taking a deep breath, she let go of the bush and grabbed the branch with her other hand. She made it! Now she was totally dependent on this branch and David's ability to pull her up the side.

"Okay, David, start me up." She looked up at him, finally. He was looking at her strangely. What was wrong?

One Man's Search for Answers

His eyes were menacing. Suddenly the truth dawned on her. David wanted her dead. It had all been an act.

"David, please. Help me up, please, oh, God, please," she pleaded, horrified by his look of malice. "I'll do anything, David, please, just pull me up."

He looked at her coldly. His eyes were glittering with hate.

"Too late, Nikki. You won't be divorcing me. Bye," he said, and let go of the branch. Nikki felt herself going backwards, spinning, falling into nothingness as she held onto the branch that was connected to nothing. She screamed and screamed and screamed—to no avail.

David watched until he could hear nothing. Quickly, he ran back down the trail and was thankful he did not run into any other hikers. As soon as he got to the bottom, he ran to the car where he'd put their picnic basket, grabbed his cell and dialed 911.

"Help! help!" he cried, panic in his voice. "Please come quickly. My wife has fallen at Long Rock," he screamed, appearing distraught. "I'm going to look for her. Hurry!" He hung up. He knew there was no way she could have survived the fall, and he didn't want to look at her, but he knew it would appear strange if he weren't hunting for her. He started around the base of the rock toward the sheer side where she had fallen. As soon as he got around the corner, out of sight of the road, he leaned on the side of the rock. What had he done? He'd followed through on his plan. Now, with Nikki gone, he could eventually marry Shelby and keep his church. The kids would be sad for a while, but they'd fall in love with Shelby, too. He wiped his face. It hadn't been as hard as he thought it would. He started walking again, and as he heard sirens, started jogging.

He came to the side where he was sure Nikki's body would be. Glancing around the corner, he got a glimpse of her blue warm-ups. He didn't want to look closely, but he needed to make sure she was dead. Slowly he walked toward her body. Oh, yes, she was dead. No two ways about it. Her body was crumpled like a rag doll's. David started running back to the entrance as he heard the emergency vehicles arrive. He ran up to them, sweaty and incoherent in his grief at the tragedy. They tried to calm him. He told them he'd seen her body and where it was. They held him there while they went to look even though he strained to go with them, protesting he had to help his wife, that it was all his fault that she had fallen; he'd tried to help her and his hands were sweaty; he'd let her drop. He never should have let her come without her hiking shoes! He was so distraught they worried about him. They found her body but kept him from seeing the pitiful-looking corpse.

He begged them, "Please make her okay, please tell me it's not true!" He asked over and over again how he could tell his kids. Finally, paramedics gave him a shot to calm him and suggested he call someone to drive him home since he was in no shape to drive. He agreed to call his friend Carl and they waited while he called, gave Carl the tragic news, and asked him to come pick him up. The ambulances left with Nikki's body. The police officer asked David where he'd called them from and David said he'd forgotten to take his cell phone with him so he'd had to get back to the bottom to get it. They seemed satisfied with his answer but told David they would eventually need to ask him some questions.

They didn't seem suspicious. That's great but then why would they? They all know who I am and know my reputation. Of course they would think it was an accident. They stayed with him until Carl arrived. They were very compassionate and caring. Carl was there in a matter of minutes. His car slid into the parking lot and he was out and running almost before the car stopped.

One Man's Search for Answers

"David," he cried. "It can't be true. Oh, God, it can't be true. Nikki can't be dead." He grabbed David and held him. David held tightly onto Carl, as if he were his lifeline. "Oh, Buddy, we'll get through this together. I don't know how, but we will," he promised. Through his tears, David thanked him. Carl took him home and told him he and Susan would come back for his car later.

Carl helped David into the house. It was obvious to Carl that David was consumed with grief. However, he told Carl he was fine, and that he could leave because he needed to tell the kids what happened. Carl said he thought he could help; David told him he didn't need him to help. That brought a strange look from Carl because David always liked to utilize his training and expertise in hard situations. Obviously, this was an impossibly hard situation! Nevertheless, David insisted, so Carl left, telling David he would be back later.

Carl knew David was in shock and denial. Still, he went home as David requested, dreading telling Susan the gory details about her dear friend. After Carl left, David thought about how to tell the kids. He knew that would be the hardest part of this whole thing. But the person he most wanted to tell was Shelby. They were free now! She would be so excited, he knew. But he couldn't risk a phone call, somehow something might get recorded. He wanted to go to her office but knew that would look strange. Or would it? What would be more normal than a person experiencing extreme grief going to see his therapist? That's what he would do! He'd have to take Nikki's car, though. He left a note for the kids asking Neil and Alyssa to come to Shelby's office as soon as they got home from school. They should be home within the hour. And she could help him tell them the news.

As soon as he got to her office, he ran into the reception area, panicked and distraught-looking. "Dr.

Cunningham, what's the matter?" the receptionist asked.

"I have to see the doctor. Something terrible, just terrible has happened. I have to see her."

It was obvious something had happened. "But she's with a client, Sir."

"Please tell her I have to see her. Tell her there's been a tragedy, and I have to talk with her." The receptionist looked at David. She'd seen a lot of crazies act like there was an emergency just to get Shelby's attention, but it was obvious this wasn't one of those times. Besides, it was Dr. Cunningham.

"Yes, sir, I'll tell her right now." Judi had never knocked on Dr. Wilkerson's door before to interrupt her in session, but this looked like it was a door-knocking time. She ran down the hall and knocked loudly on the door. It opened abruptly. "What!" Shelby demanded, unused to being interrupted during a session.

"Dr. Cunningham is here and he says there's been a tragedy," Judi gasped. "He looks terrible."

"Oh, dear God," Shelby said. "I wonder—okay, let me explain to my client I have an emergency. Tell Dav—Dr.Cunningham I'll see him in just a minute."

Judi ran back down the hall to tell David the news. Shelby closed her eyes and breathed a prayer. She was terrified something had hurt David, but he must be okay or he wouldn't be here. Okay. He was okay and that was all that mattered. She turned and looked at her surprised client. Explaining to her that there had been a tragedy, and that she was extremely sorry but that she'd need to reschedule their time together, Shelby actually ushered her out the door.

"There won't be a charge for today," she said, trying to ease the awkwardness. As her client walked down the hall, Shelby was right behind her till she left the office. She saw David in the waiting room, looking like a man possessed.

Quickly, she came back in the waiting room.
"David! What's wrong?" she asked. David looked up and saw her. *It's going to be alright. Shelby is mine now.*

"My wife has been in a terrible accident," he said. "She's dead."

Shelby's mouth dropped. "Why, that can't be true," she said, knowing that of course it could. "What happened?"

"Could we go to your office to talk?" David asked.

"Of course. How thoughtless of me to leave you standing here. Please, come back. Judi, hold all my calls, please, and cancel my next appointment." But, she just stood there looking at David. Her feelings were like a roller coaster. Certainly she hadn't disliked Nikki and could understand how she felt toward David. She certainly wouldn't have wished her dead. But, on the other hand—David was free! Free to marry her! She took a deep breath and they looked into each other's eyes. Shelby looked down first and led the way down the hall. She closed the door into her office. He desperately wanted to hold her and to be held, but she was just looking at him and making no move to be close. He knew she wanted to comfort him but wasn't sure it was appropriate at the time.

Finally, Shelby said, "David, tell me about it. Are you okay? Was it a car wreck? What happened?"

"We'd gone hiking this morning," he said.

"Hiking?" Shelby asked immediately. "Together?" Of all people, she knew how angry David had been at Nikki. "Why?" She gave him a searching glance. He looked down this time.

"I thought we could talk about things peacefully, you know, maybe come to some kind of agreement—that she'd just let me go without a huge stink."

"Let you go? You mean a divorce?" Shelby asked. "You said you'd never get a divorce because it would ruin your ministry."

In Whose Steps?

"Maybe I thought you were worth it," he said meaningfully. "Worth the stink or whatever it took to be together—to be married to you. It's no secret to you that I didn't love Nikki. Is it okay for me to show my happiness to you? Aren't you happy, too?" His eyes begged her to say yes.

"You never talked to me about a divorce," Shelby said. "You never said anything to me about marriage." She was still in a quandary. It seemed so indecent to be glad that his wife was dead, especially someone she met, someone who had tried to be so vulnerable to him. But she did love David. "Anyway, you still haven't told me what happened."

"It was horrible, actually," he said calmly. "We were hiking and she slipped. I watched her fall."

"That's incredible! How horrible for you!" Shelby gasped. "Your poor wife. Was she dead on impact?"

"I'm sure she was. She fell from a great distance. She'd insisted that we go hiking this morning although she couldn't find her hiking shoes. I told her that I didn't think it was safe. But she was distraught after we'd talked about getting a divorce. She went running up the rock and there wasn't anything I could do to stop her. I tried to stay with her. We got to the narrow ledge and she slipped going around it. I tried to grab her and missed. She hung onto a bush until I could get a branch and lower it down to her."

Shelby was listening intently, tears running down her face. Poor Nikki, was all she could think. What a horrible way to die.

David continued. "Actually, she was able to grab the branch and I started pulling her up. But this is the really horrible part, Shelby. My hands were sweaty because I was so afraid and the branch slid out of my hands. I couldn't hold her!" He started sobbing, putting his head in his hands.

Shelby moved quickly to him. "Okay, David, I understand." She took him in her arms and held him. "It's okay, it's okay, you can cry all you need to," she said, as tears continued to run down her face, too.

"Not only did you see her fall, but you must feel terribly guilty, like it's all your fault, right?" He shook his head that was on her shoulder. "You did all you could. It must be terrible that it happened right after talking about a divorce, though."

David suddenly realized he hadn't told anyone else that. In a muffled voice, his head still buried on her shoulder, he said, "I didn't tell the police we'd talked about a divorce. I was afraid they'd suspect me."

"Suspect you? You mean of killing her? That's preposterous, isn't it? They would understand how distraught she was."

"All the same, I'd rather not tell them. Do you have to tell them? Don't you have to keep what I say confidential?"

"Yes. Unless they subpoena my records, that is."

"But you don't have any records yet."

"They could ask me what you said to me. But you're acting like there's going to be a trial or something."

"No, I can't see why that would happen. They just might think it's strange if I marry my therapist after my wife's death, you know."

Shelby wasn't sure what to make of David. But she knew that people do funny things when they're in shock. She'd have some more questions to ask later.

"Shelby, I have a huge favor to ask of you."

"Of course, David, I'll do anything. Anything at all."

"I don't think I can face telling my kids. Will you do it?"

"You need to do it, David. The kids need you. You're the parent. You need to be there for them."

"I can't stand it. What if they blame me for their mother's death?" He started sobbing again.

"They love you and they know you. They're not going to blame you. Tell you what. I'll help you tell them, but I won't do it for you."

"You're wonderful," he said, as his sobbing ceased. "I left them a note to come here because I was sure you would help me. I wanted you to meet them anyway. Not under these circumstances, of course."

"Me, either, David. I can't imagine that they would ever accept me." She paused for a moment, wondering what it would be like to be a mother. She'd always wanted to have children, but Don didn't want any. Didn't want to share her with anyone. Well, she certainly hadn't wanted to start out with teenagers, but thanks to her training and experience in therapy, she knew she was good with them.

"I need you, Shelby. I need you so much. Will you just hold me until the kids get here?" he asked.

"Of course I will, Sweetheart, of course I will," Shelby answered. She was filled with compassion for him. She cradled his head in her arms and stroked his back while they waited for the children.

CHAPTER TWENTY-ONE

David arrived at the funeral home, which was already filled with flowers for Nikki's service, about an hour before visitation. They'd worked hard on Nikki, but she just didn't look right. They couldn't cover all the bruises or the way her head was tilted due to her broken neck. So, he'd decided to have a closed casket for the service. He knew it would probably be harder on the kids and thought that he might let them see her even though she looked so badly. Shelby said they might need the viewing for closure with their mom so he should ask them if they wanted to see her anyway, after explaining to them that she "didn't look like Mom." He'd ask them when they got here later. Shelby was bringing Alyssa. He hoped Neil would show.

Telling them had been harder than he could have imagined. Two days ago, they'd come running into Shelby's office, asking "What's wrong, Dad, what's wrong? Someone said Mom had an accident and that she's in the hospital! Is she okay?" He'd started sobbing again and Shelby had told them that their Mom had been in an accident and hadn't made it through, and that she was in Heaven now. Neil just stood there without shedding a tear. David knew Carl would say he was in shock. Alyssa had screamed, "I want my mother!" over and over again. No matter how much teens and parents fought, death had a way of helping them realize how much they loved each other. (Well, except for Ann, he thought. He wasn't sure it would bother her if either or both her parents died. But then his thoughts about Ann reminded him he must not be very upset about Nikki or his own children.)

Anyway, the ordeal was finally over. He was glad Shelby had been there; it had been an odd sort of bonding time for her with the kids. They had listened to her and seen her compassion and tears for their mom. Alyssa had cried herself to sleep every night. He didn't think Neil had been home since. David guessed he was at Christina's. *Do I feel guilty? Well, some; I didn't want to cause the children so much pain.* But he knew God didn't want Nikki to divorce him and ruin his church—his ministry. Of that he was sure. And after a while, Shelby would fit in beautifully. He smiled to himself. She was so willing to comfort him at this time, knowing how much he was hurting. He was glad he wouldn't have to do an Easter sermon. Certainly no one expected him to do that. Things were going well under the circumstances.

Carl and Susan came in early, Susan's eyes swollen from crying so much. They both hugged him in silence, holding him for a few minutes. Then Carl asked him, "How're you doing, David? You're handling this better than I could."

"I'm just hanging in there."

"I won't go into it in detail right now," Carl said, "but there are five stages of grief you'll have to go through. And the first one is denial. I think that's where you are now. It's not real to you yet that Nikki is gone."

David really didn't care what stage he was in but he was grateful for their support. They continued to sit with him, each lost in their own thoughts of Nikki and what would happen next. Before long, church members started trickling in, some by themselves, some in groups. No one seemed to know what to say to David. Obviously, they had all been crying. They filed by, hugging David; some offering their condolence and others just crying. David knew they loved him, no matter how inane their comments.

Surprisingly, of all the people who had been by the house, it had been Paul who had been the most comforting to his children. He had come to bring some food—adding to David's already-full table—and had taken both Neil and Alyssa in his arms and cried. Both of them had seemed to feel awkward at first. Paul looked them in the eyes and promised them that God would comfort them. He told them Scripture promised them comfort from God Himself. He seemed so sure that God's Word was true and that He would not fail them in their grief that both Neil and Alyssa seemed to latch onto Paul's calm assurance and stability. They had hung around him the whole time he was at their house. David never would have thought that Paul could—or would—be comforting, but he'd sure been there for his kids. He could see Carl wanted to talk to them about the stages of grief they needed to go through, but they never left Paul's side. Oh, well, he was grateful that he could count on Carl to be there later when they were ready to hear the truth about the grief process.

David noticed some policemen pull up outside the funeral home. More questions, he supposed. They'd certainly asked him enough already. He couldn't believe they'd come to the funeral home. As a spouse, David had known he'd be questioned. But he was so sure of his ability to pull off Nikki's death as an accident that he wasn't worried. No one would ever believe that he would do it on purpose! They didn't get out of their car, though. They just seemed to be watching. He didn't get ruffled and continued to greet the people who came to comfort him. Everyone kept saying how well he was handling himself.

Finally, it was over, and the last of his congregation and friends had gone home. Shelby had brought Alyssa and Neil had shown up with Christina. They'd all cried together, even Neil. Neil seemed to be softening toward him some, now that he had only one parent. *At least for right now but that will be changed as soon as it is decently possible.* David smiled to himself again. He'd talked Shelby into a short mourning period telling her he'd think of a way to make it look plausible. He walked out into the cool spring air to get into his car. As he opened the door, he noticed one of the policemen get out of the patrol car and walk over toward him. The patrolman seemed to look vaguely familiar, but David didn't think he'd met him before. He met so many people.

"Good evening, Dr. Cunningham," he said. "I'm Officer Butler. I want you to know I'm real sorry about what happened to your wife."

"Thank you, that's very kind of you," David responded. The man continued to look at him.

"Did you want something else?" David asked.

"Seems as though I've seen you somewhere before," he said. "I've been trying to place where it was. As you were walking out, I think it hit me. There's a restaurant that gives us cops free meals when we're working. It's called 'The Breakers.' I think maybe I saw you there last week with your wife. It was obvious you guys loved each other."

"No, I don't think so," David said without thinking. Lying was the first thing that came to his mind at the time. *Oh, God, had the cop seen him? Could he prove it?*

"Were you by yourself?" David asked.

"No, there were a couple of other officers with me. We were talking about what a romantic couple you were, over there in that corner! We were all jealous!" he laughed.

David took a deep breath. Evidently he hadn't seen Nikki's picture and thought Shelby was his dead wife. His heart began to race; he began to perspire. "I think you have me mistaken for someone else," David said. "I like the restaurant, but I haven't been there for a while, that I remember."

"I'll ask my buddies later," he said, looking at David strangely. He was sure it had been him. David was a striking looking man and not easy to confuse with someone else. They'd all looked at the lovely woman with him who seemed so infatuated with him, too, and taken bets on whether they were married or lovers. No one knew how to find out for sure because they had to leave before the couple had. He could show David's picture to the waiters and to the desk clerk and ask if any of them remembered him. Maybe they'd even stayed, he thought, and even if he'd used a false name, he could still compare the handwriting.

"Well, I guess it doesn't really make any difference, does it? I mean, whether it was you or not."

"Can't say that it does," David replied, with a sigh of relief. "Well, thanks for the condolences. I've had a long day and I think I'm ready to go home, Officer..." he didn't remember his name and looked at his badge..."Butler," he said, smiling at him.

That does it, thought Officer Butler. *I know that smile with all those pearly whites. Why would he say it wasn't him? Does he have something to hide?*

"Yessir. I imagine you have had a hard day. I'll let you go home now." Officer Butler turned to walk back to his patrol car.

David was frantic. Was there any way they could find out? If they saw Shelby, would they recognize her and know it wasn't Nikki? They hadn't seen Nikki, but they could sure find a picture of her. Should he ask Shelby not to come to the funeral in case the cops were there and then later leave town with her? Would she give up her practice for him? He thought so. Was he willing to give up his church for Shelby? Not likely. He wanted his church and Shelby, too. That's why he'd done all this. Otherwise, he could have just persuaded Shelby to marry him after he got a divorce. This young man was going to ruin all his plans.

In Whose Steps?

Sweat began pouring down David's face as he drove home. He was more afraid now than when the initial deed had been done. Both kids were in bed. Eventually, he went to bed, too, wondering what the patrolman was doing. He couldn't sleep for hours. Finally, he fell asleep to fitful dreams where cops walked up to his door and said, "You're under arrest for the murder of your wife, Nikki Cunningham. You have the right..."

With a start, he woke up from his dream. *Oh, God, I can't stand it. I can't go through the public exposure even if they can't prove what I did. I can't stand a trial. Okay, okay, calm down. Even if they saw me there with Shelby at the restaurant, and all of them testify it was me, that doesn't mean they can prove what I did. So it does give me a motive. Even if they find out Shelby and I rented a room because the clerk identifies me. And the clerk in Pendleton—she might remember my asking for Shelby. Well, that's no big deal. After all, she is my therapist. And what if they should subpoena Shelby's records? They will just show Nikki and I had marital problems, that we were unhappy. Most couples are. That doesn't prove anything. I said I was holding the branch and that it slipped out of my hand. I don't have anything to worry about. What if. What if. What if they were able to prove I was having an affair with Shelby? They might never be able to prove I killed Nikki, but they might prove the affair. Shelby might even tell the truth and what would that do to my church, to my ministry! I'd be ruined even if I didn't go to jail for murder. And what would that do to my relationship with my kids? They wouldn't have anything to do with me if they knew I was sleeping with Shelby. And they'd never accept her as their mother. And what would Shelby do if she knew I'd killed Nikki?* He tossed and turned some more. The sheets were sopping from his excessive sweating. *What am I going to do?*

One Man's Search for Answers

Be sure your sins will find you out, he thought to himself. But not with any conviction. He knew he was panicking. That dumb cop had ruined everything for him. Steady, steady. He knew if he panicked he'd say and do things that would give him away. He got up, tired of tossing and turning. The bed seemed empty without Nikki, but he planned on filling it soon with Shelby. Walking over to the window, he looked out on the moonlit night. There was a patrol car outside his house! What were they doing there? This was ridiculous. *Just a fluke. It probably has nothing to do with me.* He looked out the window again. It was gone. It hadn't had anything to do with him. He felt safer now.

Turning on a lamp in his study next to the bedroom, he noticed his Bible on his desk. He quickly turned it over. He wasn't ready to deal with God yet. But the Word seemed to call to him. He kept looking at it and then he'd turn and ignore it. He knew he wanted to continue to serve God at his church with Shelby, and he was sure God had not wanted Nikki to get a divorce. He hadn't really talked to God about any of this, but all of a sudden he burst out, "Well, King David did it, Lord! He wanted Bathsheba and he took her and he murdered her husband. And you let him live! And said he was a man after your own heart!" *But he repented,* David heard in his heart. *Like King David before you, thou art the man.*

Gingerly, as if it would bite, David picked up God's Word. He let it fall open. The first words he saw were in Romans 1: "They exchanged the truth of God for a lie..." Looking up quickly, he shut his eyes tightly. He didn't like that. He looked back down and saw, "God gave them over to a depraved mind, to do what ought not to be done." David slammed it shut. He was afraid; he was ashamed; he knew he was wrong, but he still didn't want to be convicted.

"Dad?" Alyssa called softly from her room. He walked down the hall and went in.

"Yes, sweetie?" he said.

"Are you okay? Sounds like I heard some noise. Is that you? It's still dark outside. I'm not sleeping very well."

"I know, I'm not either. We miss your mom, don't we?" Her eyes began to tear as she shook her head yes.

"But I'm okay, and you're going to be, too. Just try and go back to sleep and dream happy thoughts of your mom being with Jesus. Okay?"

She nodded her head sleepily. "Okay, Dad. Thanks. You're a good dad." He groaned at the remark.

"What now, Dad? Does something hurt?"

"Just my heart, Alyssa, just like yours does." Her calling him a good dad had knifed his heart. Maybe he still had one, he thought, beginning to get a tiny glimpse of how he'd allowed his lust to deceive him so horribly. Going back into his bedroom, he sat back down at his desk. He knew random opening of the Bible was not an effective means of knowing God's will, but he did it again anyway. Proverbs 28:13 was marked on the page he opened to: "He who conceals his sins does not prosper, but whoever confesses and renounces them finds mercy." It was more of the knife that Alyssa had started thrusting in his heart when she called him good and he knew he wasn't. Everything in him was working to conceal his sin and God plainly said if he did that, he would not prosper. His ministry wouldn't prosper. But how could he have been so deceived? He exchanged the truth of God for a lie, didn't he? So what now?

He began to cry, softly at first, then great racking sobs. He got a pillow and put his face into it, trying not to wake Alyssa. His confession poured out. *Dear Lord, I have sinned so greatly. I'm not worthy of You. Or Alyssa. Or Neil. Or even Shelby. I led her into sin. And certainly not Nikki. She just exposed my selfish desires. Oh, God, what am I going to do? Confession would be bad for the kids and the reputation of the church. That won't help God's cause. There must be another way. I must do something quickly before the cops find out about Shelby and me.*

A truck roared by, loud in the silent night. And then he had the answer to his dilemma. Quietly, he dressed and went downstairs. He left a note for Alyssa and Neil telling them he was going to Long Rock, he had to go back to where Nikki died. He thought it was best not to tell Shelby anything, or leave her any word. He went into the garage and quietly started his car. Even at this time of night, he knew there would be eighteen wheelers on the freeway and he had to go down the freeway to get to Long Rock. No one would ever know that he'd faked a flat tire and that when he got out to fix it, they would think he had slipped and fallen in front of a truck. They'd think it was an accident and it wouldn't add shame to his church or his children.

And then they'd get his insurance! It was a good plan, he thought. He knew Shelby and Carl—and Paul—would help Neil and Alyssa. Driving down the road, blinded by his own tears, he prayed fervently for a fatal accident. But nothing happened. God didn't rescue him. Slowly, he pulled off the road onto the shoulder. It was dark, with only occasional traffic going by. He reached into the glove compartment and got out his tire gauge. Without hesitation, he got out of the car and inserted it into the valve stem of the back tire on the driver's side. The air hissed loudly into the dark, silent night. When the tire was almost flat, David put the gauge back into the glove compartment. Then, going to the trunk, he opened it to get out the tire tool. Slowly and methodically, he took his time, sure of what he must do. Taking the tire tool from the trunk, he laid it beside the flat tire and then returned for the spare.

In Whose Steps?

"God, please forgive me," he said. "I have sinned greatly against You and my family. I allowed Satan and my own lust to control me and lead me into this hell-on-earth. Please find it in your heart to forgive me." He deluded himself into thinking that suicide seemed less of a sin than allowing God's name to be smeared by his ungodly deeds—not to mention sparing his children and his church from finding out what he'd done. For a fleeting moment—but only a moment—it occurred to him that taking responsibility for what he'd done would be the righteous thing to do. He hadn't been totally humbled; his desire to look good, to save face, was still greater than his desire to be righteous before God.

There was a distant whine of a large engine. His death was coming. He heaved the spare from its storage into the floor of the trunk. When the truck was close enough so that it couldn't stop, David planned to step from the curb, while clutching the spare, onto the highway. He had no question but that the stupendous impact would put him out of the misery of the wretched and contemptible existence he had brought upon himself, as well as everyone unfortunate enough to have been involved with him. The thunderous roar of the engine was more deafening by the moment; it seemed to fill his head. Wiping his clammy palms on his pants, he took a deep breath as he grasped hold of the tire and pulled it from the trunk, steadying its bounce as it hit. David sneaked a furtive look as he bent down over the tire. Just a few more seconds and it would be close enough. The headlights were coming closer and closer. He was gulping to get enough air; his heart was pounding and sweat was pouring down his face. Soon. Soon. Now, it was time! The trucker would not have any time to stop! With his hand on the tire, he stepped off the curb and onto the highway. For a split second—although it seemed much longer—it felt like slow motion as he stared at the monster's yellow eyes and steel teeth and felt the enormous heat blasted from its nostrils. David closed his eyes and screamed.

CHAPTER TWENTY-TWO

"David! David!" *Someone was calling his name. What was happening? Wasn't he dead? Someone was shaking him. Why? What was happening?* He wondered if he could open his eyes and found that he could.

"Carl! Linda!" he said in surprise. "What are you guys doing here?"

"Trying to get you awake! I've been shaking you for several minutes. You must have been having a nightmare. You were screaming. I guess you fell asleep," he laughed, until he looked at David's face.

"You're drenched in sweat, David. What's going on? Are you alright? Must have been a really bad dream!"

David looked around. He was in his study, in his chair. Carl was sitting across from him, smiling at him. Linda was looking down, worriedly. David shook his head, as if to clear it. As he wiped his face, he noticed it was wet. *What is happening?* He felt a weight in his lap and looked down. In His Steps was lying open in his lap. He looked up, in wonder. *God! I've been dreaming? I had a nightmare? It couldn't be. It was so real..*

The phone rang and Linda left to answer it.

"It's Nikki," she called. "Do you want to take it or should I tell her you'll call her back?"

Nikki. He closed his eyes. She was alive. It was a dream. *Dear God, thank you, thank you, thank you.*

In Whose Steps?

"Please tell her I'll call shortly," David said. He had to have a few minutes to think, to pray, to clear the cobwebs from his head—to find reality. He wasn't sure he could keep his composure and talk to her at the moment. Carl was staring at him.

"You look funny," he said. "Are you sure you're okay?"

"Never felt better in my life," David replied, as he jumped up and did a little dance step right there in the middle of his office. Who cared what anybody thought? The book fell to the floor, of course. He picked it up, lovingly. "I want to walk in Your steps, no doubt about it," he whispered to God. "Thank you for giving me the chance to do that."

"Who are you taking to?" Carl was getting worried. He'd been thinking David seemed depressed lately. Now he was wondering if he was bipolar, down one day and up the next—the evidence seemed to support it. He'd been wanting to talk to him about seeing someone anyway. Maybe now was a good time.

"Carl, some new things are about to happen—or maybe I should say some old things are about to re-appear," David said, as he began to pace, "like the old-time gospel. I'll need to talk with you about them. You may not like some of them. You see, we've been walking in the *world's* steps and we need to walk in Jesus' steps. And as a pastor leading his flock, I am convicted that we must do an about face."

Grandiosity, flight of ideas, impulsive, increase in activities. Yep, David was looking bipolar alright. Maybe even a bit delusional. Please—'in the world's steps'? What on earth was that about? We need to get this guy checked out for some lithium. Maybe I need to talk with the elders about him.

"David?" he ventured, "why don't you sit down and rest and let's talk about a few things..."

"Didn't you hear what I said? Aren't you supposed to be the great listener? I don't want to sit down. I'm too excited about God!"

Psychomotor agitation, Carl checked off an imaginary list.

David wasn't stopping. "I have a million ideas that I can't wait to put into effect. I hope you'll join me in walking in His steps, doing what Jesus would do."

"That's what I always try and do. Just calm down, David, okay?"

David gazed at Carl, seeing that he wasn't comprehending—at the moment, anyway—what he was saying. David thought he had to share his happiness with someone or he'd burst. And evidently it wasn't going to be Carl.

"I want to be alone awhile. Thanks for waking me up. We'll talk later."

You can say that again! "Okay, just let me know when," Carl said, as he left David's office.

The minute he left, David shut the door and fell on his face before God. "Father, I pray you'll help me to put together an Easter sermon that will turn people's hearts to you. I don't care if they like it or not or if they like me or not, as long as they are challenged to turn to you, that's all I ask. Thank you for changing my cold heart. Thank you for showing me that I'm not depressed or going through a mid-life crisis. I have been sinning because I wasn't honest about my anger, bitterness, and resentment toward Nikki, and because I was angry that I couldn't control my life, my family, and my church—that things weren't going *my* way. I repent and humbly ask Your forgiveness. I commit my life to doing things Your way as I lead my flock in your steps, not mine. I ask your forgiveness for leading them according to the world rather than according to your Word. Help me to learn and grow in your grace. In Jesus' name, Amen."

David picked up his Bible, ready—eager—to start preparing his Easter sermon. He knew his heart had been changed. But he knew just preaching the truth wasn't enough. How was what he'd experienced going to work out practically? Glancing back down at his Bible, he knew it would be good if his life started showing some change before he started preaching it to others.

Which means, I have to start being honest with others, starting with Nikki. Some of his exuberance, but none of his resolve, began to fade as he thought of being honest with Nikki. He wasn't looking forward to that experience! *Well, there's no time like the present. God, will you please give me both the desire and the courage to talk with Nikki in a kind yet truthful way, without losing my temper—or acting like I don't have one when You and I know good and well that I do?* Hmmm, it actually felt good to admit that he did have an anger problem.

Slowly, he dialed his home number. Maybe Nikki had already left although Linda had told her he would call her back. But she was home. David asked her to meet him for lunch and she agreed to come. *Okay, it's now or never. It's time to face the real music. God, will you give me what I need to speak lovingly to my wife?* David was sure God would answer that prayer but he continued to pray for help.

CHAPTER TWENTY-THREE

He was already there, waiting anxiously, when Nikki walked into the restaurant. He grabbed her—right in the middle of the restaurant crowd—and hugged her. She looked at him with a "what's-gotten-into-you-look" as they sat down to wait for a table. His eyes seemed welcoming. But she was still apprehensive, to say the least.

"David, what's going on? You're not usually—no, you're not ever," she corrected herself, "happy to see me."

"You have no idea how happy I am to see you," David said.

"Well, this is going to be a *very* interesting lunch. Did you get hit on the head or something...?"

"In a way I guess you could say I did get hit on the head. A lightning bolt to the heart, at least." He smiled at her.

"Okay, I'm scared now. You're smiling at me. You're talking lightning. Is this a set-up or what? Am I in trouble again?"

"I must have been pretty awful to you for you to be so suspicious of my motives."

"'Have been pretty awful'? Why are you using past tense? I don't know any reason to use the past tense."

"Cunningham, party of two, your table is ready," the hostess said.

David effectively ignored Nikki's comment by getting up and motioning for Nikki to go first. Obediently she followed the hostess, wondering what on earth David was up to. She was sure it wasn't good, and she didn't trust him to be honest with her. What was he going to try and manipulate her into?

David held out her chair and Nikki sat down. Strange. It almost seemed he was glad to be holding her chair—serving her—rather than just doing it because he wanted to look good in everyone else's eyes. What was happening? Could it possibly be something good? As he sat down, she looked at him, waiting for him to continue.

"I have many confessions to make, Nikki. And I'm going to need lots of forgiveness from you."

Nikki was dumbfounded. This did not sound like the David she knew. Then fear struck her heart. Even though she hadn't been happy with David for a long time, she didn't want him to have had an affair! But what else would bring about this kind of confession? And doing it in a restaurant so she wouldn't—or couldn't—get hysterical and make a fool of herself. It was a set-up, she was sure.

"Should we order first?" she asked, looking down at the menu, her mouth so dry the words would hardly come out. Maybe she didn't want to hear any confessions. She wasn't sure she was hungry anymore.

"Sure," David replied, as the waitress came up to their table to take their drink orders. Reaching his hand over and putting it on top of hers, her head jerked up and she looked at him in amazement. He said, "Want the usual?"

This had been their favorite restaurant forever for burgers, fries, and cokes, but they hadn't been here since—well, she couldn't remember the last time they'd been here together.

"Sure, that will be okay." Had the words come out correctly? Her heart was pounding and she felt dizzy with apprehension.

"Two old-fashioned's with the works, a large order of fries, one large Coke and one large diet Coke, please."

One Man's Search for Answers

"Have it out shortly," the waitress said, taking their unopened menus.

"I never do understand why you eat a fat-laden meal of burger and fries and get a diet Coke with it," David laughed.

"That's just one of many things you don't understand," Nikki said sharply, looking him in the eye. "Okay, what's this about? I know it's not whether or not I drink diet Coke."

"I'm not sure where to start."

"Obviously, the beginning would be good."

"I'm not even sure where the beginning is. In a way, it's this morning. In another, it's when we were first married. But in another, it's my whole life, Nikki."

She couldn't stand the suspense. "Just say it!" came out of Nikki's mouth. She glanced around. She hadn't meant to be so loud. "Just start somewhere, for goodness sake, before I go berserk. I have no idea what you are saying or where you are going with it." She propped her chin in her hands with her elbows resting on the table and stared at him, waiting.

David felt like squirming away from her direct gaze. Finally he replied, "Well, you couldn't know, I guess. So, here it is: I've never really been honest with you."

Nikki sat straight up, her hands clasped in her lap. She leaned forward toward David.

"Like, that's not supposed to be a revelation, is it?" she asked. "Because it sure isn't. Well, not to me, anyway. I mean, I've thought for a long time you were so used to lyi-- uh, being dishonest with yourself that you wouldn't know the truth if it hit you in the face like a freight train!" She didn't notice his wince at her mention of a freight train. She didn't know how close to true that statement was! But she was on a roll as she continued, "I must say, though, for you to confess to me that you haven't been honest is a revelation. A much-welcomed one."

David sighed. It was difficult not to get defensive. "You're right, Nikki. And the truth did hit me in the face like a freight train. Figuratively and almost literally. But God was the freight train who hit me with it."

"Now you have my full attention. Please, keep talking to me—well, just a sec. Here's our food. That was quick," she said to the waitress.

"We try to please," the waitress said, balancing the tray with one hand as she plunked down the cokes and then the two hamburger platters with the other, fries spilling onto the table. "Need anything else? Ketchup's right here."

"No, thank you, we're fine," David told her, immediately shoving his plate, untouched, to the side. "I'm not really hungry, Nikki. Not physically, anyway."

"David! Whatever do you mean?" she said, as she set down her hamburger as quickly as she'd picked it up. She sat back, crossed her arms, and raised her eyebrows questioningly.

He smiled. "I know I keep confusing you. Okay, I'll make it plain. God showed me what a jerk I've been—no amens, please—as a husband, as a father, and as a pastor. You see, I had a dream, maybe a revelation, this morning..."

"Before you left for your office?" Nikki interrupted.

"No, in my office."

Nikki started to ask, but David said, "Wait. I'm going to tell you why I had a dream in my office. Please don't ask any questions until I'm through. Is that okay?"

"Okay. Sorry. Please go ahead. I'll just quietly eat my hamburger while you talk, and then I'll decide what I think and feel." But she wasn't feeling anything anymore. Her emotions had gone up and down every time David started a new sentence because she couldn't imagine what he was going to say next.

"Thank you, Nikki. Really, thank you. I'm not being sarcastic." David took another deep breath. "Well, as I was saying, I had a dream—again, nightmare would probably be more accurate—this morning in my office. I fell asleep reading an old book about a congregation wanting to do only what Jesus would do for an entire year."

Mouth full, Nikki interrupted. "I know that book—something about walking in Jesus' steps. I read it a long time ago. I--oh, sorry," she said as David looked at her, waiting. "Please, go ahead."

"Okay. This may or may not surprise you, but I've been feeling rather blah for a while. I was thinking maybe I was depressed, going through an early mid-life crisis, whatever. I wanted to talk with Carl about it and get his feedback. This morning it was really bad. I felt like quitting the pastorate—as well as quitting being a husband and a father." He glanced at Nikki to see her reaction.

Her eyes began to water. Even though what David was saying felt scary to her, it also felt good that he was being so transparent with her. She didn't interrupt. And David could see Nikki's love for him reflected in her eyes. It had been a long time since he had seen that. He began to realize that she must have closed down or been sarcastic to him as he continually shut her out. He continued.

"I thought the answer was for me to get Carl to refer me to someone for therapy. I'd been thinking that the Bible was an old, dead book with no answers for today's—no, for my—problems. The thought of taking an anti-depressant even crossed my mind."

Nikki caught her breath in surprise but still she didn't interrupt. He had her full attention.

"Need anything?" the waitress asked, not even looking at them as she breezed by.

"No thanks," they said together, but she was halfway across the room and didn't hear.

"She didn't really want an answer, did she?" David asked.

In Whose Steps?

"That's the way I feel with you most of the time, David," Nikki ventured. "You say the right things but you don't really want any feedback—and certainly no feelings—from me."

"That's true," David admitted, hating every minute of it. Nikki was pointing things out before he even had the opportunity to confess them! "If it's okay with you, I'll come back to that issue. But I'd rather finish my story first if you don't mind."

"Okay." Nikki was surprised David hadn't reacted with anger to what he would normally perceive as an attack or accusation. "Please. I'm listening."

"You know I've talked with Carl about lots of emotional problems people have. I've heard him relate all kinds of stories about the necessity to work through your baggage from the past and the value of anti-depressants during that process. The more I learned from him, the more I thought about my own past and all the anger, rage, lies, and deception that occurred in my home. I thought about how scared I was growing up and how scared I was to say I was scared—or to have any feeling, for that matter. About how I just shut down and withdrew to keep from dealing with conflict."

"I know you do—did," Nikki said softly. She took a napkin and wiped her eyes while continuing to focus on David.

"The only way I thought I could get past all that was to have therapy, although I hadn't said it to you, Carl, or really even admitted it to myself. After all, everyone at church raves about our support groups and how helpful they are for working through problems. The Bible certainly didn't seem to have any relevant answers for me. It's true that God was trying to reach out to me through Dr. Burns, and Paul, too. But I wouldn't let God or them in. You know me. I'm the wonder boy. I can handle everything."

Nikki shook her head in agreement, tears now spilling down her face. She waited expectantly while blowing her nose on her napkin.

"I neglected to remember that God doesn't want us—me—to handle everything. He wants me to depend totally on Him as I live my life. I gave that lip service—I even thought I meant it—but I didn't really depend on Him. Nikki, I don't know what it means to depend on Him or to trust Him. And rather than grapple with what that means, theologically or practically, I realize now I started believing what it seems the whole modern Christian world seems to believe, that God can actually sanctify His church through psychotherapy rather than through His Word."

As he thought about it, David slowly shook his head. "Imagine. The God of the Universe—the God who created man, who wrote the instruction book about man—needs psychology's ideas about what makes man tick? Of course Carl would say that God in His common grace allowed those psycho guys to discover spiritual and emotional concepts about man that would enable him to be whole and healthy."

"Wow. You've been doing some deep thinking, haven't you?" Nikki said quietly, not wanting to detract David from his thoughts.

"Yes. And praying. I know you're wondering how I came to these conclusions—and, by the way, I guess I need to tell you up front that Carl thinks I'm bipolar."

"David, you've never sounded more sane to me than you are right now. Please, tell me more." Nikki was thrilled that David had at long last allowed God to invade his deepest being—and that he was also letting her in. She started feeling convicted for telling God that she'd given up hope that He could change David. Also, she was convicted for her own bad attitude toward David when he wasn't kind to her. She had justified herself to God that she didn't have to be nice to him since he, supposedly the spiritual leader of their home and her church, wasn't nice to her.

"Want me to take these plates away? Doesn't look like you ate much," the waitress interrupted.

"Go ahead," Nikki said. "You're right; we aren't very hungry." The waitress took the plates and David reached across the table and took Nikki's hands in his. Slowly he made eye contact with Nikki. Tears continued to run down her face.

"Which brings me to my relationship with you, Nick. I have hurt you and sinned against you because I've been very angry at you. I've been full of resentment and bitterness and blamed you for my unhappiness in life because you weren't meeting my needs, as the world would say."

"I knew you were angry, David, even though you kept saying you weren't."

"Well, you're right. About that and every other emotion you accused me of having and that I denied. I really didn't believe I had bad feelings toward you or anyone. I believed you were a bad person, so it was your fault I was angry. I felt justified in my anger."

"I understand."

"Thank you. So I know I need to learn to start being more transparent, more honest with you. And hopefully today is a start."

"It's a big start, David. You have no idea how much I appreciate your honesty. You've been so terribly mean to me and left me alone so many times. I couldn't talk to you about it because you wouldn't listen—just like that waitress. Acting like she wanted to help but just saying her lines."

"Alright, just wait a minute here. You were always so busy..."

"David. You're already doing it again."

"Doing what?"

"You're not listening to me. You're blaming me and justifying yourself. If you want to tell me you were angry at me, then do it. But don't blame me."

"This is harder than I thought it would be," David confessed. "I thought it was hard to ask God for forgiveness for shutting Him out. Man. It's even harder with you!"

Nikki started getting angry. "So are you saying that's my fault again?" she demanded.

David realized fear of conflict with Nikki was making him either want to run from her or strike back with strong words. He realized he had started again to handle the situation by himself. *God! I need help right now because I want to say all the mean things I can think of to hurt Nikki. I want to attack her, same as always. Please give me the desire to choose to walk in your Spirit rather than in the flesh, to say what You desire me to say rather than what I want to say to protect myself.*

He looked Nikki in the eye. "Honey," he said, choosing to say something kind rather than something evil, "I'm trying very hard not to blame you. If I'm coming across like that, please forgive me. I don't want to blame you. I want to acknowledge and take responsibility for my own feelings."

Seeing his struggle and his obvious sincerity, Nikki was immediately contrite. "I'll listen," she said.

Thank you, God. He continued to confess: "So I'm trying to practice speaking the truth in love but I'm pretty lousy at it. But I am really trying. What I was trying to say is that I've blamed you for my own unhappiness when it was my own unwillingness to make choices to do something about it—which means allowing God to transform my heart. No easy matter in my case," he admitted. The words of Jeremiah stating that the heart is deceitfully wicked never seemed more true to David than at this moment.

"Not easy for any of us, David. We all want our own way, and we all want it to be someone else's fault when we don't get it, just like Adam and Eve blamed each other. So where do we go from here?"

"I want to commit to you to be consistently honest with God and with you. To tell you when I'm angry or upset or when I feel like withdrawing rather than just doing one or the other—to talk out the problem with you without blaming you. Are you willing to give me a chance to do that?"

Nikki hesitated.

"Well?" David demanded impatiently. He'd spilled his guts. What else did she want, for crying out loud?

"It's scary for me, David. Even now, you already seem angry because I didn't immediately do what you want. Besides, I have a good bit of anger and resentment built up that I think I need to talk about with you. Maybe not. But I want you to be willing to try and understand my feelings, past and present, before I commit to any kind of telling the truth with you. Otherwise it's not a risk I'm willing to take right now. And you need to pray for me that God will give me the courage to do it because I know it's a sin not to do so."

David realized how quickly he reverted to his demanding, controlling self the minute he didn't get the response he wanted. He knew the only reason he was realizing it, though, was because he'd asked God to convict him when that happened rather than immediately switching into his blaming/withdrawing/angry mode. How hard to keep making that choice—like willingly asking someone to stab you when you goofed. Ouch! But then, life certainly hadn't been working the other way. He saw Nikki waiting with her head and eyes down. He began to understand a little of her pain rather than just his own. Reaching over, he gently took her chin in his hands and raised her eyes to his.

"Nikki, by the grace of God, I commit to trying to understand you, to hear and acknowledge your feelings when we're in conflict, before I ever ask you to hear my side. I know I'll fail many times, so I'm asking you to hold me accountable to you when I do fail and sin against you. Will you do that for me?"

Nikki was embarrassed that tears—and makeup, if there was any left—continued to flow down her cheeks in the restaurant. David's words were next to unbelievable, and it was frightening and very scary to believe him. But, she knew she would be pleasing God to trust David's words. And she so desperately wanted to trust him and to believe he would do what he said. She'd never seen him so sincere or broken.

"Okay, David. I will," she said with the solemnity of a marriage vow. "And I want to commit to you to hear and try and understand the ways I've hurt you." She wanted to say "even though that's not fair because you've hurt me more than I've hurt you," but she chose not to. "God help us."

"If He doesn't, it's a lost cause," David said. "The thing of it is, He promises to transform us if we let Him. And, He loves and cares more about us and our marriage than we do."

Looking around, they noticed for the first time that the lunch crowd was long gone. Their waitress was staring at them. David quickly put cash down and without waiting for change, he and Nikki left hand in hand. They were experiencing the hope of God, something no human could provide.

CHAPTER TWENTY-FOUR

Easter morning David woke to the steady sound of falling rain. He knew many people were going to be incredibly disappointed when they realized it was raining on Easter morning. The unwelcome wet weather would dampen their colorful spring clothes, and their kids couldn't enjoy their Easter egg hunts if it was muddy outside. But none of that fazed him. Nothing—definitely not lousy weather—could touch the abounding joy of the Lord singing in his grateful heart. His joy was compounded as his eyes drank in his lovely Nikki, asleep—and alive!—in the bed next to him.

Overwhelmed with thankfulness to God, David reached over and gently touched her tousled hair. He once again praised and thanked God for His goodness and grace to him. Quietly he slipped out of bed and went to his study to pray and to go over his sermon once more.

As he had done every day for the last two weeks, he literally fell on his face before God. "Father, my life and the message I deliver this morning are in your hands. I have nothing worth saying without the power of your Holy Spirit. Thank you for removing spiritual blinders from my eyes and showing me your truth. If anything I plan to say today contains untruth, then let me stutter and stammer rather than say it. I continue to thank you and praise your name for the opportunity you have given me to glorify you. . . ." The words caught in his throat and David started sobbing. He knew he was totally unworthy to be used as an instrument of God.

One Man's Search for Answers

Nikki woke up hearing David sobs. He was doing that a lot lately. She could hardly believe the difference in him in the last several days. It seemed God was answering her prayer to make *her* David "a man after God's own heart." It had been very painful to watch David grow cold and distant in his relationship to God—and to her—over the years. But it was evident his heart had been strangely warmed. Pushing back the cover, she got up and walked down the hall to David's study. As she reached for the door knob, she heard him pouring out his heart to the Lord. Feeling as though she were standing on holy ground, she quietly turned around and went back to the bedroom.

She'd noticed David had been studying every minute to get ready for his Easter sermon. Nikki had never seen him agonize so intensely over a sermon. He told her he had some important things to share with the church this morning—some things which might even affect their lives at the church and possibly even their friendship with Carl and Susan. David said he'd explained to Carl what he was going to say and Carl had agreed to listen—even though David knew, and told Nikki, that Carl still thought he was in a manic state.

"I hate to even think this," David had told her, "but Carl may be just one of the friends I'll lose. It's possible my message will upset Carl to the point that he and Susan might leave the church—unless, of course, the elders ask me to leave."

Nikki bravely told him, "If you think it's from God, go for it!" Then she'd countered, "But I am curious to know why you would think Carl would be upset enough to want to leave the church."

"It's a huge difference in worldview, Nikki. A worldview is the way each person looks at the world and makes sense of it. My worldview regarding soul care has changed; I no longer believe that psychological theories are necessary to counsel people. Carl believes they are, so, in his opinion the Bible alone is not sufficient to help people through their problems. But, he doesn't want to discuss what I have to say because he thinks I'm uneducated regarding counseling, I'm manic because I'm bipolar, and I should be on medication."

As Nikki pondered these things in her heart, she started praying. She knew the best way to help David was to ask God's guidance and wisdom for him and the message he was going to deliver this Easter morning.

Several hours later, David was on the platform in the church listening to the music the choir had rehearsed diligently for months. Their performance was beautiful and he knew people's hearts were touched by it. What he continued to pray, though, was for them to be moved more by God's Spirit than they were by the music.

It was time for his sermon. The congregation was poised, expecting his usual fine message. *My usual fine message that will tickle their ears—well, no more tickling.* David breathed a quick prayer under his breath: "Lord, into your hands I commend my life and words." He knew this could be the last sermon he'd preach as pastor of the church and was immediately struck with the irony that he might lose his job because he was going to talk about the sufficiency of the Bible to help hurting people. Something, indeed, was wrong with that picture!

He stepped into the pulpit. It was very quiet in the auditorium. David took a deep breath and began speaking. "The title of my message today is *Jesus, the Wonderful Counselor: Walking in His Steps.* As you turn in your Bibles to Job 33:14, I'll first tell you why I've chosen this message for an Easter Sunday."

David heard the rustling of pages as they turned in their Bibles to the passage. As he began reading, he prayed his unusual nervousness didn't show:

"For God does speak—now one way, now another—though man may not perceive it. In a dream, in a vision of the night, when deep sleep falls on men as they slumber in their beds, he may speak in their ears and terrify them with warnings, to turn man from wrongdoing and keep him from pride, to preserve his soul from the pit, his life from perishing by the sword.

The congregation looked up expectantly as he began his sermon. "Two weeks ago, God gave me a terrifying dream which I believe was for the purpose I just read in Job: to turn me from wrongdoing and keep me from pride. I know I may sound somewhat melodramatic, but through what God showed me in my dream, He began my rescue from pride and brought me back to His Word and His way of doing things.

"This is how it happened. Lately, I'd been feeling somewhat depressed and started wondering if I was going through a mid-life crisis. I wasn't excited about God, life, or anything else. Then I just happened—of course, I don't think it really 'just happened'—to pick up an old book, In His Steps, from my bookcase. I'm sure many of you are familiar with the story of the pastor who challenged himself and his people not to do anything for a year without first asking, 'What would Jesus do?' You may have even seen some of our teens wearing the 'WWJD' bracelets based on that book. Anyway, as that congregation began to study Scripture in order to find out what Jesus would do, their lives were transformed.

"God convicted me right then that I had no idea what it would mean if we were to do the same thing at our church. Sadly, I realized I had no idea what Jesus would do! And as I continued to think about it, I fell asleep—and that's when I had the horrible dream. Through the dream, God showed me what could happen if I kept going down the same prideful road I was on. He showed me I was trying to get my emotional needs met by seeking others' approval rather than His. I was literally addicted to approval and just like any other addiction to sin, one always needs more. I had peaked out on your approval and I became fearful you'd think I was slipping. Then I started feeling depressed because my approval god was no longer working for me. I began to wonder if I needed therapy for what I thought must be a mid-life crisis. I was not walking in His steps, if you will."

It was silent. The congregation was not used to David being honest about himself and definitely not in a negative way. A few disapproving eyebrows were raised and David could almost hear their thoughts: "These are not really Sunday morning topics and besides it's Easter and we've brought visitors." But he gulped and continued.

"In this dream, God graciously allowed me to learn what happens when a person starts focusing on himself to get his emotional needs met and forgets about others; even worse, what happens when he begins to focus on serving himself more than serving God. And that's really seriously sinful when you're the pastor of the church! I know it's hard to believe that you can convince yourself that you're doing God's will when you're actually sinning—but you can! Some shameful, terrible things occurred in the nightmare which opened my spiritual eyes—things I would be ashamed to share, even though they aren't true, thank God!

"Through my dream, I came to understand that my desire for approval meant I was controlled by what the Bible calls 'fear of man.' Among other Scriptures regarding fear of man, the writer of Hebrews tells us 'The Lord is my helper; I will not be afraid. What can man do to me?' (13:6). Well, I knew what man could do to me: disapprove of me, and I was petrified you were going to do that. The disapproval of others has always created terrible fear in me. I learned early in life that I was very capable and I have always depended on that capability to feel good about myself. But when I began to feel less capable, and therefore less worthy of approval, I did not know where to turn. I did not know how to turn to God and I became depressed. I realized that if I did not know what it meant to depend on God myself, how could I teach you to do so?

"Jesus said in Matthew 22:29 'You are in error because you do not know the Scriptures or the power of God.' That means I, your pastor, was in error because I did not know the Scriptures or the power of God in a way that made a difference in my life. I had never learned to turn to God as my helper because I didn't actually need Him; I'd always been capable on my own. Certainly I believed in God, but basically, I gave Him lip service. Jesus said in Matthew 15:8, 'These people honor me with their lips, but their hearts are far from me.'

"Of course I never believed I could get to heaven on my own. Years earlier, God showed me I was a sinner and I gave my heart to Christ when I depended on His death, burial, and resurrection for salvation. However, as far as Him making a difference in my everyday life, I was far from Him. What I did not realize at the time was how much I allowed the approval of others to influence the decisions I made each day. Because of my lust for that approval, when what seemed like modern, scientific sanctification-by-psychology came along, I wanted to keep up with the world's wisdom. I did not search Scripture; instead, I believed and taught you to believe, there was more power in the psychological theories of men than in the truth of God.

"But what does it mean to know 'Christ and the power of His resurrection,' as Paul states in Philippians 3:10? What does it mean that Jesus died to pay the penalty for our sin and that He was resurrected from the dead? That's what we celebrate on Easter Sunday: the power of Christ's resurrection which brings us salvation. However, I also want you to consider that His power does not stop with salvation—as totally glorious as that is. The power of the resurrection also pertains to sanctification, God's continuing work of grace in our hearts to make us holy.

In Whose Steps?

"I realized I did not believe, or rather, I did not function as if I believed the power of the resurrection had anything to do with sanctification—that is, with the process of making us holy. That process happens as we learn to depend on the Lord throughout our lives in practical problems we must face every day—problems such as depression, anxiety, worry, fear, anger, alcohol, drugs, food, sex, and shopping. Those are the problems to which the theories of psychology claim to have answers. Some have called it sanctification by psychology. However, the Bible claims to answer these problems as well. On this resurrection Sunday I want you to think about whether or not the biblical process of sanctification has been taken captive by psychology—that is, are Christians sanctified by walking in Christ's steps or by walking in the steps of psychological techniques?

"While I think that we would all give the right spiritual answer, I believe that functionally we live our Christian lives based on our belief in the world's wisdom of psychotherapy. But here is what God's Word tells us in 2 Peter 1:3-4 about living our everyday lives:

> His divine power has given us everything we need for life and godliness through our knowledge of him, who called us by his own glory and goodness. Through these he has given us his very great and precious promises, so that through them you may participate in the divine nature and escape the corruption in the world caused by evil desires.

"That says it all, doesn't it? His divine power has given us <u>everything</u> we need for life and godliness through our knowledge of Him. But how do we access everything we need? Through our knowledge of Him! Not a superficial knowledge, but a deep, intimate knowledge of Him which we receive as we get to know Him better. The more we study the Word, the more we know God. The more we know God, the more we can trust Him and believe His great and precious promises which enable us to escape the corruption of the world. We don't need medicine to make us feel happy; we need Jesus. Scripture is truth, and truth works even though it doesn't make sense to the world—and sometimes not even to us. However, God doesn't call us to understand everything; He calls us to obey. Do we think that people living in Peter's time had it so easy that Christ was enough for them, but He's not enough for us because we know more and are more sophisticated? We've just learned how to sin in a more sophisticated way.

"Of course, we have no problem believing His divine power has given us all we need for so-called spiritual things like teaching and preaching, but we think we need the world's wisdom to help us with problems like addictions. Yet Colossians 2:8 warns us: 'See to it that no one takes you captive through hollow and deceptive philosophy, which depends on human tradition and the basic principles of this world rather than on Christ.'

"What do we usually tell people who are having problems: go talk to the pastor, a friend, or a therapist? Our advice is based upon our belief in what helps us. Sadly, what we think helps us—and temporarily it may—is often hollow and deceptive philosophy based on the world's wisdom rather than on Christ. One pastor stated, 'If you were to walk into a room and see Sigmund Freud, Carl Rogers, Carl Jung, Abraham Maslow, and Jesus Christ seated together, to which would you go for what you consider your greatest problem needing a solution? Your answer to the former is dependent largely on how you answer the latter.'[1]

"Many Christian counselors believe it is necessary to integrate the world's wisdom of psychological theories with God's Word in order 'to form a better counseling system. One

In Whose Steps?

Christian psychologist calls this approach spoiling the Egyptians. He compares this adaptation of secular concepts to the Israelites' taking of Egyptian goods as they made their exodus.'² But there is a problem with this comparison:

> The Israelites were taking gold, silver, and other material objects, while integration is appropriating concepts, philosophies, and worldviews that are hostile to God's plan for man. It is more akin to the adoption of Canaanite practices than spoiling the Egyptians. . . . The all-too-common but disastrous result is that we tend to look at Scripture through the eyeglasses of psychology when the critical need is to look at psychology through the glasses of Scripture.³

"We are not looking at psychology through the glasses of Scripture if we believe that psychological techniques can be substituted for the work of the Holy Spirit. Listen to this report:

> A respected Christian psychologist argued that the fruit of the Spirit. . .could be produced by psychological techniques alone. There was no need to wait for the Holy Spirit to develop these. . . .They could all be duplicated by any competent psychologist. . . .In his opinion, spiritual maturity and psychological health are really the same thing. They can be produced either psychologically or spiritually.⁴

"First of all," David exclaimed, "this report reminds me of Pharaoh's magicians who were able to perform the same miracles by magic that Moses performed by the power of God. Obviously, their magic power came from a different god than the God of Moses. Secondly, if psychological techniques can sanctify us, we can all go home right now because Christ's death and His resurrection are not necessary."

David noticed that he seemed to have everyone's rapt attention—so far, anyway. *Or maybe they're just in shock at what they're hearing me say?* He swallowed hard and continued.

"People are looking desperately for answers to life's problems, but the answers they want—and the ones I wanted, also—are the ones that gratify us, not ones that require spiritual battle. Our culture, including our Christian subculture, wants easy answers. Although I didn't set out with the goal of easy answers, that was the end result. For that reason, I must take responsibility for allowing this church to turn aside to the world's wisdom because I was not willing to speak the truth to you. I believed that I could help you find the answer to your felt needs by referring those of you with emotional problems to a person I believed was better qualified than I was to help you with those problems. I didn't want to call anything you did or anything I did by its rightful name—sin.

"I want to add at this time that I believe most Christian counselors are people who genuinely care about and want to help people. However, I want to challenge them, also, to pray about the things I am saying and to examine their own hearts in the light of Scripture to see if they, too, may have been deceived into believing Christ is not sufficient for the problems of life."

David wanted the congregation to know he was not accusing any counselors, especially his dear friend, Carl, of trying to deceive hurting people. He knew Carl's heart was to help people. However, now that he'd brought up the word "sin," David believed many people would automatically turn him off. They believed "sin "and "help" were mutually exclusive. It was definitely not a politically, psychologically—

or, heaven forbid, even spiritually—correct word. People seemed to be of the opinion that if you used it you were uncaring and perhaps even un-Christian. How could he convince them that he was showing them love by calling sin "sin" rather than using a psychological term? He was going to try!

"I hope I haven't lost those of you who hate the word 'sin' because it has been misused to bash you and others in the Body of Christ. I pray I can help you understand that by not using it, I have been unloving to you! Let's say a doctor who had no bedside manner spoke to you bluntly as he told you had a tumor which must be removed in order for you to get well. Then let's say another doctor spoke to you compassionately as he told you he was sorry you were sick but he'd be there for you. Since he didn't want to hurt you, he didn't tell you the truth about your tumor—that you would die if it was not removed. Which doctor would be actually showing you the most love? Perhaps the first one needed to learn good bedside manners, but that didn't mean he needed to change his message or that he didn't care. He would be willing to hurt your feelings for you to get well. The same is true for spiritual doctors. Why?

> [Because] if sympathy is all that human beings need, then the Cross of Christ is an absurdity and there is absolutely no need for it. What the world needs is not a little bit of love, but major surgery. . . . If a person can get to God in any other way, then the Cross of Christ is unnecessary. . . .[so] a worker cannot always be charming and friendly, but must be willing to be stern to accomplish major surgery. We must be willing to examine others as deeply as God has examined us [by] sensing Scripture passages that will drive the truth home, and then not be afraid to apply them.[5]

"I am confessing that I have not been willing to tell you the truth, much less apply it. I have tried to be kind, caring, and compassionate, which is good and right, but these are not sufficient. All of us must have a surgical operation of the heart. I thought I could do that by encouraging the elders to make sure we had psychologically-oriented self-help groups. But do you see the irony in that? The reason Christ came was to save us from ourselves because we cannot help our selves! Isn't that an oxymoron? Self-help groups in our church?

"I did not tell you the truth about your 'tumor' of sin because I didn't want to hurt your feelings. I didn't want you to be angry with me. I didn't want you to disapprove of me. I didn't want you to think I was uneducated in the field of science. Without realizing it, I quit speaking the truth in love. I wasn't meaning to, you understand. I was deceived into believing the world's lies. I allowed Satan and the world's philosophies to neutralize me. I am sorry to say I made the 'Cross of Christ an absurdity.' Or as the authors state in "In *The Power of the Call,*

> If I were Satan, scanning the horizon in search of my competition, the person who would interfere most with my work would, of course, be the pastor. How would I neutralize his effectiveness? One way would be to talk him into turning away from his Bible and fill his mind instead with every possible kind of reading material. I would try to persuade the pastor that he needs to be knowledgeable in many fields, especially psychology, psychiatry, sociology, anthropology, economics, world affairs, social work, mental health, etc. Why, if I were Satan, would I recommend these fields to study? Because the writings are dominated by authors who reject God. . . [and who] are redefining sin. If I were Satan, I would attempt to persuade the pastor to put the

Bible on trial—measure it against these other writings. If the Bible does not agree with them, then go along with these other writings. Better yet, just put the Bible aside. Above all, get our seminaries to study other books for guidance in life. . . . Generally speaking, our nation has followed the leading of the social scientist, who has sought to produce a Godless, valueless, permissive society as the answer to our needs. We have tried it for a half century. Where has the trail led us? We are headed for the rocks with multitudes of ministers guiding the ships.[6]

"I must confess and ask your forgiveness for being one of those ministers guiding the ships to the rocks rather than to the Rock of Ages," David confessed. "I became convinced the social sciences had the answers to life's problems, and that the Bible was only sufficient for spiritual life, not sufficient for us to live our everyday lives. I became a 'disciple of humanists, even though I kept studying my Bible.'[7] I did not believe that 'the power of the resurrection' could give us the necessary power for the everyday experience of sanctification.

"Until recently, I could never have verbalized this because I was blind to it. Now I realize that functionally, I placed my faith in the power of psychological theories to live my life and I taught you to do the same! Psychological theories seemed necessary for sanctification. Somehow I thought you and I needed to get our emotional needs met before Christ could begin the process of sanctification in us. But, as David Powlison points out, 'With increasing frequency the pulpit, the pew, and Christian publishing houses are speaking the same psychological language when they attempt to explain human experience and solve life's problems.'[8] In fact, psychological theories dominate explanations of human actions so that even the humanists are worried:

There are no longer sinners, only addictive personalities... The traditional list of the seven deadly sins... has been transformed into behavioral problems that require treatment, not castigation. For example, take lust: those who might once have been denounced as lustful are now said to be 'addicted' to sex and in need of therapy. Gluttons, likewise, are suffering from an eating disorder. Uncontrolled anger now takes forms such as 'road rage' and calls for stress management techniques. Greed and envy have become a form of 'shopaholism'. Even some forms of sloth have been medicalized. As for the last of the seven deadly sins, pride, this has actually been turned into a virtue: almost all problems today are blamed on a lack of self-esteem.[9]

Are people still listening? Well, they're definitely not restless! Every eye seems glued to me. Of course, two of modern man's favorite words, "needs" "and "emotions," seemed to keep their interest piqued. Praying silently for God to open his flock's eyes in the way his were being opened, he continued speaking.

"I have neglected the power of my call and my mission. I have been more like the director of a cruise ship, helping all aboard find what they think they need to be happy. But this is what Scripture commands me to do: 'Preach the Word; be prepared in season and out of season; correct, rebuke, and encourage—with great patience and careful instruction' (2 Timothy 4:2).

"My brothers and sisters in Christ! I was exhausted in both patience and instruction. But it was because I was not teaching God's Word. I was teaching what the world had to say and baptizing it with a few Scriptures. You just listened to God's mandate to me as your shepherd, delineating my responsibility to you. But I have fed you the world's platitudes and the world's answers to your problems. I believed the world's ways offered more compassion than God's ways. No wonder He caused my heart to be heavy. Again, I praise His name for His grace in bringing me back to His truth. I pray you will allow Him to do the same for you.

"I have so much to learn about all this; I've just begun this journey back to Christ and His Sufficiency," David continued to elaborate. "I have neglected to give you the Bible's definition of your problems. Although I didn't use the clinical definition the mental health professionals use from their text called *The Diagnostic and Statistical Manual of Mental Disorders*,[10] known as *The DSM-IV* for short, I used the same definitions in laymen's terms. I believed the 'diagnoses' or 'labels' in the book actually defined something. However, they only describe behaviors. Listen to what one Christian psychologist has to say about the DSM: 'That publication is filled with descriptions of sinful behavior redefined as sickness.' Then, he gives an example of a diagnosis that is behavior-driven."

David knew many in his congregation might feel defensive when he started talking about children and mental health; nevertheless, he began to read from the psychologist's book:

> A concerned mother asked me to observe her grade school age son. It seemed to me that he was an intelligent boy who could out-argue a confused single parent. Her son was on Ritalin and was diagnosed as oppositional defiant disorder. The *DSM* describes this illness as a pattern of *negativistic, defiant, disobedient, and hostile behavior toward authority figures.* Social scientists would say that these people are sick; they need therapy. A look at 2 Timothy 3:1-4 turns up the following words: *lovers of themselves, disobedient, unforgiving, and headstrong.* This is behavior.

One Man's Search for Answers

These people need to be saved, cleansed, renewed, and empowered by the Holy Spirit. This is the minister's territory.

David looked up from the book to see if the congregation appeared to be listening; they did, so he kept reading:

Another mother asked me to observe her son who was diagnosed with Attention Deficit Disorder [ADD]. This boy, as I observed him, was a normal, rebellious child who was running wild because his parents were arguing with each other over many issues. Neither parent was able to focus on child training.

Again, using the same Scripture, none of these people were sick. They were sinful. *Unthankful, unloving, without self-control,* and *haughty* were descriptive words that applied. This is sinful behavior. They need to be led to the truth by a faithful, loving minister. Relief from [these problems are] available. It is a relief to talk about one's problems. Listening to music, reading a book, exercise, and alcohol and drugs can have a calming effect. This world offers many sources that give relief. The cure for these symptoms is to recognize them as sin—which is easily solved by coming to the Savior for help.[11]

"And I'd like to add psychiatrist Peter Breggin's definition of ADD," David said, "although it may seem like he's stepping on some toes. Dr. Breggin labels ADD as 'D.A.D.D.: Dad Attention Deficit Disorder'[12] in his book, *Toxic Psychiatry*. Nevertheless, we are still drawn to the mental health professional's definitions as if their diagnoses were based on truth and scientific research, and as if they had the same type meaning as 'diabetes' or 'cancer,' since that is how they are explained.

"Research psychologist Paula Caplan wrote an expose of the process by which the mental-health elite judge us all. In her expose, she assessed 'the astonishing extent to which scientific methods and evidence are disregarded as the DSM is developed and revised' to decide who is normal.[13]

"Doesn't it seem strange to you that we would rather accept DSM diagnoses and be called 'crazy' or 'mentally ill' than to accept God's diagnoses and be called sinful? God tells us plainly what causes our problems and behaviors in Matthew 15:19-20: 'For out of the heart come evil thoughts, murder, adultery, sexual immorality, theft, false testimony, slander. These are what make a man unclean.' Mark 7:21-23 states the same: 'What comes out of a man is what makes him unclean. For from within, out of men's hearts, come evil thoughts, sexual immorality, theft, murder, adultery, greed, malice, deceit, lewdness, envy, slander, arrogance and folly. All these evils come from inside and make a man unclean.' Luke 6:45 tells us that 'The good man brings good things out of the good stored up in his heart, and the evil man brings evil things out of the evil stored up in his heart. For out of the overflow of his heart his mouth speaks.'

"Other biblical diagnoses of our 'mental health condition' can be found in Galatians 5:19-21: 'The acts of the sinful nature are obvious: sexual immorality, impurity and debauchery, idolatry and witchcraft; hatred, discord, jealousy, fits of rage, selfish ambition, dissensions, factions, and envy; drunkenness, orgies, and the like.' 'And the like' would include additional works of the flesh such as fear, worry, anxiety, unforgiveness, greed, arrogance, brutality, violence, rebellion, disobedience to parents—the list goes on and on. But there is hope in Christ! There is a cure because all these acts are sins which originate in our own hearts; they are not sicknesses, diseases, or addictions. Also, as we just saw, we must remember Jesus said it was out of our own hearts that these things come. That means it's not someone else's heart that causes us to behave in sinful ways. Can another's sinful behavior influence us and create stumbling blocks for us? Definitely! But another cannot cause or make us to sin. No, of course I am not saying that we sin when someone hurts us. I am saying we are responsible for how our hearts respond to being sinned against in these verses from Romans 12: 'Bless those who persecute you; bless and do not curse. . . .Do not repay anyone evil for evil. . . . Do not be overcome by evil, but overcome evil with good' (14; 17; 21). Notice that Scripture doesn't say we must spend years in therapy before we decide we can do what's righteous.

"As we all know, there is only one person who knows the heart and only he can transform it: We read in Jeremiah 17:9-10: 'The heart is deceitful above all things and beyond cure, who can understand it? I the Lord search the heart and examine the mind.'"

"Amen! Praise the Lord!" David was taken aback as he heard the "amen" but quickly recognized Paul's voice. No one had ever said "Amen" during his message. No one ever said anything; it wasn't considered appropriate. To his surprise, David found himself actually energized by the "amen." He was happy, too, that as far as he knew no one had walked out yet.

Gathering his thoughts, David continued. "So you see, brothers and sisters, if we attempt psychotherapy with these problems we've just read about in Scripture, we are actually doing therapy with the 'flesh.' But that is impossible, because no matter how long we work through problems, the flesh never gets cured! It has to die. Even though we may have been led to believe that our emotions are neutral, nothing about us is neutral. We are always worshiping God, the world, the flesh, or the devil. Where does this leave us? We have a choice.

In Whose Steps?

We can give our emotions relief through therapy or some other worldly answer, or we can allow God to transform our hearts by bringing those emotions into conformity with His will for our lives. He does that as He changes our motivations to worship Him and live for His glory rather than our own.

"Many of you may be willing to concede, at least on some level, that there is some truth in some of the issues I'm discussing. Maybe what you thought were real 'mental health illnesses' might truly be behaviors motivated by what's in the human heart. But then you may wonder what you do about something like spousal abuse or child abuse. So I'd like to insert here that I will be talking about these kinds of sins in more detail in future sermons. I am going to suggest we set up a structure where mature men in the Body of Christ are willing to go into homes where abuse occurs to 'speak up for those [abused persons] who cannot speak for themselves, for the rights of all who are destitute' as Proverbs 31 tells us to do. If we hear of someone in the Body with unrepentant sin, we will go in the spirit of Galatians 6:1 [and Matthew 18 if necessary]. I am not saying to ignore sins like abuse and do nothing to help, as James warns against in 2:16. We will accompany our words with actions.

"But as I was saying, some of you might take issue with me on the mental illnesses which you believe originate in the brain, those the professionals call organic disorders such as depression, bipolar disorder, obsessive-compulsive disorder, and anxiety disorders—disorders it seems as if people have no control over. I acknowledge that depression and anxiety can be debilitating. I will be discussing these problems, along with all the others I have named, in much more detail on following Sundays. I want to emphasize that I am not saying, 'just do it' without helping you know how. I promise I will follow up on this.

"Most people who have been diagnosed as depressed will tell you their doctor diagnosed them with a 'chemical imbalance.' However, 'the biochemical-imbalance theory is merely the latest biopsychiatric speculation presented to the public as a scientific truth. . . . The ironic truth is this: The only known biochemical imbalances in the brains of nearly all psychiatric patients are those caused by the treatments.'"[14]

David read on without looking up, all the while praying he would be able to provoke his people to think and pray about what he was presenting: Christ is the wonderful sufficient counselor.

"'The reasoning is this,'" David continued. "'If you give a person a drug that you think increases a certain neurotransmitter such as serotonin or dopamine, and then he feels better, then he must be low on that neurotransmitter.' But that kind of reasoning is the same as thinking that if aspirin makes your headache better, you must have an aspirin deficiency! After all, 'it doesn't take a broken brain to respond to a drug; it just takes a brain.'[15]

"As neuropsychologist Ed Welch reminds us, 'A person whose brain has been altered by disease or drugs cannot excuse sin by saying that the brain or the drugs made me do it. A dysfunctional brain can make it very difficult to understand what is going on, but it can't create sin. It can only reveal things that were previously hidden in the heart.'[16] Do you realize that more and more we are excusing all sinful behaviors as being caused by genetics? May I remind you, however, in David Powlison's words, that

> . . . what God has said about human nature, our problems, and the only Redeemer is true. It is True Truth. His truth is reliable. What the Bible says about people will never be destroyed by any neurological or genetic finding. The Bible is an anvil that has worn out a thousand hammers. Neurology and genetics are

finding lots of interesting facts. New findings will enable doctors to cure a few diseases, which is a genuine good. More power to them, and we will all be the beneficiaries. But biopsychiatry cannot explain, nor will it ever explain, what we actually are. All people are in the image of God and depend on God, body and soul. The ability even to figure out the human genome or design a PET scan is God-given. Furthermore, all people are morally insane with sin, living as if we were gods, even while God restrains sin's logical outworking. That's why the implications, applications, and hopes of neurobiologists' findings combine the good with the terrifying and perverse. Biopsychiatrists and microbiological researchers interpret their findings and determine the implications through a grid that is bent with sin. . . .God's children are in Jesus, and learn to love Jesus, changing gradually from insanity to wisdom. The Bible's presuppositions are not contrary to the facts of neurobiology, any more than they are contrary to the facts of suffering, socialization, war, sexuality, emotions, or history.

Christianity is the grand 'synthesis,' the unifying 'theory,' the truth' . . . [So,] when the gene mapping is complete, when the folks on Prozac still can't get along with their spouses, when the fountain of youth still does not arrive in a bottle, when money and achievement fail to satisfy, and when your clone grows up to hate you, sinners will yet find Christ to be the one we need.[17]

"What all this means is that we must use a biblical worldview to interpret all other research in order to come up with the biblical conclusion I just read: 'sinners will yet find Christ to be the one we need.' If we use another worldview to interpret our lives, the answer will never be Christ."

While studying for his sermon, David had learned there could be severe repercussions for people to come off psychiatric medication and he wanted to make sure no one in the congregation who was taking anti-depressants thought he was telling them to get off their medication. For that reason, he emphasized strongly, "I have no doubt many of you are taking anti-depressants. YOU MUST HEAR ME SAY THIS LOUD AND CLEAR: I AM NOT ENCOURAGING YOU TO GET OFF YOUR MEDICATIONS. ANY CHANGE IN MEDICATION SHOULD ALWAYS BE DONE UNDER THE SUPERVISION OF A PHYSICIAN. My goal is simply to encourage you to do some research and understand psychotropic drugs are not a cure.

"Perhaps you're wondering at this point why I am preaching on this subject. It is not to put you on a guilt trip or judge you in any way. What I want to do is to help you understand that by taking an anti-depressant or an anti-anxiety drug, you may be masking the problem in your heart which only God can cure. People may feel better taking these medications—but, again, they are not cures. It is not wrong to want to feel better. But is feeling better our only goal? As Christian Americans we are prone to think one of our rights is not to suffer! We forget or ignore what Paul tells us in Philippians 2:20: '. . . it has been granted to you on behalf of Christ not only to believe on Him, but also to suffer for Him.' God states that He uses suffering in our lives, and the emotions it brings up, such as anger, bitterness, resentment, sadness, fear, anxiety, worry, etc., to bring about Christ-likeness in us. As John MacArthur writes in *Our Sufficiency in Christ*:

> I am convinced that many who submit to various kinds of extrabiblical therapy do so precisely because they are looking for a way of solving their problems without surrendering to what they know God's Word requires of them. Scripture hasn't failed them—they've failed Scripture. Many have never learned to let the Word of Christ richly dwell within them, as Paul instructs in Col. 3:16. They have treated Scripture in a

cursory way and never plumbed its depths. Their sinful neglect inevitably bears the fruit of doctrinal confusion and spiritual impotence. Because they never disciplined themselves to life according to biblical principles, they're now abandoning Scripture for worldly alternatives. They turn to psychoanalysis to solve their problems, to science to explain the origin of life, to philosophy to explain the meaning of life, and to sociology to explain why they sin. Churches, schools, and seminaries have thus made themselves vulnerable to the influence of such teachings.[18]

"Does God have anything to say when we suffer with painful emotions? Are we to refer those who experience troubling emotions to the professional experts? One pastor comments:

> Jesus never made referrals to anyone else. He and His Father were present to bring all the help they needed. . . . Psalm 50:15 is very real to me: *Call upon Me in the day of trouble; I will deliver you, and you shall glorify Me.* How much honor has been denied our Lord when we make referrals to the world and do not call on Him? A lady once asked, *How do you know when a person needs big time help?* She was asking how to know when to refer to a person to someone greater than God! How much more big time can you get than God![19]

"Psychologist Dr. Brandt adds, 'The biblical counselor, then, will refer a counselee to a clinically trained person or to a physician if the person has rejected turning to God and has chosen to live with the sinful nature—and has turned to the world for help [since, as we said previously], relief is relief wherever you find it. That is true. The relief that the world gives seems interchangeable with the relief God gives. Be advised that the source is not the same.'"[20]

Emphatically, David stated, "I want you to understand God is our 'big time help.' I'm not asking you to live in denial of your feelings in the sense that you ignore what's really going on in you. I want to make what the Bible says very practical. I do not intend to beat you over the head with it. I do intend, with love and compassion, to share it with you to give you hope for a cure. Why is God's Word a cure? Because 'there is no human remedy for sin.' There is no alternate source of a new response to evil deeds. . . . The Spirit, however, produces in human life fruits such as these: love, joy, peace, patience, kindness, generosity, fidelity, tolerance and self-control.'[21] I hope you will come and hear the series before making a final decision about what I'm saying.

"Again, I know many of you are thinking you tried Scripture and it didn't work for you. I challenge you to think about it like this: What have you ever done you didn't have to practice and then learn to apply? As Christians, we often think if we memorize God's Word, we will automatically change. But we must apply what we learn. What if you memorized a book about how to ride a bicycle? To swim? To do math? To cook, sew, paint, type, repair a car, style hair? I could go on and on. I'm sure you would agree you must practice—over and over again!—what you learned before it works. The same is true with Scripture. You can memorize it from cover to cover—but it doesn't work if you don't practice it! I think this is exactly where we go astray. Jesus tells us:

"Therefore everyone who hears these words of mine and puts them into practice is like a wise man who built his house on the rock' (Matthew 7:24). Most of us do not know how to practice applying God's truths to real life so we exchange God's truths for psychology's theories and apply them to our lives. But, remember Brandt's words, 'the source is not the same.' I will help you learn to apply God's Word and you will find that it does work."

Thinking he heard sniffling on the front row, David looked down and saw Nikki there, smiling and wiping her tears at the same time. As she pushed her hair back, she gave him a small smile through her tears. He was encouraged.

"Thinking I was headed for a mid-life crisis, I tried to improve myself without God. I applied self-esteem concepts and found that pride loves self-help. By the way, it is possible we can improve ourselves and/or our relationships without Him—but unless He changes our hearts, those behaviors will be temporary because the flesh does not improve. The flesh would love to talk about itself in therapy for years.

"The term 'flesh' brings up another hot topic: low self esteem. Later I'll do a sermon on that topic, but for now, I'll give you a report from the famous California task force on self-esteem which was done to prove the damage low self-esteem could do. The researchers had to confess:

> One of the disappointing aspects of every chapter in this volume is how low the associations between self-esteem and its consequences are in research to date. Nowhere in Scripture are we told to have self-esteem, self-confidence and faith in ourselves—only to have esteem, confidence, and faith in God. . . . the very self that modern psychology exalts is the fallen self . . . Scripture cannot be reconciled with the modern self-love/self-esteem movement.[22]

David knew many people in the church felt their problem was one of low self-esteem—he could certainly understand since he'd believed that about himself and he'd been worried about causing low self-esteem in his children. But he knew he was deceived and so were others who believed developing a high self-esteem was the answer to their problems.

He knew it was getting late for an Easter Sunday, but a quick glance at his watch convinced him he had a little more time. "I will close soon," he said, smiling at his congregation. "Thank you for your patience. I'd like you to hear an excerpt from an article by psychiatrist Jeffrey Boyd. In his article titled *An Insider's Effort to Blow Up Psychiatry,* Boyd states that he 'believes the Bible is the greatest textbook of psychiatry ever written, and that humans cannot be understood apart from the God-human relationship.' He contends that 'the secular mental health movement and Christianity are in competition [and] psychotherapy [has won and has become] the central way of understanding the soul in America.'[23]

"And this isn't just because mental health professionals are altruistic; Boyd relates that 'secular psychological treatment is approximately a one-hundred-billion dollar-per-year industry in the United States.' What bothers Boyd the most, however, and what he can't figure out, is

> . . .Why the pulpits of America are not ringing out with the message that appears so obvious, namely, that this is absurd. Were fifty thousand clergy each to preach a sermon saying that psychotherapists treat the soul, but are incompetent because they fail to appreciate most of what constitutes the soul, America would change profoundly within a year. But I have never heard a single sermon on the subject [although] the clergy have it easily within their reach to destroy this secular self-concept which plagues America, and bring lay people back to a biblical self-concept.[24]

In Whose Steps?

"I want to be one of those clergy to destroy this secular self-concept," David proclaimed. "And today is the beginning of my attempt to ring out the message that the power of the resurrection gives me—and you—the power to live a life of peace and joy, not a life of learning to love myself so that then I can love you. I pray, as Paul did in Galatians 4:19, that you, 'my dear children, for whom I am again in the pains of childbirth until Christ is formed in you' will understand, with me, that Christ set us free to be free indeed, 'not free from everything except a therapist.'[25]

"Like Paul, I pray that I 'have not become your enemy by telling you the truth' (Galatians 4:16). I hope you will return and give me the opportunity to teach and challenge you further in the area of sanctification as we come to understand together that Christ alone possess the power of salvation and sanctification. Listen to Hebrews 2:10-11: 'In bringing many sons to glory, it was fitting that God, for whom and through whom everything exists, should make the author of their salvation perfect through suffering.' Even Jesus had to suffer and we are given the same privilege, as we saw earlier in Philippians.

"Because of Jesus Christ's payment for our sins, we can experience eternal life, which Jesus described as an intimate, never-ending relationship with God the Father and God the Son. Now it is my contention on this resurrection Sunday that we have forgotten what Christ has done for us and the resources He has given us to live life for Him. We are reminded of Peter's words: 'For if you possess these [Godly] qualities in increasing measure, they will keep you from being ineffective and unproductive in your knowledge of our Lord Jesus Christ. But if anyone does not have them, he is nearsighted and blind, and has forgotten that he has been cleansed from his past sins' (2 Peter 1:8-9).

"We have forgotten that He is the wonderful Counselor who makes us effective and productive in our knowledge of our Lord Jesus Christ. We have exchanged His incredible truth for the lie that we can receive healing through another counselor. We must repent and put God in His rightful place as both Savior and Counselor. We must remember our identity is in Him.

"In Galatians 3:1-3, Paul states emphatically, 'You foolish Galatians! Who has bewitched you? Before your very eyes Jesus Christ was clearly portrayed as crucified. I would like to learn just one thing from you: did you receive the Spirit by observing the law or by believing what you heard? Are you so foolish? After beginning with the Spirit, are you now trying to attain your goal by psychotherapy—oops, I mean, human effort?'" David couldn't resist the sarcasm.

"We all believe by grace through faith that Jesus was crucified for our salvation and He is our wonderful Savior. But I want you to realize Jesus was also crucified for your ongoing sanctification, that He is the wonderful Counselor who has given us, by His grace and divine power—as we read earlier—'everything we need for life and godliness through our knowledge of him who called us by his own glory and goodness. Through these he has given us his very great and precious promises, so that through them you may participate in the divine nature and escape the corruption in the world caused by evil desires' (2 Peter 1:3-4). Remember earlier we saw that Peter doesn't say we escape corruption through the world's wisdom? We escape it through our knowledge of Christ. Yet, we are in the middle of a recovery culture which provides us with its so-called knowledge which says the knowledge of Christ is not sufficient: we need to 'Celebrate Recovery' as we work through our problems and addictions by acknowledging we are powerless over them. This totally contradicts the knowledge about Christ found in Philippians

4:13: 'I can do everything through him who gives me strength.' And what about Paul's list of 'addictions' found in I Corinthians 6:9-11? 'Do not be deceived. Neither the sexually immoral nor idolaters nor adulterers nor male prostitutes nor homosexual offenders nor thieves nor the greedy nor drunkards nor slanderers nor swindlers will inherit the kingdom of God. And that is what some of you <u>were</u>. But you were washed, you were sanctified, you were justified in the name of the Lord Jesus Christ and by the Spirit of our God.'

"When we say we are in recovery, we have become 'nearsighted and blind, and have forgotten that we have been cleansed from our past sins' (2 Peter 1:9). Our identity is no longer who we are in Christ but it is in our behavior; that is, 'I'm _____ and I'm an alcoholic (or whatever addiction we are in bondage to). We should say, 'I'm _____ and I am a child of God—who sometimes struggles with (whatever addiction we are in bondage to). Christ died to make us his. In John 1:12 we read, 'Yet to all who received him, to those who believed in his name, he gave the right to become children of God' and in I John 3:1 we read, 'How great is the love the Father has lavished on us, that we should be called children of God! And that is what we <u>are</u>!' When we identity ourselves with a behavior, we are denying who we are in Christ!

"I repeat: we are not in recovery! If we are in Christ, we are recovered. We must celebrate Christ, not recovery, or we 'pervert the gospel of Christ' with a different gospel (Galatians 1:7)! Luke 15 tells us the story of the prodigal son who thought he could find life away from his father. Once he 'came to his senses' and remembered who he was, however, he repented and returned home to his father. Repentance is not the same as recovery although

> The recovery movement appeals to the same . . . universal desire of going home. Through recovery [we are promised], we can go home again . . . but the

ultimate issues are: Which self do we reach when we come to ourselves? Which guide home from the far country do we trust? Which home are we going to? And which father will be waiting for us? [26]

"Because we are looking for relief from our emotional pain, we need to be reminded again and again of this earlier statement: 'Relief is relief wherever you find it. That is true. The relief that the world gives seems interchangeable with the relief God gives. Be advised that the source is not the same.' However, when God is our source,

> the acts of the sinful nature are not beyond His ability to heal. Nor are these acts beyond the biblical counselor's level of competency. If you want God's help . . . you have access to His resources. Then the Biblical counselor can help. If you turn [to the world's counselor], you put yourself in the world's hands. We are not talking about competence. We are talking about unrelated disciplines. In which will you put your trust? [27]

"If you want to be whole, don't put your trust in 'a different gospel, which is really no gospel at all. Evidently some people are throwing you into confusion and are trying to pervert the gospel of Christ' (Galatians 1:6). Our source must be in someone totally trustworthy, our Savior and Lord Jesus Christ who died for our sins. That is the gospel. However, as I heard a pastor say,

> I am absolutely convinced that most Christians believe that the gospel ignites the Christian life but fail to believe that the gospel is the fuel that keeps us going and growing every day. Realizing that the gospel is for Christians is something relatively new in the church today. Christians conclude we get in the door via the

gospel, but once we're in, we're to advance to deeper theological waters and in essence leave the gospel behind. The gospel does not simply ignite Christian life; it's the fuel that keeps it going. Christian people, converted people, are to be making a beeline for the finished work of Jesus every day, looking back at what Christ accomplished for sinners, by his life, in his death, with his resurrection, and then applying that secured reality to every area of life today, to every part of our experience today, believing that he is the answer to the greatest human problems and dilemmas we face today.[28]

"Since Christ is the trustworthy source of all we need for life and godliness, why would we ever desire to walk in the steps of the world? I ask you, 'am I now trying to win the approval of men, or of God? Or am I trying to please men? If I were still trying to please men, I would not be a servant of Christ' (Galatians 1:10). I think it is obvious to you I am no longer trying to win the approval of men or I wouldn't be saying these things to you. As your shepherd, I must give account to God for whether or not I present you with truth.

"God willing, no longer will I water down the gospel. No longer will I be a pastor who does not 'correctly handle the word of truth' (2 Timothy 2:15). I take responsibility for not being the kind of shepherd I should have been to you. In Ezekiel 34, the Lord said:

> Woe to the shepherds of Israel who only take care of themselves! Should not shepherds take care of the flock? You eat the curds, clothe yourselves with the wool and slaughter the choice animals, but you do not take care of the flock. You have not strengthened the weak or healed the sick or bound up the injured.
>
> You have not brought back the strays or searched for the lost. You have ruled them harshly and brutally. So they were scattered because there was no shepherd and

when they were scattered they became food for all the wild animals. My sheep wandered over all the mountains and on every high hill. They were scattered over the whole earth, and no one searched or even looked for them.

"I have not been the kind of shepherd who searched and looked for you," David confessed. People looked at him with questioning eyes. They did not seem to grasp why he was so passionate. As he continued to speak, his voice broke. "You'd likely say I haven't been that bad. You might even say that I've been a good shepherd to you. But God has shown me my heart, and I have not been the kind of shepherd who 'strengthens the weak, heals the sick, binds up the injured, brought back the strays, or searched for the lost.' Perhaps I was not 'harsh and brutal' in a physical sense. But in a spiritual sense, I have been. I have asked God to forgive me, and now I ask you for the same forgiveness. I will be happy to speak with any of you who are holding an offense against me because I have not been there for you in a way that pleased God because I was looking to the world's ways of ministering rather than God's ways of ministering.

"I thought I was on guard against error, but I was deceived. I don't even know when I got caught up in error. But as your shepherd, I am guilty of using, and allowing other leaders to use, psychological theories, techniques, and recovery programs as the means of your sanctification. I was wrong, I am wrong, and I have sinned against you; I ask your forgiveness," David said in closing, as tears streamed down his face. Most of his congregation had their head bowed, probably out of embarrassment for him.

Choking back his tears, David said, "May we close in prayer? I'd like to pray for you, my beloved sheep, from Colossians 1 and 2." David began to pray, "Heavenly Father, first of all, I would like my flock to hear me ask your forgiveness for allowing them to wander over the mountains without a shepherd and for not tending to their hurts or strengthening them when they were weak. I confess I delegated my job to others when you placed me here to be their teacher, shepherd, and counselor and to train others to do the same.

"Along with the apostle Paul, my desire is that I will never

>cease to pray for [this congregation], and to ask you that they may be filled with the knowledge of His will in all wisdom and spiritual understanding; that they may walk worthy of the Lord, fully pleasing Him, being fruitful in every good work and increasing in the knowledge of God, strengthened with all might, according to His glorious power, for all patience and longsuffering with joy; giving thanks to the Father who has qualified us to be partakers of the inheritance of the saints in the light. He has delivered us from the power of darkness and conveyed us into the kingdom of the Son of His love, in whom we have redemption through His blood, the forgiveness of sins.'

"Lord, I also ask that they will 'continue to live in Christ, rooted and built up in him, strengthened in the faith as they were taught, and overflowing with thankfulness so that no one will take them captive through hollow and deceptive philosophy, which depends on human tradition and the basic principles of this world, rather than on Christ.' May each of these who have heard me speak search the Scriptures daily to see if these things are so in order to walk in the steps of our wonderful counselor Jesus Christ. I ask these things in His name; Amen," David said, as he ended his prayer and sermon, absolutely dripping with perspiration. Looking up, he added quickly, "I have provided a list of the references I used this morning should you want them."

David stepped down from the pulpit as people started stirring. Happily, he saw Nikki's face as she smiled at him. Then he searched faces to find Paul's, who gave him a quick thumbs-up. *I'm totally exhausted but so happy to have started this journey. I'm so grateful for Nikki and Paul's support, Lord. Please let there be some others to encourage me.*

Picking up his Bible, he headed for the front door. People would certainly notice him standing at the door to greet them since he normally left out a side door. He was beginning to realize that his calling from God was to spend time shepherding his sheep, and he intended to do just that. As the congregation poured out in their Easter dress, they seemed more intent on getting to their lunch reservations than anything else. The sky had cleared, and it was going to be a beautiful day for Easter egg hunts. *Lord, will you please let them understand the importance of Scripture to live their lives? It looks like all that's on their minds is beating the Easter crowd to the restaurants or rushing home to hide the Easter eggs. Doesn't anyone care? Please let them remember our discussion today throughout the week as they read Your Word. Reveal your truth to them!*

Just then, a bright pink hat caught his attention although he couldn't see the lady wearing it. His attention was deflected immediately as Alyssa grabbed his arm and demanded his attention. "Dad! May I go to Tim's and Cindy's house for lunch today? They've invited all the youth group over."

"On Easter? Alyssa, I think it would be nice if we could be together as a family—" David began.

"You always have an excuse not to let me do something, Dad. Come on, all the others are going, please, please, please?"

"It would have been nice if they'd planned it earlier. But okay, I guess you can go." Before he could get out, "We'll miss you, though," she was gone, blowing a kiss as she ran.

"Dad," Neil said as he came up and grabbed his dad in a bear hug.

Wow. This hug feels good. "You want to go to Tim's and Cindy's, right?"

"How did you know?"

"Your sister just asked to go. I'm surprised you want to go if she's going to be there, too."

"Well, you know she's not the only girl who'll be there, Dad," Neil said, smiling.

"Okay, your mother and I will do without either of you today. Please bring Alyssa home when you come. I guess you want my car keys, too?"

"Well, yes, since you and Mom came separately, I thought maybe you'd let me take your car."

"Sure, that's fine. I'll find Mom. Have a good time, Son," David said as Neil grabbed the keys. Before he lost his nerve, David asked, somewhat hesitantly, "Uh, Neil, what did you think of my message today?"

Neil turned back to his dad and a smile lit up his face. "Far out, Dad. I liked it. You really gave it to us! And I'm not saying that just because you're letting me use your car."

David immediately thought of his dream when Neil asked to talk to him about Christina. *Maybe I should approach him about it this week even though it would be pretty uncomfortable. I owe it to him, though, so I think I'll ask him if he'd like to talk about his dating life.*

Nikki came up and kissed him on the check. "David, you did a great job today. I was praying for you to present truth in a way they could be understood, in the way you've been talking to me this last week. I think you did." She was still smiling.

Things are different between us for sure. I'm falling in love with my wife again! That's a blessing. I can see she's really trying even though I don't deserve it. Thank you Lord!

One Man's Search for Answers

"It's just us for Easter lunch, Nikki. I told the kids they could go out with Tim and Cindy. I hope you're okay with that."

"Sure. I think it'll be fun to go out alone with my husband."

"Pastor, thank you for your sermon today," Jack interrupted their conversation as he stuck out his hand to shake David's. "I don't how to say this other than just blurt it out. My family's asked me to go to a psychiatric hospital and I was wondering if I should. What you said today made me wonder if that's the best thing for me to do. Could I talk to you about it this week?"

What? Did I hear right? "Sure, Jack, give me a call and we'll set up a time to talk." *Why was Jack thinking of going to a psychiatric hospital? In his dream, Jack was depressed and an abuser. What could this be about?*

Patiently, Nikki waited for David, thinking he'd be through soon. Then, much to her surprise, Carl walked up. She held her breath to see what he would say.

"David."

"What, Carl?" David asked.

"I guess we need to talk, don't we?"

"Yes, we do. Would you and Susan like to go to lunch with us today and let's start dialoguing? Our kids are gone for the afternoon."

"I'm not sure if Susan has plans or not. Also, I'm not sure I'm ready to start talking yet. You said a lot today that I will admit made me think. At the same time, my clinical experience doesn't agree with what you've said. You've not seen what I've seen."

"So, lunch or not?" David asked as Susan walked up.

"Susan, do we have plans for lunch?" Carl asked.

"Yes, don't you remember? We're going to Mother's," she replied.

In Whose Steps?

"You heard the boss, "Carl said. "Look. How about this: come to one of my groups at the church this week and listen to some of the women we have in this very church who have been emotionally, physically, and/or sexually abused. Hear them out and then we'll talk and see if you can show me how the Bible would help these women. Okay?"

What's going on? This is uncanny. Was God preparing me for this? "Okay, "David replied. "I'll do that. Just let me know when and where."

"Great," Carl replied. "I'll be more willing to talk with you once you've seen what mental illness and abuse really look like. I do think you're naïve, David. But, I am willing to talk to you about it because I did feel some conviction from the Lord, and I want to please Him. I'll give you a call to set up our time."

"What, no bipolar lecture?" David couldn't help saying. "You don't think I'm manic anymore?"

"I'm holding off on the diagnosis till we talk more," Carl replied, smiling at him as he and Susan waved goodbye to David and Nikki.

What else is going to happen? Who else wants to talk to me? Well, that's what I wanted but I sure didn't think it would happen like this!

Paul approached him with a beaming smile, slapped David on the back and grabbed him for a hug. "Wonderful, Pastor, that was just wonderful how you talked about the sufficiency of God's Word to handle our problems through sanctification!" he boomed.

"Thank you, Paul; I knew I could count on you. All the books you've loaned me and the biblical counselors you introduced me to have been really helpful. I look forward to learning more from you and from them. And I know you were praying for me and the congregation. I am very grateful to you for all your support. You are truly a dear friend," David finished.

One Man's Search for Answers

"My pleasure, David, my pleasure. I'm just thankful you'll listen to an old man. But hey, look, here's Anita waiting to talk with you. Maybe you and I can talk more next week."

Sure enough, Jack's wife Anita was standing behind Paul. As she walked up to David, he saw she was mostly dragging her daughter Ann with her. *What gives now?*

"Pastor, Jack told me he's going to talk with you this week. I'm so glad because he's got to do something about his depression. Ann's really tired of her dad's moping, and she's getting more depressed herself being around him."

"Mom! You don't have to tell everything you know," Ann snapped. "Dad just needs to get some help from Pastor Carl, and if that means putting him in the hospital, you'll just have to get over it."

She certainly does sound angry. I'm sure there is no truth to my dream about her being sexually abused by her dad, though. I've got to listen and pray and check it out. It's just too strange that all the people I dreamed about are coming up and talking with me.

"Would all of you as a family be willing to come to my office this week and we'll talk about what's going on? I believe God has something to say to each of you which will be helpful. Please say you'll come." *I can't believe I'm actually asking people to come to me for counseling! But I am because I am confident God can help!*

"It would be wonderful to do that, "Anita said, turning to Ann. "Honey, would you be willing to go with us to talk with Pastor David this week?"

Caught off guard, Ann flipped her hair and eyed her mom coldly. Suddenly she replied, "Sure, Mom, what can it hurt? I already see Dr. Carl but I'm willing to go with you to talk."

Anita smiled broadly. "Okay, Pastor, we'll see you this week. I'm certainly looking forward to the rest of your message. And see? I've got your handout so I can look up all the Scripture you quoted today as well as a list of the references you gave."

"That's awesome, Anita. Then I'll see all of you later this week."

David turned to find Nikki but evidently she'd drifted off during his conversations. He suddenly realized a lady was shaking his hand and talking to him.

"I'm sorry, could you please repeat that?" he asked her.

"You just keep shaking my hand while I'm trying to talk to you. I'm not sure where your head is," the lady replied with a laugh.

"Oh, I'm sorry," he said, as he released her hand and realized it was the lady with the pink hat he'd seen earlier. *What a pleasant laugh; sounds familiar—I guess it reminds me of someone else.* Although he was looking down at her, he couldn't see her face for her hat.

"What I said was, I'm a Christian therapist who is going to have to think long and hard about what you said in today's message. I'm not sure if I'm mad because you're naïve and don't understand what you're talking about regarding mental illness, or whether I'm convicted about what you presented regarding the sufficiency of God's Word for counseling. I guess I'll just have to make an appointment to meet with you so we can discuss it!" She looked up at him and smiled.

Then David saw her face. His brain froze. *This can't be; it's impossible. God, what's happening? This lady isn't real; she's a nightmare. God, please help me!*

"My name is . . . ." she began.

"Shelby Wilkerson," David finished for her.

She looked up in surprise. "Have we met?" she asked.

"Not exactly," he replied. "Not exactly."

(See endnotes for chapter 24 after appendices)

APPENDIX A: Additional Information on the Sufficiency of the Gospel for Counseling

The Bible, Sin and a Pastor's Responsibility

Integrated counselors (those who integrate Scripture and psychological theories) often say that the Bible does not go 'deep' enough into our psyche to heal us so we need psychological insight into our souls. That is the exact opposite of what God tells us in Hebrews 4:12:

> For the word of God is living and active. Sharper than any double-edged sword, it penetrates even to dividing soul and spirit, joints and marrow; it judges the thoughts and attitudes of the heart. Nothing in all creation is hidden from God's sight. Everything is uncovered and laid bare before the eyes of him to whom we must give account.

Obviously, God knows about every single sin in our hearts. But did you know that there are secular psychologists who have questioned the Church about their dismissal of the word sin? One psychiatrist and past President of the American Psychological Association, O. Hobart Mowrer, actually

> ...challenged the church to get back to its responsible duty of counseling. He declared that psychopathology (which is another term for mental illness) was a moral problem which has gravitated into medical hands by default and complacency on the part of the Christian Ministry. ... He demanded to know

whether Evangelical religion had sold its birthright for a mess of psychological pottage as well as stating that so long as Protestant clergymen preached the gospel on Sundays and then on weekdays had recourse to secular psychotherapy for help in the management of their own lives, their message will have little force or effect in stemming the tide of personal and social disorganization in our time.

Mowrer said further that if the Church refused to go all the way with the person who was in that emotional and moral crisis which we call 'neurosis' and 'psychosis,' it would lose its very excuse for existence and would cut itself off from all essential sources of inspiration and validation. As soon as the Church turned such a person over to some agency or professional to deal with them, it would sign and seal its own death warrant.

Continuing, he maintained that today's clergyman could only save himself by the radical expedient of returning to the full-fledged business of saving, rescuing, redeeming others. And only when the clergy did this would the Pulpit theology recover substance and stability which it was lacking today. Mowrer calls mental illness a moral problem which should be handled by Christian clergy (Bowden & Law, 1999, p. 12).

Therefore, shepherds need to return to the full-fledged business of saving, rescuing, and redeeming others; they need to return to being pastors and shepherds:

> Many pastors have replaced being shepherds using biblical and theological models and [instead] clamored after sociological and psychological ones. While they continued to insist that the Bible is the final rule of faith and practice, in reality they [relied] on more

practical tools fashioned in the worlds of business or academia. . . . They [forgot] the primary duty of those whom God calls to lead his church is <u>caring for the sheep</u>—not managing, not directing, not vision-casting, not anything else.

    Shepherds who fail to care for their sheep—that is, who neglect to strengthen the weak, heal the sick, bind up the injured, bring back the strays, or search for the lost—are in danger of losing their privileged position and of incurring the discipline of God (Wagner, 1999, p. 56; 47).

These shepherds who fail to care for their sheep are not the kind of shepherd Jesus talks about. Here is how he describes himself:

> I am the good shepherd. The good shepherd lays down his life for the sheep. The hired hand is not the shepherd who owns the sheep. So when he sees the wolf coming, he abandons the sheep and runs away. Then the wolf attacks the flock and scatters it. The man runs away because he is a hired hand and cares nothing for the sheep. (Jn. 10:12; 14).

Pastors are to care for their sheep and to feed them truth. Elizabeth Schaeffer writes that poison can be deceptive enough to be taken into the body without recognizing it. Without realizing one is ingesting it, a person then ends up dying from the poison. As bad as it is to take poison into one's physical body, however,

> there is another pollution, the most dangerous of all, the pollution of true truth, the pollution of the absolute Word of God, the pollution of the Bible. . . . Satan

In Whose Steps?

whispers, *'Hath God said'* over and over again in different tones of voice and with fresh sneers, as he speaks *not through a serpent* but through pastors, professors, teachers who lend themselves to Satan's twisting of the Word of God (1977, p. 33).

This was written in 1977. I think if Elizabeth Schaeffer wrote it today, she would include the word "psychologists" so that her list would read that Satan speaks through "pastors, professors, teachers, and psychologists who lend themselves to Satan's twisting of the Word of God."

Only the Word of God gives light to see through pollution and evil: "And we have the word of the prophets made more certain, and you will do well to pay attention to it, as to a light shining in a dark place until the day dawns and the morning rises in our hearts" (2 Peter 1:19).

Schaeffer relates that one of her friends lived in a concentration camp during her childhood and of course she missed out on basic nutrition. Noting that when one is hungry s/he will eat almost anything, Schaeffer describes her friend's food: "A certain amount of some kind of grain—mixed with castor oil, so that digestion was prevented and starvation was assured." Even more deadly than a food which does not sustain physical life is food which does not sustain spiritual life. This happens when unbelief is added to God's Word, a

> *mush* [made] with the castor oil of liberalism and unbelief—mixed with phrases from God's Word that are true. A mush of biblical quotations—mixed with castor oil of denial and dished out in the same bowl. A murky, oily mélange of God's truth and Satan's lies spooned into open mouths by the same Satan who wanted to purse all the truth from Eve's system in the first place. Mush—cancelling out spiritual nourishment (p. 74).

This mixing of untruth with the truth of God's Word happens in many Christian places: "With increasing frequency the pulpit, the pew, and Christian publishing houses are speaking the same psychological language when they attempt to explain human experience and solve life's problems" (Powlison, 1997, p. 72). This is because our biblical worldview has changed to an almost completely psychological worldview. In other words, as Powlison states further,

> through books, articles, seminars, videotapes, and radio broadcasts [psychologists have become] the evangelical authorities for solving problems in living. . . . The seminar and conference circuit, both in person and on video, finds psychologists filling roles once filled by Bible expositors [so that] psychologists, not pastors or theologians, maintain cultural authority in the evangelical church with respect to people and their problems. They are the experts, with the authority to define what is right and wrong, true and false, good and bad, constructive and destructive (1992, p.197).

Integrationists envisioned and sought to rationalize professional counseling as a legitimate activity by Christians, separate from the direct oversight of the pastoral ministry. . . . 'Bible-believing evangelical' became one flesh with 'professional psychologist.' 'Christian psychotherapy' could now be a legitimate calling. . . . Conservative churches in most major population centers no longer needed to refer troubled members to secular therapists. Christians trained in psychology could treat their own (pp.196; 198).

Psychological Worldview

Our culture is proliferated by a psychological worldview of

In Whose Steps?

almost every problem we can imagine. For instance, we don't think, "What does the Bible have to say about 'Attention Deficit Disorder'? We think, "What does psychology have to say about Attention Deficit Disorder? Perhaps you're thinking that we of course don't ask what the Bible has to say because it doesn't speak to such a disorder. But read what secular psychiatrist Peter Breggin writes in his book, *Talking Back to Ritalin* about ADD/ADHD: "The notion of a biochemical imbalance in the brain of children diagnosed with ADHD is wild speculation. Meanwhile, we know with certainty that every child treated with a stimulant will suffer from multiple drug-induced biochemical imbalances" (1998, p. 173).

Dr. Fred Baughman, an adult and pediatric neurologist with 35 years experience in his field, writes in his book, *ADHD Fraud: How Psychiatry Makes Patients of Normal Children* that his told his

> . . . psychiatrist colleagues who are given to waxing biologic that they do not do general physical examinations, or neurological examinations, or laboratory, x-ray, or scanning diagnostics. How, then, can they possibly claim to demonstrate organic, biologic, or chemical abnormalities, the very things necessary to diagnose actual diseases? But diagnose they do, in violation of the most basic precepts they learned in medical school. . . . The role of psychiatry was defined in 1948 when neuropsychiatry was divided into two specialties. One was neurology, dealing with organic/physical diseases of the brain. The other was psychiatry, which addressed emotional and behavioral conditions in normal human beings after all possible physical diseases had been ruled out. There was, therefore, no such thing as a psychiatric disease then, and there is not today, either (2006, pp. 98-99).

Even with such profound statements from the secular world, the biblical counselor is still accused of denying the reality of mental health disease. The majority of people in our culture accept the theory of mental illness as a fact but that does not make it one. In fact,

> this is the same logic that says believers deny the existence of Santa Claus or the Ester Bunny. Many people believe they exist, so does that make them real? Since mental illness is a theory and not a fact, biblical counselors do not deny the existence of something that has been proven to exist by empirical data gained in the laboratory. There is no need to deny the existence of something that does not exist [as Dr. Baughman states above] (Smith, 1994, p. 375).

That is why we will find no cure for these problems in psychotherapy. Although people may feel better temporarily, they are not cured. In fact, "there is mounting evidence that psychology is yet another 'sick physician' that has failed to cure itself. The eminent British psychologist made the point bluntly. 'The success of the Freudian revolution seemed complete. Only one thing went wrong: *The patients did not get any better*" (Guinness, 1992, p. 131).

The reason people do not get any better is because sin is not a disease, an illness, or an addiction (except as it relates to slavery, as in 2 Peter 2:19: ". . . for a man is a slave to whatever has mastered him" and in Romans 6:16: "Don't you know that when you offer yourselves to someone to obey him as slaves, you are slaves to the one whom you obey?"). The flesh is not curable. Where we err is thinking we should base our decisions on our fleshly emotions, i.e., what we feel is right. We feel like hypocrites if we deny what we are feeling. One author states, "Emotions are the cry of the soul. They expose what we are doing with the sorrow of life and in turn reveal what our heart is doing with God. . . [therefore] every emotion is a theological statement" (Allender, 1994, pp. 31; 34). Emotions reveal where our heart is in relation to God, that is, they show us whether we are seeking, avoiding, or denying him. But their purpose is not to rule our decision-making.

Generally, we seek help when we are hurting. We want to feel better and so we seek temporary relief through therapy. The psychological culture teaches us we are victims of our painful emotions and we should not have to experience them. I am in no way saying there are not people who have been victimized in our culture. We are called to mourn with those who mourn. We are also to comfort others with the comfort we ourselves have received from God. But the recovery movement encourages both continuing victimization and the need of everyone in America to be in a recovery group to deal with one's problem (otherwise one is in denial of one's problem/dysfunction). But is that helpful?

> The very act of constantly looking at and talking about one's past can generate new forms of psychological pathology and exacerbate old problems. . . . Seeing oneself as a victim frequently results in an increase in resentment and a deeper hatred toward the people responsible for one's suffering. The status of victimhood often gives rise to a strong sense of moral superiority, not only toward the particular perpetrators of the client's traumas but to similar people in society at large. . . . We conveniently forget that those who hurt us were often, themselves, abused in childhood too (Guinness & Seel, 1992, p. 103).

The apostle Paul encourages us to forget "what is behind and [strain] toward what is ahead" so that we can "press on toward the goal to win the prize for which God has called me heavenward in Christ Jesus" (Philippians 3:13-14). He also encourages us in Philippians 4 to rejoice in the Lord always, to pray about everything without anxiety, and to think about godly things.

Positive Psychology

Is thinking about godly things the same as the fairly new entry into the psychological world called "Positive Psychology"? Positive Psychology teaches "authentic happiness" and introduces the

> revolutionary, scientifically based idea of focusing on strengths rather than weaknesses, asserting that happiness is not the result of good genes or luck. [Author] Seligman teaches . . . that happiness can be cultivated by identifying and using many strengths and traits [people] already possess. By frequently calling upon their 'signature strengths' in all the crucial realms of life, readers will not only develop natural buffers against misfortune and the experience of negative emotion, they will move their lives up to a new, more positive plane' (Seligman, 2002, inside cover).

What Seligman presents is that one should focus on good rather than bad. That doesn't mean positive thinking (such as looking in the mirror and saying, "I'm a good person"), but thinking positively because of one's usable signature strengths. What is particularly interesting is that early in his career, Seligman developed the theory of "Learned Helplessness," the concept that nothing one does matters, so one gives up—a victim mentality.

Neither Scripture, Positive Thinking nor Positive Psychology encourages others to have victim identities. What is totally different in Scripture, however, is that Christians focus on a sovereign God who gives us strength. That strength is not found by looking positively in the mirror and saying good things to ourselves or by finding our "signature strengths." It's strength from who we are in Christ. Have you considered that unlike "Jesus Christ, the same yesterday and today and forever" (Heb. 13:8), psychological theories change continuously? One small example would be Dr. Seligman's theory changing from "Learned Helplessness" to "Learned Optimism." In addition, it is really helpful to copy the world's victim mentality? Some researchers believe that creating a culture of victims is actually for the purpose of obtaining clients.

Manufacturing Victims and Real Victims

A research psychologist wrote the book *Manufacturing Victims: What the Psychology Industry is Doing to People*. In this book, the author shows that psychology is an industry in search of "victims" who need psychological treatment in spite of the facts that scientific studies prove:

- therapy is not effective
- it is no better than friendship
- higher paid professionals do not do a better job than minimally trained counselors
- training and experience do not improve a therapist's skills
- therapy is not always helpful and safe
- professionals do not know more about human nature than anyone else
- people do not naturally get worse without professional treatment (Dineen, 1996, p. 154).

The majority of our culture believes that the above statements are false. But the facts just given are some of the very few statements which have been scientifically proven! Yet they are uniformly ignored by the profession and the culture. You can see why: If psychotherapists are no better at helping someone (even from a worldly standpoint) than a good friend is, what is the point in having them?

We must not forget that there have been some real victims who suffered greatly. Although they were persecuted, they were overjoyed to suffer for their Savior. This is how they responded to being victimized:

> Others were tortured and refused to be released, so that they might gain a better resurrection. Some faced jeers and flogging, while still others were chained and put in prison. They were stoned; they were sawed in two; they were put to death by the sword. They went about in sheepskins and goatskins, destitute, persecuted and mistreated—the world was not worthy of them. They wandered in deserts and mountains, and in caves and holes in the ground. These were all commended for their faith, yet none of them received what had been promised (Hebrews 11:15-39).

These victims weren't seeking treatment for a disease. Instead, they found meaning and purpose in their suffering. Another great example of godly suffering is found in the book *Fair Sunshine: Character Studies of the Scottish Covenanters* by Jock Purves. This book contains incredible stories of men, women, and even children who died gloriously for the sake of Christ. Here is a description of one of the martyrs on the gallows:

> Brave, composed, ecstatic, full of faith and of the Holy Ghost, John Dick was going Home with joy. Amid the shameful drumming din he sang the 2nd Psalm. . . . Ezekiel, chapter nine, was his reading, and among his

last words were these: 'I am come here this day, and would not change my lot with the greatest in the world. I lay down my life willingly and cheerfully for Christ and His cause, and I heartily forgive all mine enemies. I forgive all them who gave me my sentence, and them who were the chief cause of my taking; and I forgive him who is behind me [the executioner]. I advise you who are the Lord's people, to be sincere in the way of godliness, and you who know nothing or little of the power thereof, to come to Him, and trust God, He will not disappoint you. I say trust in the Lord, and He will support or strengthen you in whatever trouble or affliction you may meet with.'

The strong, young eyes gazed up intently at the gallows, then out across the crowds, and a light of adoration came upon his face. 'Now blessed be the Lord,' he said, 'here is the sacrifice and free-will offering. Adieu, farewell all friends' (2003, pp. 147-148).

This young man had been running and hiding from those wishing to kill him for the sake of the gospel. Can you imagine asking him if he would like to go to a self-help group, or perhaps if he would like an antidepressant? It's likely he would laugh in our faces and ask us if we were sure we knew Christ.

Author Os Guinness has similar thoughts about real victims:

> Victim-playing is a wrenching, poignant issue to me because I have vivid boyhood memories of Chinese Christians preparing for their baptism of fire—persecution under Mao Tse-tung after the Communist victory in China in 1949. Forty years and countless martyrdoms later, we can see the results of their

unfathomable courage—the blood of the martyrs has once again become the seed of the church. But this was no comfort to them at the time. Theirs was a courage that could afford few illusions and no self-indulgence. Without rights, redress, or respite, they were truly victims, but their sole cry as victims was to God. To their captors and persecutors they were like their Master—steadfast and forgiving (1992, p. 92).

Taking on the identity of a victim does not heal us. Healing comes as we allow God to transform our hearts and make us new creatures in Christ. Then we learn not to stay bitter, to choose to forgive, and to love our enemies. Our emotions no longer rule us but come into conformity with His will for our lives. God changes our motivations so that we worship Him and live for His glory rather than our own. He changes our focus from ourselves to what He desires as we accept His sovereignty in our lives. We are willing to pray with Jesus, "My Father, if it is not possible for this cup to be taken away unless I drink it, may your will be done" (Matthew 26:42).

For those who mean evil toward us, God wants us to be willing to say what Joseph said: "You intended to harm me, but God intended it for good" (Gen. 50:20). Romans 8:28 also becomes very real to us: "And we know that in all things God works for the good of those who love him, who have been called according to His purpose."

What does Romans 8:28 look like in a practical way? If we are,

> for instance, destitute, despised, depressed or angry, are we really willing to let God take us through times of defeat and despair, when we experience communion with Him in His crucifixion? The wonder of God's goodness is that He can use these crosses for our sanctification, just as He used the death of Jesus to advance His redemptive plan"

(Pearcy, 2004, p. 359).

The Cure for Our Blues

For the majority of us, we find the wonder of God's goodness (sadly) when we feel good and look good. If we're not feeling good or looking good, we often seek psychotropic medication as a cure for our blues (think of all the TV ads: "Depression hurts. [This antidepressant] can help.") But let's consult Dr. Breggin again: "If you give a person a drug that you think increases a certain neurotransmitter such as serotonin or dopamine, and then he feels better, then he must be low on that neurotransmitter." He emphasizes that is the same logic as thinking that if aspirin makes your headache better, you must have an aspirin deficiency! After all, "it doesn't take a broken brain to respond to a drug; it just takes a brain" (Breggin, 1994, p. 33). And did you know that "antipsychotic medications work independently of the presence or absence of any biological or psychological disorder? They have the same pacifying, subduing effect on normal individuals and, indeed, on animals'" (Farber, 1999, p. 126).

Psychiatrist Valenstein argues similarly:

> The claim that psychotherapeutic drugs correct a biochemical imbalance that is the root cause of most psychological problems rests on a very shaky scientific foundation. These ideas are simply an unproven hypothesis . . . [which is] heavily promoted as a well-substantiated explanatory theory. Because these ideas have enormous implications, there is a great need to examine the evidence and basic assumptions much more critically than has been done up to now (1998, pp. 1; 3).

Another psychiatrist reports, "there is no established biochemical imbalance for depression. There is no established gene for depression. . . Medical ethics, not business standards, need to prevail in health care" (Glenmullen, 1998, p. 336).

Neuropsychologist Ed Welch reminds us, "A person whose brain has been altered by disease or drugs cannot excuse sin by saying that the brain or the drugs made me do it. A dysfunctional brain can make it very difficult to understand what is going on, but it can't create sin. It can only reveal things that were previously hidden in the heart" (1998, p. 58).

The Bible states that problems happen due to what is found in our hearts (*see* Matthew 15:16-20; Luke 6:45; Mark 20-23), but the world's wisdom states that problems happen due to what is found in our brains. More and more we are excusing sinful behavior, attributing it to bad genes. After all, if our genes make us do it, we aren't responsible. In a tongue-in-cheek article, "The Gods are Anxious: The Delightful Rise of Genetic Polytheism," the author states:

> there is not, if you think about it, that much difference between saying 'The gods are angry' and saying 'He has the gene for anger.' Both are ways of attributing a matter of personal agency to some fateful and mysterious impersonal power. . . .The dream of finding an extra-personal explanation for the course of human life is very old, and it promises relief from the burden of responsibility that each person feels in making a choice and taking the risk that it will be a bad one (Menand, 1998, p. 43).

Biblical Worldview

As you can see, how we interpret our problems makes a big difference in how we look at life. Many, probably most, of us like the idea of not being responsible for ourselves and having someone or something else to blame. However, having a biblical worldview means interpreting everything in our lives through God's eyes rather than our own. It means we use weapons to fight with that "are not the weapons of the world. On the contrary, they have divine power to demolish strongholds. We demolish arguments and every pretention that sets itself up against the knowledge of God, and we take captive every thought to make it obedient to Christ" (2 Corinthians 10:4-5). We evaluate everything by its agreement or disagreement with God's Word and whatever does not agree with it (whether genes, emotions, or anything else), we take captive to Christ. Also in our biblical worldview,

> we must be alert to medical advances, especially those in psychiatry and the brain sciences, and be prepared to interpret this data through a biblical lens. Too often we envision a huge chasm between our Christian beliefs and issues in medicine. But Scripture addresses all areas of life, and medical sciences, especially when they discuss human behavior, cannot help but take some kind of religious stance (Welch, 1992, pp. 17).

Having a biblical worldview also keeps us from believing what Pearcy calls "false visions of redemption" such as "New Age methods of meditation and guided imagery applied to the classroom (redemption through cultivating a higher consciousness) or therapeutic techniques (redemption through psychological adjustment)" (2004, p. 130). Furthermore, Pearcy writes,

> Christians cannot counter the spirit of the age in which they live unless they develop an equally comprehensive biblical worldview—an outlook on life

that gives rise to distinctively Christian forms of culture—with the important qualification that it is not merely the relativistic belief of a particular culture but is based on the very Word of God, true for all times and places.

Genuine worldview thinking is far more than a mental strategy or a new spin on current events. At the core, it is a deepening of our spiritual character and the character of our lives. It begins with the submission of our minds to the Lord of the universe—a willingness to be taught by Him. The driving force in worldview studies should be a commitment to 'love the Lord your God with all your heart, soul, strength, and mind' (Luke 10:27).

The worldview behind psychology and psychiatry

As Christians—pastor, elder, teacher, counselor, or layperson—it is imperative to have a biblical worldview when we think about how to help others in our midst. As we just read, even science must come under a biblical worldview. If it doesn't, we accept blindly what we are told because of our belief that science never errs, including the supposed science of psychiatry and psychology. Yet the worldview behind psychiatry and psychology is that there is no morality, no right or wrong.

For example, in 1945, psychiatrist Dr. G. Brock Chisholm, first head of the World Federation of Mental Health, in a meeting of psychiatrists and high government officials, said this about morality:

> What basic psychological distortion can be found in every civilization of which we know anything? The only psychological force capable of producing these perversions is morality—the concept of right and wrong

are the belated objectives of nearly all psychotherapy. If the race is to be freed from its crippling burden of good and evil it must be psychiatrists who take the original responsibility. . . . The people who have been taught to believe whatever they were told by their parents or their teachers are the people who are the menace to the world (Stormer, 1998, p. 155).

This "science" is not neutral. And does it represent the kind of worldview you want your children to have? Additionally, in 1973, Harvard psychiatry professor Chester Pierce told educators:

Every child in America entering school at the age of 5 is mentally ill because he comes to school with certain allegiances to our founding fathers, toward our elected officials, toward his parents, toward a belief in a supernatural being, and toward the sovereignty of this nation as a separate entity. It's up to you as teachers to make all these sick children well—by creating the international child of the future (Stormer, 1998, p. 155).

Now that we are in the 21st century, many of our five-year-olds (and younger) <u>are</u> diagnosed as mentally ill! Read this sobering story:

Meet Alex. Alex could be anyone's partner, parent, child, brother, or sister. He or she has a nervous problem of some sort. Many of us do. Throughout human history, we have struggled to understand just what might be involved when we have a nervous problem. Do we have a disease or are we stressed because we are caught in a crisis or does our malaise have a spiritual origin? In order to get by, we need answers or at least hypotheses. . . The complexity is particularly apparent for the kind of nervous problem that Alex had, which was finally diagnosed as manic-depressive illness or bipolar disorder.

Alex's story is a modern one. The time spent in treatment with psychotropic drugs occupied 75 percent of his or her life. This simple fact dates the story to the 1960s or later. That a clinician settled on a diagnosis of bipolar disorder after trying and rejecting a number of other possibilities dates the story somewhere closer to the 1990s. While being treated with one of the antipsychotics released since 1996, Alex dropped dead. She died aged two years old (Healy, 2008, p. xvi).

Now thousands of us, from two to ninety-two, receive a mentally ill diagnosis (not even counting our dogs which take Prozac). And right and wrong as well have basically gone out the door, including the Church's door.

Psychology's deception–Exchanging God's Truth for a Lie
Evolution took theology out of creation. Psychology has taken it out of salvation and sanctification. Just as evolutionists wanted to explain the creation of man without reference to God, psychological theorists wanted to do the same as they created theories to explain who man is and why he does what he does with no reference to God. Being independent from God started in the Garden of Eden when the serpent convinced Adam and Eve they would be better off without God. Satan is still attempting to convince everyone else, using all means possible, how much better off we are without God. Francis Schaeffer explains it well:

The freedom that once was founded on a Biblical consensus and a Christian ethos has now become autonomous freedom, cut loose from all constraints. Here we have the world spirit of our age—autonomous man—setting himself up as God, in defiance of the knowledge and the moral and spiritual truth which God has given [creating] moral breakdown in every area of life. The titanic freedoms which we once enjoyed have been cut loose from their Christian restraints and are becoming a force of destruction leading to chaos (Howse, 2009, p. 336).

We believe the worldly spirit of our age, ignoring the fact that it leads to destruction. We also ignore the old, old story from Scripture which brings us life and freedom:

> For the message of the cross is foolishness to those who are perishing, but to us who are saved, it is the power of God. For it is written: 'I will destroy the wisdom of the wise; the intelligence of the intelligent I will frustrate.' Where is the wise man? Where is the scholar? Where is the philosopher of this age? Has not God made foolish the wisdom of the world? For since in the wisdom of God the world through its wisdom did not know him, God was pleased through the foolishness of what was preached to save those who believe. . . .
> For the foolishness of God is wiser than man's wisdom and the weakness of God is stronger than man's strength. . . . God chose the foolish things of the world to shame the wise; God chose the weak things of the world to shame the strong . . . so that no one may boast before him. It is because of him that you are in Christ Jesus, who has become for us wisdom from God—that is, our righteousness, holiness, and redemption. Therefore, as it is written: 'Let him who boasts boast in the Lord' (I Corinthians 1:19-31).

Obviously, God does not want to share His glory with anyone. He does not want any psychological theories of man to receive glory for their supposedly wise explanations regarding who man is and why he does what he does. God is man's creator and tells us why he does what he does. But how we love to read psychological theories supposedly explaining man's behavior which leads us to say, "Wow, so that's why I do what I do!"

Autonomous men continue, in their worldly wisdom, to set themselves up as God: "For although they knew God, they neither glorified him as God nor gave thanks to him, but their thinking became futile and their foolish hearts were darkened. Although they claimed to be wise, they became fools and . . . exchanged the truth of God for a lie" (Romans 1:21; 24).

Returning to a Biblical Worldview

When our hearts choose to exchange God's truth for a lie, we no longer look at things the way He does. That is why we need to repent and return to a biblical worldview. For instance, believing there is a medication for every distressing emotion is based on a worldview that unhappiness is a disease. One doctor calls this medication worldview "artificial happiness" which began, he states, "with a sincere effort on the part of doctors to help people with everyday psychological trouble [but] it has evolved into something troublesome, even scandalous" (Dworkin, 2006, p. 2). In his opinion this

> . . . new ideology articulated a new worldview, one that aspired to benefit society as a whole [and which] rested more on faith than on proven knowledge. This new ideology, which envisioned unhappiness as a disease, led to an enormous increase in psychotropic drug prescriptions, meaning drugs with mood-modifying effects, including antidepressants, antianxiety drugs, stimulants, and narcotics. . . .

In Whose Steps?

> Artificial Happiness's distinctive feature is its power to resist life. When people enjoy Artificial Happiness they manage to avoid feeling miserable when life is miserable. Measure their misery by degrees during a painful life experience and it never reaches the boiling point. No matter how bad things get, a person with Artificial Happiness goes on feeling well; you can't arouse in him the feeling of total hopelessness.
>
> Enough Artificially Happy people exist now in the United States to make for a new class of Artificially Happy Americans, or Happy Americans for short. These people live full and busy lives, except that what they get from life doesn't penetrate them very deeply. Religion may make them moral, work may satisfy their ambition, but medicine is the real guarantor of their happiness, not life. Rather than mine happiness from their daily activities, some of these Happy Americans get it from the medicine cabinet through antidepressants like Prozac and Zoloft. Happiness comes to them unawares, like sleep, and stays with them until some preappointed time determined by the drug's half-life. How they live and how they feel have little to do with one another (Dworkin, 2006, pp. 4-5).

As you just read, this doctor has a strong opinion that people are giving up on life unless they have medication to help them through it and while that is often true, **there can be severe repercussions for people who abruptly quit taking their psychiatric medication. One should never stop taking medication without the advice of a physician.**

Dr. Dworkin continues to speak bluntly on the subject of medicine, pastors and religion. He basically agrees with Mowrer that evangelical religion has sold its birthright for a mess of psychological pottage. How did this happen?

One Man's Search for Answers

In the 1950s, clergymen used psychology to further core religious ideas; by the 1970s psychology was a core idea, as many clergymen exchanged traditional notions of sin, evil, and damnation for psychology's odyssey of self-discovery, reinforcing psychology as life's organizing principle for millions of Americans (p. 173) [they exchanged the truth of God for a lie].

. . . Clergymen began to doubt their own paradigm, putting psychology ahead of theology [such as when I watched a minister] sell himself [to a doctor to get referrals for his counseling practice]. It was painful enough [to watch] from a human perspective but even worse from an historical perspective. The tradition of Western religious training stretches back two thousand years . . . [as] clergymen inspired people to see life in a new way, guiding worshippers toward an idea that was clear and eternally significant. Yet here was this minister, heir to the tradition of Saint Augustine, Thomas Aquinas, Martin Luther, and John Calvin, pathetically begging a doctor for patients so he could teach them biofeedback and meditation. This minister had ceased to be the representative of a glorious tradition; he was now the emissary of a defeated and humbled power (p. 232).

Yes, these are strong statements which I pray will provoke us to think about what has happened in our country, in our churches, and to our pastors. But it is wrong when one's goal in life is simply "happiness." Happiness is dependent on circumstances which change all the time. We need to compare fluctuating happiness with ongoing fruits of the Spirit such as joy and peace. That is why James 1:2 tells us we can "consider it pure joy, my brothers, whenever you face trials of many kinds, because you know that the testing of your faith develops perseverance" such as the heroes of the faith cited above.

In Whose Steps?

God's Word is the Foundation

How will each of us make a decision about how to persevere? Where will we find answers to life and in whose steps we will find them, God's or the world's? God's Word is the foundation upon which we stand and which will give us the courage to change. Real heart change doesn't happen by following the twelve-steps, however. It happens as we learn to trust the God who has shown his great love to us:

- This is love: not that we loved God, but that he loved us and sent his Son as an atoning sacrifice for our sins (I Jn. 4:10).
- And so we know and rely on the love God has for us. God is love. Whoever lives in love lives in God, and God in him (I Jn. 4:16).
- There is no fear in love. But perfect love drives out fear, because fear has to do with punishment. The one who fears is not made perfect in love (I Jn. 4:18).
- We love him because he first loved us (I Jn. 4:19).
- How great is the love the Father has lavished on us, that we should be called children of God! And that is what we are! (I Jn. 3:1).
- . . . God has poured out his love into our hearts by the Holy Spirit, whom he has given us (Rms. 5:5).

It is because of His love that we begin to practice walking in His steps:

- In view of God's mercy . . . offer your bodies as living sacrifices, holy and pleasing to God—this is your spiritual act of worship. Do not conform any longer to the pattern of this world, but be transformed by the renewing of your mind' (Rms. 12:1-2).

- Whatever you have learned or received or heard from me or seen in me—put it into practice. And the God of peace will be with you (Phil. 4:9).

Here are some of the things the Philippians observed in Paul which he told them to practice:

> ...I have learned to be content whatever the circumstances. I know what it is to be in need, and I know what it is to have plenty. I have learned the secret of being content in any and every situation, whether well fed or hungry, whether living in plenty or in want. I can do everything through him who gives me strength (4:11-13).

And Christ Himself tells us to practice: "Therefore everyone who hears these words of mine and puts them into practice is like a wise man who built his house on the rock. . . . But everyone who hears these words of mine and does not put them into practice is like a foolish man who built his house on sand" (Matt. 7:24; 26).

Self-esteem vs. self control

As opposed to putting God's Word into practice, we have become foolish, substituting high self-esteem for walking in godliness. Why? Because we have read and heard that for decades, psychologists "have viewed self-esteem as the panacea for many of individuals' and society's woes," writes Dr. Roy Baumeister, a psychologist and former self-esteem proponent. After years of study, he came to the following conclusion:

> After scrutinizing the accumulated research on self-esteem, these studies show not only that self-esteem fails to accomplish what we had hoped, but also that it

can backfire and contribute to some of the very problems it was thought to thwart. For instance, self-esteem does not make people popular or altruistic; does not keep children from indulging in sex, drugs, and alcohol; and is a result, not a cause, of good schoolwork. Enhancing self-esteem is therefore a waste of time in the pursuit of health and well-being. . . . The most promising human strength is self-control [and] although the research on self-control is newer, the evidence already looks much better than the case for self-esteem ... [and] interventions that boost self-control have shown remarkable and sweeping benefits (Chang, 2006).

Isn't it interesting to read that "interventions that boost self-control [not self-esteem!] have shown remarkable and sweeping benefits?" The latest scientific research shows it's better to have self-control than self-esteem. Yet, biblically speaking, self-control is a fruit of the Spirit. So if we are walking in His steps, the Holy Spirit empowers us with self-control.

Another research psychologist reports that even though sixty-five hundred studies have been done on self-esteem,

> all that has been discovered concerning global self-esteem are very unimpressive correlations, and they—as well as higher ones involving specific areas of self-esteem—can be easily accounted for on the basis that self-esteem reflects reality. The California task force has performed a valuable service, but not the one it intended. Rather it created a volume of work demonstrating that the Holy Grail of pop psychology is nothing more than a mirage (1994, Dawes, p. 243).

Ankerberg & Weldon remind us that "nowhere in Scripture are we told to have self-esteem, self-confidence and faith in ourselves—only to have esteem, confidence, and faith in God. . . . the very self that modern psychology exalts is the fallen self . . . Scripture cannot be reconciled with the modern self-love/self-esteem movement" (1995, p. 41).

Do you realize the world's wisdom is now reporting that low self-esteem is not our biggest problem? Yet there are still many Christian writers and teachers who believe having good self-esteem is a necessary part of being a Christian, regardless of what the Bible states (or even what the world is saying). Often they believe the scriptural command, "You shall love your neighbor as yourself" (Matthew 19:19) means you must love yourself before you can learn to love your neighbor.

Jay Adams critiques this concept:

> In truth, this verse says nothing of the sort. Consider the facts. First, there is no command here (or anywhere else in the Bible) to love yourself. . . To hear self-image leaders talk, you would think the Bible contained little else. But in fact there is no command here or elsewhere in Scripture to love yourself" (1995, p. 67).

Here's a statement from a professor at a Christian college about the importance of the self:

> If our sin is viewed as causing the death of Jesus on the cross, then we ourselves become victims of a psychological battering produced by the cross. When I am led to feel that the pain and torment of Jesus' death on the cross is due to my sin, I inflict upon myself spiritual and psychological torment' (Matzat, 1992, p. 256).

And former New Ager Warren Smith reports that Dr. Robert Schuller's "second reformation within the Church [is] to move it away from its message of fear and guilt, retribution, and damnation, and toward a theology of self-esteem" (2009, p. 25).

Unification of Psychology and Theology

Smith also quotes Norman Vincent Peale's biographer as stating, "No matter what people think about his theories, they have to acknowledge Peale's <u>remarkable unification of psychology and theology</u>. Without that unification, mega churches wouldn't exist today" (p. 50). Dr. Schuller relates that the most important question facing the Church today is: "What are the deepest needs felt by human beings? . . . Religious institutions who ignore this question will remain dying churches" (2009, p. 26).

After reading books regarding the unification of psychology and theology, or integration as it's called, it is plain that this union has been the impetus to bring people's psychological "felt needs" into the church.

Psychology, New Age and Carl Jung

Much of psychology is based on New Age concepts. Did you know, for example, that psychologist Carl Jung

> was one of the founding fathers of modern-day New Age psychologies. His many encounters with seemingly supernatural forces were a part of the collective unconscious, a type of collective human mindfield maintaining all aspects of human experiences and psyche makeup. It was only at the end of his long career that he felt that he was being overpowered and possessed by forces beyond his control. He finally admitted that his invisible friend, named Philemon, was

an 'independent spirit-entity [who] at times seemed to me quite real, as if he were a living personality. I went walking up and down the garden with him, and to me he was what the Indians call a guru (Baer, 1989, p. 157).

Another researcher on Jung writes,

> One of the most powerful modern forms of Gnosticism is without question Jungian psychology, both within or without the Church. Carl Jung explicitly identified depth psychology, especially his own, as heir to the apostolic tradition, especially in what he considered its superior handling of the problem of evil. . . . [His] direct and indirect impact on mainstream Christianity—and thus on Western culture has been incalculable. It is no exaggeration to say that the theological positions of most mainstream denominations in their approach to pastoral care—as well as in their doctrines and liturgy—have become more or less identical with Jung's psychological/symbolic theology (Sundquist, 2009, p. 244; 248).

Psychologists like Jung seem to have more influence on the body of Christ than our Savior does. And that's only one psychologist out of all the others whose theories we believe. For instance, did you know that Freud wanted to get rid of all pastors and to replace them with a nation of secular priests? To a great degree, he seems to have accomplished his goal as priests and pastors have surrendered to psychological worldviews.

Many Christian leaders have not heeded the instructions and warning to them from the Apostle Paul which he gave to the Ephesian elders in Acts 28:30:

In Whose Steps?

> Keep watch over yourselves and all the flock of which the Holy Spirit made you overseers. Be shepherds of the church of God which he bought with his own blood. I know that after I leave, savage wolves will come in among you and will not spare the flock. Even from your own number men will arise and distort the truth in order to draw away disciples after them.

In verse 31 he concludes, "So be on your guard! Remember that for three years I never stopped warning each of you night and day with tears." How many of us are concerned enough to warn those to whom we minister, much less to do it night and day with tears? If a professional counselor did that, s/he would be considered an enabler and co-dependent with his/her client. And what does that make Paul? John Piper warns ministers who long to be professionals: "Brothers, we are not professionals. We are outcasts. We are aliens and exiles in the world. Our citizenship is in Heaven, and we wait with eager expectation for the Lord. The world sets the agenda of the professional man; God sets the agenda of the spiritual man. The strong wine of Jesus Christ explodes the wineskins of professionalism" (2002, pp. 2-3).

Christ is the wonderful Counselor, not a professional counselor. Is it possible we have exchanged this incredible scriptural truth for the lie that we can receive healing through "another" counselor who is preaching "another" gospel as Paul states emphatically in Galatians 3:1-3?

> You foolish Galatians! Who has bewitched you? Before your very eyes Jesus Christ was clearly portrayed as crucified. I would like to learn just one thing from you: did you receive the Spirit by observing the law or by believing what you heard? Are you so

foolish? After beginning with the Spirit, are you now trying to attain your goal by human effort?

Alcoholics Anonymous, Jung and 12 Steps

God calls us to follow Him, not to walk with human effort in the steps of Alcoholics Anonymous. Many people believe A.A.'s founder, Bill Wilson, was a Christian and therefore his twelve-steps are, also. In his biography, Wilson said the thought of a God of love who could "watch innocent children starve" made him furious. Facts were all that mattered to him so he did not "believe in . . . God, or in heaven and hell . . .[it was] the church making people believe through fear and medieval superstition. . . . He refused ever to be solaced by anything his rational mind could not accept" (Thompson, 1975, p. 350). The author of Wilson's biography continues:

> At this time [Wilson] knew he was a drunk and was going to die if something didn't happen to him. One day, his drinking buddy Ebby shocked and surprised him with the news that he was sober because he 'got religion.' He had gone to the Oxford Group who had told him he had to 'admit you were licked [and then] to pray to whatever God he believed there might be.' As Ebby called God a 'higher power,' Bill felt expectant as if something were going to happen to him. He went on a three day binge, 'lost and terrified' about what was going to happen to him. With his 'last vestige of pride, the last trace of obstinacy crushed out of him [and he realized] he wanted to live. O God,' he cried. 'If there is a God, show me. Give me some sign.'
>
> As [Bill] formed the words, in that very instant he was aware of a great white light that filled the room. He seemed caught up in ecstasy he would never find words to describe. Everywhere now there was a wondrous

feeling of Presence akin to but far beyond what he had sensed [before]. Nowhere had he ever felt so complete, so embraced. This happened as suddenly and definitely as a shock from an electrode. When it subsided—and whether it was in minutes or longer he never knew—the Presence was still there about him, within him. And with it there was a sense of rightness. No matter how wrong things seemed to be, they were as they were meant to be. There could be no doubt of ultimate order in the universe.

Now, in place of the ecstasy, he was filled with a peace such as he had never known. He had heard men say there was a bit of God in everyone, but this feeling that he was a part of God, himself a living part of the Higher Power, was a new and revolutionary feeling. And it was a feeling that he wanted to hang on to whatever had happened (p. 362).

Wilson's biographer states that at the end of Bill's life, his thoughts were that he had not aligned A.A. with any church and that left the door open for people of any faith: "But he had tried. He had studied religions, ancient and modern; and it sometimes seemed that what he was seeking was deeper and far simpler than anything they offered" (p. 425). In addition to studying all religions, Wilson wrote Carl Jung that he was indebted to him for the critical role he had played in the foundation of A.A. after reading Jung's *Modern Man in Search of a Soul*.

Whatever he believed for sure, Wilson's white-light-ecstasy experience from a "Presence" which assured him he "was a part of God" (p. 362), sounds very much like a New Age/spirit guide experience. And out of that experience, Wilson wrote the twelve-steps philosophy, which has become the bible for millions. His bible is not based on the truths of God's Word.

One Man's Search for Answers

In a similar experience from the New Age, Randall Baer writes that when he was a young person, no one would answer his questions about Christ, so he started looking for other areas of spirituality. Eventually, he too, received a vision which

> was ecstatic. [He] felt that God had answered [his] spiritual cry and that [his] experience confirmed his life was going in the right direction. [He felt that truth had been revealed in a very special way, and that [he] was one step closer to personal healing and spiritual enlightenment (1989, p. 19).

That is, he believed it until the night his "spirit was roaming some of the farthest reaches of heavenly light that he had ever perceived" (p. 19). Listen to how he describes his experience:

> During my experience [of heavenly light] I was surrounded by a virtually overwhelming luminosity—it was if I was looking straight into the sun. Waves of bliss radiated through my spirit. I was totally captivated by the power (p. 55).

Evidently, these kinds of experiences are very powerful. Here is the experience of another New Ager who

> related an incident in which a group of Christians confronted him and tried, as he put it, to save [his] soul. He told them to come back and talk to him when they've had the same wonderful mystical experiences he has had. The point he was trying to make was that these naïve Christians had no idea what the metaphysical life is all about and if they did, they would want what he

had rather than trying to convert him to their way of thinking (Youngen, 2007, p. 141).

These ecstatic, out-of-body experiences must be very difficult to give up. Those who experience them describe experiences and things we cannot even imagine and which boggle our mind. But just because feelings are wonderfully mystical, it does not mean they necessarily come from God; that's why we are told we must test every spirit (I John 4:1).

Baer, cited above, did not test the spirits he encountered which captivated him with their power and bliss; that is, he did not test them until he had another experience, this one not so blissful:

> Suddenly, another force stepped in. It took me by complete surprise. In the twinkling of an eye, it was like a supernatural hand had taken me behind the scenes of the experience that I was having. I was taken behind the outer covering of the dazzling luminosity and there saw something that left me literally shaking for a full week. What I saw was the face of devouring darkness! Behind the glittering outer façade of beauty lay a massively powerful, wildly churning face of absolute hatred and unspeakable abominations—the face of demons filled with the power of Satan. In absolute stark terror I felt powerless to stop what appeared to be inevitable doom. Horror filled me like a consuming flame. Then, miraculously, the same supernatural hand as before deviled me from the jaws of this consuming darkness. . . . What I didn't know at the time was that it was Jesus who intervened by His greater grace into my life. . . . Over the following months, [I] found a Way, a Truth, and a Life that I had never known before—Jesus Christ (Baer, 1989, pp. 55-56).

Out of that experience, Baer wrote *Inside the New Age Nightmare*. After he came to know the Lord, he certainly would agree with the following statement:

> What it comes down to is the preaching of the higher self versus the preaching of the Cross. The New Age is saying that God is the higher self in man—that God is just a meditation away. . . . If a belief system is not the preaching of the Cross, then it is not the power of God (I Cor. 1:18). If other ways are correct, then Christ died in vain, His blood shed unnecessarily (Yungen, 2007, p. 179).

A young lady who grew up in India also became involved in the New Age practices of meditation, centering prayer, and visualization. Although she loved her visualizations and the power they gave her, they began to control her. Looking for help, she tried psychotherapy but that didn't last long when she discerned it wasn't that different from her New Age practices:

> On a daily basis in dozens of Christian counseling sessions, the same [New Age] practices are being used. Jesus is visualized, animating the mind of the patient, and sought for counsel. When this visualized Jesus speaks, his words are accepted as the very words of God. . . . Can we mentally create an 'envisioned Jesus' to speak to us at our whim? What makes us think we can manipulate the God of the universe to appear at our every request? How can we be sure we've contacted the real Jesus? . . . Never is there a report in Scripture of His being mentally pictured, soon materializing with sage advice (Matrisciana, 2008, p. 168).

Or, as one pastor asks, "Is the devil willing to trade healing for heresy, deliverance for deception, emotional health for doctrinal confusion? I believe he is" (Matzat, 1987, p. 140). Perhaps the devil is willing to help addicts and those with emotional pain get better emotionally while deceiving them as to the source of their help. Only God knows whether Bill Wilson really became a Christian when the light he experienced brought him ecstasy, but we do know the result of his experience did not bring glory to God.

In Christ or in Recovery?

If we functioned as though we believe Jesus gives us power to live our lives, we would not be living in a recovery culture. How can white light ecstatic knowledge received from the twelve-steps of A.A. or Celebrate Recovery honor and glorify Christ? They direct us to work through our problems and addictions by acknowledging we are powerless over them (contradicting Philippians 4:13: "I can do everything through him who gives me strength") while at the same time using human effort.

Paul lists the works of the flesh (i.e., "addictions") in 1 Corinthians 6:9-11: "Do not be deceived. Neither the sexually immoral nor idolaters nor adulterers nor male prostitutes nor homosexual offenders nor thieves nor the greedy nor drunkards nor slanderers nor swindlers [now that's a list of addictions if I ever heard them!] will inherit the kingdom of God. And that is what some of you were. But you were washed, you were sanctified, you were justified in the name of the Lord Jesus Christ and by the Spirit of our God." Do you hear the past tense? We are not <u>in</u> recovery! We are no longer the people we <u>were</u>. If we are in Christ, we are recovered. We must celebrate <u>Christ,</u> not recovery, or we "pervert the gospel of Christ" (Galatians 1:7).

But in the recovery movement, one can find what Paul Vitz calls the addiction of "recovery from recovery." That is,

> . . . just because a recovery group has driven out a devil of addiction does not mean that seven new and worse devils cannot come to take its place—and one of the worst of these new devils may be spiritual pride. . . . There are people for whom the recovery group process itself becomes an addiction. They replace their dysfunctional family for a dysfunctional recovery group; they become, once again, an enabler and defend and cling to the recovery group as they once defended and cling to their family (1992, p. 109).

Psychological recovery groups are believed by many to improve Christianity as well as to help the church grow by marketing the groups

> . . . in a way that will bring it in line with the latest intellectual and cultural beliefs while not compromising biblical integrity. The goal is to bring more people under the preaching of the Gospel. Psychology, they thought, was one way to give Christianity a 'scientific' relevance and make it more attractive. Sadly, biblical integrity and, therefore, the Gospel, have been enormously compromised. The Church's fear of irrelevance in the postmodern world has led to uncritically accepting man's wisdom and denying God's (Tyler & Grady, 2006, p. 16).

As the above authors state, the goal of bringing people under the preaching of the gospel was good. But when psychology watered it down with man's wisdom, it became a mush which was not effective or helpful for salvation or sanctification. We're back to the fact that psychological theories do not and cannot explain how to deal with sin:

Dealing with Sin Biblically

> As a potentially powerful master, sin is undaunted by those things we consider powerful, such as logic, intelligence, money, or even human love. Nothing human can break its hold on life. For true change to occur, it must be preceded by something much more dynamic. It must be empowered by Christ, enabling us to respond to him in faith, repentance, and obedience. This truth is the heart and goal of all [biblical] counseling (Welch, 1991, pp. 19-20).

True godly change, empowered by Christ, is what we should desire. For that to happen, we must understand that we must have God's truth in our lives. A biblical counselor

> . . . can offer God's wise perspective through Scripture. He brings more than just opinion, research, experience, or training. He brings a confidence in (and a submission to) the Word of God that will expose and penetrate the counselee's blindness. The biblical wisdom he offers will be pure, peace-loving, considerate, submissive, full of mercy, full of good fruit, impartial, and sincere (James 3:17) (Tripp, 2002, p. 292).

So as followers, pastors, teachers, and counselors of Christ who want to build on God's Word for the truth and grace to help others, we must say, "For God's sake, an end to all idolizing of psychology" (Guinness, 1992, p. 132). Idolizing psychology really means we are idolizing ourselves.

> For followers of Jesus Christ, breaking with idols and living in truth are finally not a test of orthodoxy, but of love. That is why idolatry is worse than apostasy—it is adultery. Love is the final expression of truth, just as

loyalty to truth is the vital test of love. Thus . . . followers of Christ who have the consuming passion to be His, entirely His, at all costs . . . [learn] God is testing us through him to discover whether we love the Lord our God with all our heart and soul. May we who call ourselves by the name of the gospel be found true to the gospel by which we are called (Guinness & Seel, 1992, p. 216).

Only the gospel of Christ cures our biggest problem: sin. Only the gospel of Christ brings us salvation. Only the gospel of Christ sanctifies us as we live our daily lives walking in His steps. The gospel of Christ is the answer to our problems in living. Nancy Leigh DeMoss. in her foreword to *Will Medicine Stop the Pain,* states:

> The authors raise important questions about a way of thinking in relation to emotional pain that has become deeply engrained in our culture. Even many committed Christians have unwittingly been influenced and co-opted by widely accepted beliefs about this subject without holding those assumptions up to the scrutiny of Scripture. [The authors'] book will challenge some deeply and passionately held beliefs of sincere, well-meaning people, including many mental health and medical professionals, counselors and therapists, Christian authors, speakers and leaders. It will challenge the choices and conclusions of many who suffer emotional pain, as well as the counsel of friends and family members who seek to help them.
> So why tackle the topic? Why swim upstream against the strong, prevailing current of much of the medical and therapeutic establishment? Because the Truth sets people free (Fitzpatrick & Hendrickson, 2006, p. 9).

In Whose Steps?

The Church and Soul Care

Sadly, we as Christians have neglected that Truth which sets people free and have succumbed to the world's wisdom to help our hurting brothers and sisters in Christ. So let's change that by being what the Church of Jesus Christ is supposed to be. The author of *Unholy Madness: The Church's Surrender to Psychiatry* challenges the Church about how to be the body of Christ in relation to those considered mentally ill:

> What a terrible abdication of duty for Christians . . . [to] abandon [individuals] to mental health professionals. . . . If the church is to become a vital force for social and spiritual transformation it must reach out to individuals in their time of crisis. Professionalism has undermined the church's autonomy from dominant social institutions and compromised its ability to act as a prophetic critic of the social order. . . . What does this mean for the church? In the first place, Christians should stop regarding mental health professionals as scientifically trained specialists uniquely suited to help individuals deal with life's problems (Farber, 1999, p. 132).

> Psychology and the Christian psychology movement constitute obstacles to the development of the body of Christ. They create an artificial hierarchy of the expert over the client and discourage Christians from ministering to each other. At the slightest feeling of discomfort mental health professionals inside and outside the church encourage Christians to seek the help of professionals. At its best psychotherapy is rent-a-friend, but usually it's rent-a-service....A true friend in Christ is of far greater value than a paid psychotherapist or paid biblical counselor, not only

because the love is freely given, but also because the love is biblically given in a biblical setting: the body of Christ.

It is imperative that Christian ministers and counselors stop promoting long-term relationships with 'professionals' and start encouraging Christian disciples to minister to each other. The goal should be to build up the Christian community, not to create another industry committed to the maximization of profit. Furthermore I heartily endorse the Bobgans' recommendation that the biblical counseling movement discontinue all counseling centers that operate *outside* a church—and thus are not accountable to any church (p. 137).

This author encourages the church to "immediately establish places of retreat, healing and transformation for individuals who are undergoing spiritual crises, that is, the seriously mentally ill" (p. 138). We know it is biblical to reach out to those in our midst who are hurting. However, for those of you who think only professionals should take care of those hurting people, there is scientific precedence for non-professionals to take care of the mentally ill. Soteria House was set up to treat schizophrenics humanely, without either drugs or psychiatrists, although a psychiatrist headed up the experiment. They had phenomenal results (Whitaker, 2001, pp. 120-126). Can't the church have even more phenomenal results, considering that we have the Truth and the power of the Holy Spirit?

In addition, the entire Spring 2007 *Journal of Biblical Counseling* is devoted to the subject of the Church's responsibility to soul care. Welch comments,

> Biblical counseling has gone on record as being committed to counseling practice as a church-based

ministry. It should be overseen by pastors and elders, done by church ministers and members. Such a position pushes against the cultural tide of professionalism. It re-centers the jurisdiction of pastoral care away from secular licensure and accrediting agencies to denominations and local churches. The details of this principle, however, have been left to the imagination (p. 55).

Does the Church not have a loving responsibility for soul care to our brothers and sisters in Christ, whether they suffer from the pain of schizophrenia, bipolar disorder, depression, or addictions of every sort? We must reclaim this territory which belongs to the Church so that

> Counseling . . .will cohere intellectually and structurally with every other form of the church's ministry: worship, preaching, teaching, discipleship, child rearing, friendship, evangelism, mercy works, missions, and pastoral leadership. Counseling ought to operate within the same worldview and with the same agenda that all ministry for Christ must have.
>
> The church is in trouble when its designated experts in the cure of souls are mental health professionals who owe their legitimacy to the state. Cure of souls is a decidedly *pastoral* function, in the broadest and deepest sense of the word. It is deeply problematic to operate as if the Word of God is useful, necessary, and sufficient for public ministry—preaching, teaching, worship, sacraments—but that training and credentialing in secular psychology are necessary for private ministry. . . Graduates of psychology programs should not have rights and honors to teach the church about the human

condition. Fee-for-service psychotherapeutic professionals should not have the rights and honors to practice the cure of souls. They have the wrong knowledge base, the wrong credentials, the wrong financial and professional structure.

According to the Bible, caring for souls—sustaining sufferers and transforming sinners—is a component of the total ministry of the church, however poorly the contemporary church may be doing the job. There is no legitimate place for a semi-Christian counseling profession to operate in autonomy from ecclesiastical jurisdiction and in subordination to state jurisdiction. The Lord whose gaze and will the Bible reveals lays claim to the cure of souls. If counseling is indeed about understanding and resolving the human condition, if it deals with the real problems of real people, if it ever mentions the name Jesus Christ, then it traffics in theology and cure of souls; it ought to express and come under the church's authority and orthodoxy. Psychotherapists are 'ordained' by the state, not by the church. From the church's standpoint, they are lay persons, not professionals. They attempt exceedingly significant and delicate work in people's lives in a dangerously autonomous way, without guidance or checks from the church that has responsibility for those people's lives. . . . In effect, functional authority over the souls of Christ's sheep is being granted to a semi-secular, unaccountable parapastorate. . . .The mind of the church about counseling is being shaped, and largely misshaped, by Christians of presumably good intentions who have their primary education and their professional identity outside of the church they claim to serve. Psychotherapeutic professionalism is a defective institutional structure for cure of souls. (Powlison, 2007, pp. 31; 35).

In Whose Steps?

Powlison is not the only one who thinks counseling should not operate in autonomy from the church. In 1913, B. H. Caroll wrote, "Paul says that Jesus set the apostles, prophets, evangelists and teachers *in the church:* that is where He put them; they are not turned out loose in the world like wandering stars: they must have anchorage; they must hail from some port and must be going to some port" (1913, p. 357). No, Dr. Caroll didn't mention "counselors" in his list but I doubt they existed (at least by that name) in his day and time. If he wrote now, I believe he would include them in his list of people who should be anchored in the church.

Fellow believers who care about the cure of souls, with God's help, we can do this! It will take pastoral leadership, however; men who are not intimidated by the psychological profession. Pastors have been told they are incapable and incompetent to counsel their flocks and therefore they need to refer them to professionals. And professionals encourage that thinking as they "epitomize neo-gnosticism, claiming to have secret knowledge for solving people's real problems. . . . The distressing result is that pastors, biblical scholars, teachers of Scripture, and caring believers using the Word of God have been made to feel they are not qualified to counsel people" (MacArthur, 1994, p. 11). The pastors, elders, leaders/ministers of the Church heard that message loud and clear. Most now believe they have no more right to counsel their flocks than to presume to perform surgery on them!

Hopefully and prayerfully, church leaders will do their own research so they will not be intimidated by mental health professionals. They will learn there are no medical or blood tests which show mental illness. Chemical imbalance is a *theory*. Treatment is based on subjective identification of symptoms and on whether a particular medication makes you feel better.

That is not to say there may not be some physical causes of distorted thinking, reasoning, etc., which look like mental health problems. It is wise to research diet and nutrition because they could be a physical cause of the problem. In the "Further Reading" section, you will find references to websites and books which address some of these kinds of problems. Our bodies are the temple of the Holy Spirit and we should find out how to take good, godly care of them!

But we must not turn to unbiblical means for sanctification. Isaiah 50 gives us encouragement and warning:

> Who among you fears the Lord and obeys the word of his servant? Let him who walks in the dark, who has no light, trust in the name of the Lord and rely on his God. But now, all you who light fires and provide yourselves with flaming torches, go, walk in the light of your fires and of the torches you have set ablaze. This is what you shall receive from my hand: you will lie down in torment (10-11). If we light our own fires by worldly wisdom, God tells us we will lie down in torment. If we trust and rely in God, He promises to give us light: "God is light; in him there is no darkness at all. If we claim to have fellowship with him, yet walk in the darkness, we lie and do not live by the truth. If we walk in the light, as he is in the light, we have fellowship with one another, and the blood of Jesus, his Son, purifies us from all sin" (I John 1:5-7). Not only that, we are a chosen people, a royal priesthood, a holy nation, a people belonging to God, that you may declare the praises of him who called you out of darkness into his wonderful light. Once you were not a people, but not you are the people of God; once you had not received mercy, but now you have received mercy (I Peter 2:9).

This brings us back to where we began in 2 Peter 1:3-12 with the following promises:

In Whose Steps?

His divine power has given us everything we need for life and godliness through our knowledge of him who called us by his own glory and goodness. Through these he has given us his very great and precious promises, so that through them you may participate in the divine nature and escape the corruption in the world caused by evil desires. For this very reason, make every effort to add to your faith goodness; and to goodness, knowledge; and to knowledge, self-control; and to self-control, perseverance; and to perseverance, godliness; and to godliness, brotherly kindness; and to brotherly kindness, love.

For if you possess these qualities in increasing measure, they will keep you from being ineffective and unproductive in your knowledge of our Lord Jesus Christ. But if anyone does not have them, he is nearsighted and blind, and has forgotten that he has been cleansed from his past sins. Therefore, my brothers, be all the more eager to make your calling and election sure. For if you do these things you will never fall and you will receive a rich welcome into the eternal kingdom of our Lord and Saviour Jesus Christ. So, I will always remind you of these things, even though you know them and are firmly established in the truth you now have.

Leaving Psychology Behind

What greater promises can we have than these? Life, truth, and power have been given to us to live effective and productive lives for our Lord and Savior. So why have I put all this together? Why do I want to remind Christians to be firmly established in the truth? Well, "dear friends, I felt I had to write and urge you to contend for the faith that was once for all entrusted to the saints" (Jude 1:3). But who am I to urge you to contend for the faith? One reason is that as a Christian counselor with two state licenses, I finally recognized that

> Psychology, like any secularized discipline, is both a dangerous catalyst to the church and a target for reinterpretive ministry. While denying that the unbeliever holds ultimate truth, the believer is challenged by what the non-Christian points to. The believer attempts to understand it from God's perspective. Such an understanding then challenges the unbeliever. Though this sounds difficult, it simply involves learning to develop a Christian world view (Smith, 1996, p. 20).

Eventually, I found that all the psychological theories I'd learned and which had seemed so enticing to me as a means of explaining who man is and why he does what he does, did not work to change others for any length of time. I had been challenged by these theories because they seemed to make sense (more sense than God's Word, actually). However, after a few years of emptying myself into my clients and only seeing temporary change, God brought Adams' *Competent to Counsel* (1970) into my life. I read the following passage:

> It is astonishing how often a conservative pastor blatantly denies his theology by his practices in counseling. It seems that the presuppositions of counseling rarely have been discussed by Evangelicals. Consequently, the pulpit and the study often have become quite disjunctive. An eloquent (or at least authoritative) preacher standing behind the pulpit proclaims God's message with power. Yet he abruptly dons another hat and closes his mouth as he shuts the

study door. He uneasily slips into the uncomfortable role of a listener, nondirectively guiding a counselee. It is an uncomfortable role because it violates his convictions, his conscience, and his calling. He acts as if God had nothing to say to the counselee (p. 78).

When I read that paragraph, I wrote in the margin: "Yes! This is what has killed me as a counselor—not caring too much, but keeping my mouth shut while everything in me is being violated—my convictions, my conscience, and my calling. I act like God has nothing to say to my counselee. I'm denying the gifts God has given me because I know I can't use them and be ethical as a counselor!" This initial unveiling started my journey into biblical counseling. I had not understood previously that Christianity and psychology, just like oil and water, could not be mixed. Adams helped me see why:

> It is impossible to destroy the foundation and preserve the superstructure. Because non-biblical systems rest upon non-biblical presuppositions, it is impossible to reject the presuppositions and adopt the techniques which grow out of and are appropriate to those presuppositions. Rogers 'acceptance' and Freudian 'transference' techniques fail because of the fallacies of the Rogerian philosophy of autonomy and the Freudian ethic of irresponsibility upon which they rest. [For instance, if a counselor uses transference], s/he becomes a party to the client's sin, so that counselor and counselee both sin in employing such transference . . . and sin is condoned. . . . Acceptance of sin is sin (p. 102).

While I had worked many overtime hours at in-patient hospitals, I realized my problem wasn't just fatigue—it was conviction of sin! As I started grappling with what I'd done, I came across Ed Bulkley's *Why Christians Can't Trust Psychology*. My spiritual eyes were being opened at a fantastic pace. When I came to chapter 12, "A Biblical Foundation for Counseling," my knees hit the ground. First I read Bulkley's description of what "The Psychological Counselor" says:

> We are not questioning the sufficiency of Christ. We are merely saying that the Bible does not address many of the problems facing contemporary human beings, and that we need the valid findings and insights available from psychology to help hurting souls (1993, p. 258).

Then I read Bulkley's description of what "The Biblical Counselor" says:

> There are no truly unique problems that modern man experiences. Sexual, verbal and physical abuse have been with us since the days of Cain. Marriage problems, poor self-esteem, addictions of every sort, Attention Deficit Disorder, jealousy, violent rage, depression, and virtually every other psychological dysfunction are recorded in biblical case histories (p. 258).

At this point, I was almost gasping for air as the differences in the foundation of the two views became more and more real to me. Then I read the Scripture for chapter 12 (one you have seen in this paper): "His divine power has given us everything we need for life and godliness through our knowledge of him who called us by his own glory and goodness" (2 Peter 1:3). I was convicted by the sure knowledge of Him who called me by His own glory and goodness that His divine power had given me everything I needed for life and godliness <u>and</u> that He had given me everything I needed to help others live godly lives. What had I been thinking???? Now I knew that "if any of these other authorities differ from

Scripture, they are to be judged by the Bible and rejected, rather than it being the other way around" (Johnson, 2001, p. 4).

I learned the true purpose of counseling was sanctification, not just helping people feel better. So, if that was the purpose, I needed to be equipped to disciple others to grow in sanctification:

> Christ has given a unique call, mission, and authority to the church to counsel God's people. The ultimate purpose of counseling is to sanctify—set apart, reserve specially for God, make holy—God's people, positionally and experientially. In other words, biblical counseling is concerned with leading a person into salvation, whereby God considers that person holy due to his position in Christ (positionally sanctified), and into a personal daily walk with God, whereby one actually experiences a holy lifestyle (experientially sanctified). God has not authorized any other organization to carry out that responsibility (p. 287).

If the church is the only organization which is to carry out that responsibility, then I decided I needed to give up my state licenses. In addition, I did not want to be unethical to my (previous) profession and share my faith in God with my clients (unless I was asked to do so). I wanted to be in a position where I could respectfully share Christ and his promises whether I was asked to do so or not.

So now you know that I was a Christian counselor who, by the grace of God, repented for looking to worldly wisdom and mixing it with Scripture to (try and) help my brothers and sisters in Christ. I am someone whose eyes God graciously opened so that I could learn to counsel biblically (actually, a better word for what I do is "disciple"). I am someone who has

One Man's Search for Answers

"no greater joy than to hear that my children are walking in the truth" (3 John 4). I am also someone who desires greatly to contend for the faith. Many brilliant biblical scholars have written wonderful books to help me grow as a biblical counselor. I owe a great debt of gratitude to all of them. I cannot add anything to what they have said; nevertheless, I, also, want to

> help a psychologized church to think and practice more biblically. A significant number of books and articles describe the problem of a psychologized church. I wonder, though, how broadly we have been able to cast our net. . . . What audiences are currently in the church? I believe that the church is filled with integrationists, both conscious and unconscious, yet little is written to reach this population. Do we understand their worlds enough to penetrate them and to point to the riches we have discovered? Do we approach them to win them or to win arguments? It is unconscionable to treat our brothers and sisters as enemies, especially when they need what we have been blessed to receive.
>
> [I know that I am] part of a relatively small, privileged group that has been given the chance to see clearly in this age of fog. With that privilege comes responsibility. To the one who has been given much, much will be expected. I urge you, as I urge myself, to use that privilege well (p. 20).

I am incredibly grateful to God for opening my eyes. It is nothing I did myself. I believe I have been given much in the sense that God rescued me from captivity to the psychological world and reminded me who I am in Christ. I feel a responsibility to share what I have been given; I want to walk in His steps and help others to do the same.

In Whose Steps?

You can read more of my story in Appendix B if you so desire. May God give you a passion to believe and share His Word with those to whom you minister and have influence.

"For from him and through him and to him are all things, to him be the glory forever! Amen" (Romans 11:36).

REFERENCES

Adams, J. (1970). *Competent to counsel.* Grand Rapids: MI.

Adams, J. (1995). *The Biblical view of self-esteem, self-love, self-image.* Eugene, OR: Harvest House.

Allender, D. & Longman, T. (1994). *The cry of the soul: How our emotions reveal our deepest questions about God.* Colorado Springs: Navpress.

American Psychiatric Association. (1994). *Diagnostic and Statistical Manual of Mental Disorders* (4th ed.). Washington,, DC: Author.

Ankerberg, J. & Weldon, J. (1995). *The facts on self-esteem, psychology, and the recovery movement.* Eugene, OR: Harvest House.

Baer, R. (1989). *Inside the new age nightmare.* Lafayette, LA: Huntington House.

Baughman, F. (2006). *The adhd fraud: How psychiatry makes "patients" of normal children.*

Blackaby, H. (1997). *The power of the call.* Nashville: Broadman & Holman.

Brandt, H. & Skinner, K. (1995). *The Word for the wise.* Nashville: Broadman & Holman.

Breggin, P. (1991). *Toxic psychiatry.* NY: St. Martin's Press.

Breggin, P. & Breggin, G. (1994). *Talking back to Prozac: What doctors aren't telling you about today's most controversial drug.* NY: St. Martin's Press.

Boyd, J. (19997). An insider's effort to blow up psychiatry. *The Journal of Biblical Counseling,* V. 15, #3, 21-31.

Bulkley, E. (1993). *Why Christians can't trust psychology.* Eugene, OR: Harvest House.

Caplan, P. (1995). *They say you're crazy.* NY: Addison-Wesley Publishing Co.

Carroll, B. H. (1913). *The book of Revelation.* Nashville: Baptist Sunday School Board.

Chambers, O. (1992). The right kind of help. *My utmost for his highest,* 12/20. Grand Rapids: Discovery House.

Chang, H. (2006). Self-esteem causes more problems than it solves, argues controversial article in Stanford Social Innovation Review: http://www.ascribe.org/cgi-bin/behold.pl?ascribeid=20060301.114808&time=12+24+PST&year=2006&public=1 (Accessed Mar. 10, 2010).

Dawes, R. (1994). *House of cards: Psychology and psychotherapy built on myth.* NY: The Free Press.

Dineen, T. (1996). *Manufacturing victims: What the psychology industry is doing to people.* Montreal: Robert Davies.

Dworkin, R. (2006). *Artificial happiness: The dark side of the new happy class.* NY: Carroll & Graf Publishers.

Farber, S. (1999). *Unholy madness: The church's surrender to psychiatry.* Downers Grove, IL: InterVarsity.

Fitch, D. (2005). *The great giveaway: Reclaiming the mission of the church from big business, parachurch organizations, psychotherapy, consumer capitalism, and other modern maladies.* Grand Rapids: Baker Books.

Fitzpatrick, E. & Hendrickson, L. (2006). *Will medicine stop the pain? Finding God's healing for depression, anxiety, & other troubling emotions.* Chicago: Moody.

Glenmullen, J. (2000). *Prozac Backlash: overcoming the dangers of prozac, zoloft, paxil, and other antidepressants with safe, effective alternatives.* NY: Simon & Schuster.

Guinness, Os. (1992). America's last men and their magnificient talking cure. In Os Guinness & J. Seel (Eds.). *No god but God* (pp. 81; 111-132).

Guinness, Os. (1992). More victimized than thou. In O. Guinness & J. Seel (Eds.), *No god but God.* (pp. 81-93). Chicago: Moody.

Healy, D. (2008). *Mania: a short history of bipolar disorder.* Baltimore: Johns Hopkins University Press.

Johnson, G. (2001). The eclipse of the reformation in the evangelical church: much ado about nothing? In G. Johnson and R. White (Eds.), *Whatever happened to the reformation?* Phillipsburg, NJ: P&R.

Kaminer, W. (1993). *I'm dysfunctional, you're dysfunctional: the recovery movement and other self-help fashions.* NY: Vintage Books.

Kilpatrick, W. (1983). *Psychological seduction.* Nashville: Thomas Nelson.

Law, R. & Bowden, M. (1999). *Breakdowns are good for you.* Bromley, Kent: Sovereign Publications.

MacArthur, J., Jr. (1991). *Our sufficiency in Christ.* Dallas: Word.

Matrisciana, C. (2008). *Out of India. A true story about the new age movement.* Silverton, OR: Lighthouse Trails.

Matzat, D. (1987). *Inner Healing: Deliverance or deception?* Eugene, OR: Harvest House.

Matzat, D. (1990). *Christ-esteem: Where the search for self-esteem ends.* Eugene, OR: Harvest House.

Matzat, D. (1992). A better way: Christ is my worth. In M. Horton, (Ed.), *Power religion: The selling out of the Evangelical church?* Chicago: Moody Press.

Menand, L. (1998). The gods are anxious: the delightful rise of the new genetic polytheism. *The Journal of Biblical Counseling,* V. 16, #2, 42-43.

Pearcy, N. (2004). *Total truth: Liberating Christianity from its cultural captivity.* Wheaton: Crossway.

Powlison, D. (1992). Integration or Inundation? In M. Horton (Ed.), *Power religion: The selling out of the evangelical church?* Chicago: Moody.

Powlison, D. (1997). Does Biblical counseling really work? In Eyrich, H. & Hindson, (Eds.), *Totally Sufficient.* Eugene, OR: Harvest House.

Powlison, D. (1999). Biological psychiatry. *The Journal of Biblical Counseling,* V. 17, #3, 2-8.

Powlison, D. (2007). Educating, licensing, and overseeing counselors. *The Journal of Biblical counseling,* V. 25, #2, 29-36.

Purves, J. (2003). *Fair sunshine: Character studies of the Scottish covenanters.* Carlisle, PA: Banner of Truth Trust.

Schaeffer, E. (1977). *A way of seeing.* Old Tappan, NJ: Fleming H. Revell.

Seligman, M. (2002). *Authentic happiness: Using the new positive psychology to realize your potential for lasting fulfillment.* NY: Free Press.

Smith, B. (1996). Authors and arguments in biblical counseling: a review and analysis. *The Journal of Biblical Counseling,* V.15, #1, 9-20.

Smith, R. (1994). Frequently asked questions about biblical counseling. In J. MacArthur and W. Mack, *An introduction to biblical counseling.* Dallas: Word.

Smith, W. (2009). *A 'wonderful' deception: The further new age implications of the emerging purpose driven movement.* Silverton, OR: Lighthouse Publishing.

Sundquist, J. (2004). *Who's driving the purpose driven church?* Rock Salt Publishing.

Stormer, J. (1998). *None dare call it education.: The documented account of how education 'reforms' are undermining academics and traditional values.* Florissant, MO: Liberty Bell Press.

Thomsen, R. (1975). *Bill W.* Harper & Row.

Tripp, P. (2002). *Instruments in the Redeemer's hands: People in need of change helping people in need of change.* Phillipsburg, NJ: P&R.

Tyler, D. & Grady, K. (2006). *Deceptive diagnosis: When sin is called sickness.* Bemidji, MN: Focus Publishing.

Valenstein, E. (1998). *Blaming the Brain: the truth about drugs and mental health.* NY: The Free Press.

Vitz, P. (1992). *Leaving psychology behind.* In O. Guinness & J. Seel (Eds.). *No god but God* (p. 109).

Wagner, E. (1999). *Escape from church, inc.: The return of the pastor-shepherd.* Grand Rapids, MI: Zondervan.

Welch, E. (1991). *Counselor's guide to the brain and its disorders: Knowing the difference between disease and sin.* Grand Rapids, MI: Zondervan.

Welch, E. (1998). *Blame it on the brain: Distinguishing chemical imbalances, brain disorders, and disobedience.* Philipsburg, NJ: Presbyterian & Reformed.

Welch, E. (2001). *Addictions: A banquet in the grave.* Phillipsburg, NJ: P&R Publishing.

Welch, E. (2007). When independent counselors do pastoral care. *The Journal of Biblical counseling,* V. 25, #2, 55-60.

Whitaker, R. (2007). *Mad in America: Bad science, bad medicine, and the enduring mistreatment of the mentally ill.* NY: Basic Books.

Yungen, R. (2007). *For many shall come in My name.* Silverton, OR: Lighthouse Trails.

For Further Reading/Research:

Adams, J. (1979). *A theology of Christian counseling: More than redemption.* Grand Rapids: Zondervan.

Angell, M. (2005). *The truth about the drug companies: How they deceive us and what to do about it.* NY: Random House.

Armstrong, T. (1995). *The Myth of the ADD Child: 50 ways to improve your child's behavior and attention span without drugs, labels, or coercion.* NY: Dutton.

Barber, C. (2008). *Comfortably numb: How psychiatry is medicating a nation.* NY: Vintage.

Bass, A. (2008). *Side effects: A prosecutor, a whistleblower, and a bestselling antidepressant on trial.* Chapel Hill: Alonquin Books.

Block, M. (2001). *No more ADHD: 10 steps to help improve your child's attention & behavior without drugs!* Hurst, TX: The Block System.

Boice, J. M. & Sasse, B. E. (Eds.) (1996). *Here we stand! A call from confessing evangelicals for a modern reformation.* Phillipsburg, NJ: P&R.

Breggin, P. (1998). *Talking back to Ritalin: What doctors aren't telling you about stimulants for children.* Monroe, ME: Common Courage Press.

Breggin, P. (1999). *Your drug may be your problem: How and why to stop taking psychiatric medications.* Cambridge, MA: Perseus.

Conrad, P. (2007). *The medicalization of society: On the transformation of human conditions into treatable disorders.* Baltimore: The Johns Hopkins University Press.

Cornish, C. & Fitzpatrick, E. (Eds.) (1997). *Women helping women.* Eugene, OR: Harvest House.

Critser, G. (2005). *Generation Rx: how prescription drugs are altering American lives, minds, and bodies.* NY: Houghton Mifflin.

Dalrymple, T. (2008). *Romancing opiates: pharmacological lies and the addiction bureaucracy.* NY: Encounter Books.

Eyrich, H. & Hines, W. (2002). *Curing the heart: a model for biblical counseling.* Christian Focus Publications, Ltd.

Fitzpatrick, E. (2001). *Idols of the heart: Learning to long for God alone.* Phillipsburg, NJ: P&R.

Glenmullen, J. (2000). *Prozac Backlash: overcoming the dangers of prozac, zoloft, paxil, and other antidepressants with safe, effective alternatives.* NY: Simon & Schuster.

Gotkin, J. & P. (1975). *Too much anger, too many tears: a personal triumph over psychiatry.* NY: Quadrangle.

Healey, D. (1999). *The antidepressant era.* Cambridge: Harvard University Press.
Healey, D. (2002). *The creation of psychopharmacology.* Cambridge: Harvard University Press.
Healy, D. (2004). *Let them eat prozac: the unhealthy relationship between the pharmaceutical industry and depression.* NY: New York University Press.
Horowitz, A. & Wakefield, J. (2007). *The loss of sadness: How psychiatry transformed normal sorrow into depressive disorder.* Oxford: University Press.
Horton, M. (1994). *Beyond culture wars.* Chicago: Moody.
Howse, B. (2009). *Grave influence: 21 radicals and their worldviews that rule America from the grave.* Collierville, TN: Worldview Weekend Publishing.
Hutchings, N. (2008). *The dark side of the purpose driven church.* Bethany, OK: Bible Belt Publishing.
Jeremiah, D. (1995). *Invasion of other gods: the seduction of new age spirituality.* Dallas: Word.
Johnson, E. & Jones, S. (Eds.) (2000). *Psychology & Christianity.* Downers Grove, L: InterVarsity Pres.
Kassirer, J. (2005). *On the Take: how medicine's complicity with big business can endanger your health.* Oxford: University Press.
Kirkpatrick, W. (1985). *The Emperor's New Clothes: the naked truth about the new psychology.* Westchester, IL: Crossway.
Lane, C. (2007). *Shyness: How normal behavior became a sickness.* New Haven: Yale University Press.
Lane, T. & Tripp, P. (2006). *How people change.* Winston-Salem, NC: Punch.
MacArthur, J. (Ed.) (2003). *Think Biblically! Recovering a Christian worldview.* Wheaton, IL: Crossway.
Oakland, R. (2007). *Faith undone: the emerging church . . . a new reformation or an end-time deception.* Silverton, OR: Lighthouse Trails.

O'Meara, K. (2006). *Psyched Out: how psychiatry sells mental illness and pushes pills that kill.* Bloomington, IN: authorhouse.

Peele, S. & Brodsky, A. (1991). *The truth about addiction and recovery: Why alcoholism, drug abuse, smoking, overeating, and other addictions are not diseases.* NY: Simon & Schuster.

Peele, S. & Brodsky, A. (1995). *Diseasing of America: How we allowed recovery zealots and the treatment industry to convince us we are out of control.* NY: Lexington.

Petersen, M. (2008). *Our daily meds: How the pharmaceutical companies transformed themselves into slick marketing machines and hooked the nation on prescription drugs.* NY: Farrar, Straus and Giroux.

Powlison, D. (2003). *Seeing with new eyes.* Phillipsburg, NJ: P&R Publishing.

Powlison, D. (2005). *Speaking the truth in love: counsel in community.* Winston-Salem, NC: Punch.

Ritchie, M. (2000). *Spirit of the rainforest: a Yanomamo shaman's story.* Chicago: Island Lake Press.

Ross, C. & Pam, A. (1995). *Pseudoscience in biological psychiatry: Blaming the body.* NY: John Wiley & Sons.

Sande, K. (1991). *The peacemaker: A biblical guide to resolving personal conflict.* Grand Rapids: Baker.

Scull, A. (2003). *Madhouse: a tragic tale of megalomania and modern medicine.* New Haven: Yale University Press.

Scott, T. (2006). *American Fooled: the truth about antidepressants, antipsychotics and how we've been deceived.* Victoria, TX: Argo Publishing.

Stein, D. (2004). *Stop Medicating, Start Parenting: real solutions for your 'problem' teenager.* NY: Taylor Trade.

Tripp, P. (2000). *War of words: Getting to the heart of your communication struggles.* Phillipsburg: P&R.

Tripp, P. (2004). *Lost in the middle: Midlife and the grace of God.* Wapwollopen, PA: Shepherd Press.

Tripp, p. (2007). *A quest for more: living for something bigger than you.* Greensboro, NC: New Growth.

Tripp, P. (2009). *Broken-down house: living productively in a world gone bad.* Wapwollopen, PA: Shepherd Press.

Welch, E. (1997). *When people are big and God is small.* Phillipsburg, NJ: P&R Publishing

Welch, E. (2007). *Running scared: fear, worry, and the God of rest.* Greensboro, NC: New Growth.

Wells, D. (1993). *No place for truth Or whatever happened to evangelical theology?* Grand Rapids: Eerdmans.

Wells, D. (1998). *Losing our virtue: Why the church must recover its moral vision.* Grand Rapids: Eerdmans.

Whitaker, R. (2007). *Mad in America: Bad science, bad medicine, and the enduring mistreatment of the mentally ill.* NY: Basic Books sermon:

Wilson, D. (1991). *Recovering the lost tools of learning: an approach to distinctively Christian education.* Wheaton: Crossway.

Wurtzel, E. (1995). *Prozac nation: a memoir.* NY: Riverhead.

WEBSITE Resources

www.christiancounseling.com
The Association of Biblical Counselors.

http://ccef.org/home.htm
The Christian Counseling and Education Foundation

http://www.iabc.net/
International Association of Biblical Counselors

www.nanc.org
National Association of Biblical Counselors

http://www.christiandiscernment.com/Psychology.htm
The purpose of this website is to provide educational materials to churches, pastors, biblical counselors, and other Christians concerning the conflict between the Bible and the theories/methods of modern psychology.

www.cchr.org
The Citizens Commission on Human Rights. Excellent resources on medication and the rights of the "mentally ill."

http://www.youtube.com/watch?v=PH1_v0zh_gk
Dr. Abram Hoffer; Nutrition and Addiction

http://www.amazon.com/How-Live-Schizophrenia-Abram-Hoffer/product-reviews/0806513829
Dr. Abram Hoffer; Curing Schizophrenia with Nutrition

http://www.youtube.com/watch?v=eNNzh5ICy64
Dr. Abram Hoffer interviewing actress Margot regarding her recovery from bipolar disorder using nutrition.

http://www.moshersoteria.com/
Treatment of Acute Psychosis Without Neuroleptics: Two-Year Outcomes From the Soteria Project by John R. Bola, Ph.D., and Loren R. Mosher, M.D.

http://www.newswithviews.com/West/marshaA.htm
"Because of what we know about Carl Jung, it would be wrong for Christians to 'seek after' his dangerous worldview," states Marsha West on her website. Marsha is a freelance writer specializing in Christian worldview.

http://www.24-7pressrelease.com/view_press_release.php?rssID=13573 "New Study Confirms No Blood Tests for Any Mental Disorder in Psychiatry's Billing Bible" from 24/7 Press Release website; reference to psychologist/critic Dr. Tana Dineen.

http://colorado.indymedia.org/newswire/display/6928/index.php A short summary of *Let them Eat Prozac: The Unhealthy Relationship between the Pharmaceutical Industry and Depression* (2004) by David Healy, M.D.

http://www.prozacbacklash.com/prozacBacklash.html
A website about a book by psychiatrist Joseph Glenmullen, M.D., who wrote *Prozac Backlash: Overcoming the dangers of Prozac, Zoloft, Paxil, and Other Antidepressants with Safe, Effective Alternatives.*

http://www.illinoisloop.org/selfesteem.html
A website of Illinois education presenting summaries of literature on the self-esteem myth: Want to build real self-esteem? Expect, even insist on, competence. Don't pretend it's there when it isn't.

http://www.pbs.org/wgbh/pages/frontline/shows/terror/techniques/ceci.html
Expert interviewer Stephen Ceci's comments on how to interview a child, particularly when the interview relates to suspected sexual abuse.

http://www.peacemaker.net/site/c.aqKFLTOBIpH/b.937085/k.A1EB/First_Visit_Please_Read_This.htm
This ministry, based on Matthew 18, is devoted to providing educational and training resources you can use to improve your personal conflict resolution skills and teach peacemaking to others. They also provide a conciliation service to churches.

http://resources.christianity.com/details/mrki/20061101/5d7d3f08-63cc-4941-8c7e-20ed969b4fdb.aspx
One of the counselors from Christian Counseling and Educational Foundation (CCEF), neuropsychologist Ed Welch, is interviewed on *9Marks* website.

http://www.antidepressantsfacts.com/2004-01-26-NetWorker-Kids-Meds-Suicide.htm
The *Psychotherapy Networker* website offers a recent article, "Kids, Meds, & Suicide." The article reports new research regarding suicide among children and teens who are taking antidepressants.

http://www.viryours.com/showcase/ocd/ocf1410l.htm
Information regarding treating Obsessive Compulsive Disorder with cognitive-behavioral changes (Dr. Jeffrey Schwartz).

http://sites.silaspartners.com/CC/article/0,,PTID314526%7CCHID598014%7CCIID2326652,00.html
"Where Does Your Congregation Turn for Help?" by Deepak Reju asking why Christians don't look to the Scriptures for life and guidance.

One Man's Search for Answers

His Divine Power Has Given Us Everything We Need for Life and Godliness Through our Knowledge of Him
by Cathy Wiseman, M.A.
September 2006

I burned out as a counselor after only a few years. Granted, I'd been counseling 60-70 hours per week (mostly inpatient) since I'd gotten my Master's Degree and I was physically and emotionally tired. No matter how hard I tried or how much I gave, many of the counselees I saw were still severely depressed, cutting on themselves, attempting suicide, hearing voices, starving themselves, experiencing panic attacks—generally very self-destructive and not getting any better. The psychiatrist with whom I worked required all therapists to be on call 24/7, but even our consistent availability didn't matter. Sometimes it seemed it made things worse, because, apart from God, **all of us** are bottomless pits, demanding to be filled with something or someone. So, when we don't allow Him to be our God, and obediently live life His way, we make other people and other things into idols to fill us. At this point in my life (I didn't know it then), I would say we therapists enabled the counselees' idol making (and what were our own idols that we were willing to try and be their saviors?)

What I didn't realize, however, was the fact that I was **spiritually** starved and exhausted. God graciously gave me another job which provided lots of time for me to get back into His Word. In light of all I'd been through, a particular passage I read absolutely astounded me with its brilliance and brought God's light and life back into my starved soul:

> *His divine power has given us **everything we need for life and godliness** through our knowledge of Him who called us by his own glory and goodness. Through*

> *these he has given us his very great and precious promise, so that through them you may participate in the divine nature and escape the corruption in the world caused by evil desires.*
>
> *For this very reason, make every effort to add to your faith goodness; and to goodness, knowledge; and to knowledge, self-control; and to self-control, perseverance; and to perseverance, godliness; and to godliness, brotherly kindness; and to brotherly kindness, love. For if you possess these qualities in increasing measure,* **they will keep you from being ineffective and unproductive in your knowledge of our Lord Jesus Christ. But if anyone does not have them, he is nearsighted and blind, and has forgotten that he has been cleansed from his past sins.**
>
> *Therefore, my brothers, be all the more eager to make your calling and election sure. For if you do these things, you will never fall and you will receive a rich welcome into the eternal kingdom of our Lord and Savior Jesus Christ (2 Peter 1:3-11).*

I thought about all my secular studies and wondered how my life and the lives of those I counseled would have been different had I spent that time studying and learning to better apply God's Word.

I was astounded and humiliated for having been deceived into believing that God wanted to use what I'd learned in college and in the field from other (even Christian) counselors and books to help people change. Functionally, I **had** forgotten I'd been cleansed from my past sins and I had become ineffective and unproductive in the knowledge of my Lord. I had forgotten God wrote the Book on how people change. I am so grateful to Him for opening my eyes to the foolishness of man's wisdom which says people can change without Him. Of course, it is true that they can change externally without Him. But the only change that matters to God is heart change, because that is where the motivation of why we do what we do is found. No secular theories or secular theories plus Scripture can change our hearts. Godly heart change comes from God alone.

    I am so sad to say that I actually believed that there was "a lack in the content of biblical Christianity itself which requires the addition of psychology" (Matzat, 1990, p. 10). Because at first, I saw counselees get better (short term, as it turned out!) and thought, "It works!" But, "Is the devil willing to trade healing for heresy, deliverance for deception, emotional health for doctrinal confusion? I believe he is," Pastor Matzat states emphatically (1987, p. 140), and I agree. What I also didn't realize was that my problem showed ". . . *evidence of [my] failure to grapple with and seek the Lord for an understanding of His Word . . . [because] it is only fair to point out that it is far easier to borrow from psychology than it is to grapple with the theology of the New Testament, especially with the Apostle Paul" (1990, p. 10).*

    With a repentant heart, I eagerly began to grapple with and seek wisdom from God's Word with the same studiousness I had from my worldly sources:

> *If you accept my words and store up my commands within you, turning your ear to wisdom and applying your heart to understanding, and if you call out for insight and cry aloud for understanding and if you look for it as for silver and search for it as for hidden treasure, then you will understand the fear of the Lord and find the knowledge of God. For the Lord gives wisdom and from his mouth come knowledge and understanding (Proverbs 2:1-6).*

I realized that no matter how much people hurt, trying to help them find emotional health apart from God so they can then get right with God doesn't make any more sense than a person trying to be good so he can come to God for salvation. With that conviction, I repented and confessed to God in sorrow and grief that I had exchanged His Words of life for a lie: the lie that effective heart change in His people (who are His Body!) comes through the wisdom of the world (which He says is foolishness); the lie that life can be found apart from God.

The only prerequisite for godly change is a repentant heart. As I continued to repent and to study, learn, and apply God's wisdom to my own life, I was led to go to my counselees and to ask their forgiveness for teaching them lies. Thankfully, they were very forgiving and most said I'd helped them know God better. While it helped me "feel better" to hear that (since it had been my true motivation), I still knew in my heart that I'd used the wrong methods to do it. I knew I had sinned against them and needed to ask their forgiveness. Only God's method (applying His Word through the power of the Holy Spirit) can effect Godly change in our hearts.

But, guess what! As I began counseling from God's Word, many, many counselees got **well** (some of them had been hospitalized and/or in therapy for years!). Their various diagnoses included multiple personality disorder (MPD; now called DID), major depression, eating disorders, borderline personality disorder, PTSD, schizo-affective disorder, panic disorder, alcohol/drug addictions, etc. As God says in I Corinthians 6:11: "And that is what some of you **were,** but you were washed, you were sanctified, you were justified in the name of the Lord Jesus Christ and by the Spirit of our God." They found true freedom in Christ—not through denial of their problems, "magic" or "just say no," but through learning to apply His truth to their lives (through true spiritual warfare: the "blood, sweat, and tears of dying to oneself and listening to God" [Powlison, 1995, p.123]) and they gained **true** wisdom.

Of course, not all (even Christian) counselees wanted Biblical counseling and those I referred to other counselors. Over the years (now around 20 since this first started), some Christians with the same diagnoses, after seeing their friends get well, have come to talk about getting well themselves. When they find out getting well has to do with doing things God's way, they shake their heads sorrowfully or rebelliously and say, "my problem has nothing to do with God" and are not willing to try His way, other than how they have defined His way themselves (rather than how He defines it). For instance, a person who says, "I know God wants me to be happy so He wouldn't want me to have to [whatever He calls them to do]," doesn't really know—or care--what God wants. They too have bought into the cultural, psychological, and spiritual lie that God wants what **they** want. It's an age of self, not God.

I thank God for His intervention in my life, and I thank Him for using many people who were willing to stand up for His truth through their preaching, teaching, and writing. I listened and read people such as John MacArthur, Jr. (I'd always listened to MacArthur on the radio, but I remember when I first started doing formal counseling and was hearing him talk about psychology, I said to him [well, I said it to the radio], "I love your preaching, Dr. MacArthur, but this is one place where you're just wrong!" It was years later before I saw I was the one who was **badly** in error.), Jay Adams, NANC, CCEF (I **love** *The Journal of Biblical Counseling*), IABC (Ed Bulkley), Deborah Dewart of Christian Discernment—are some of the authors and speakers to whom I owe a debt of gratitude for helping me out of the quicksand of theoretical psychology. Praise God that "His divine power has given us everything we need for life and godliness through our knowledge of Him who called us . . . "

Bibliography:

Matzat, D. (1987). *Christ esteem: where the search for self-esteem ends.* Eugene, OR:
    Harvest House.
Matzat, D. (1990). *Inner healing: Deliverance or deception?* Eugene, OR: Harvest
    House.
Powlison, D. (1995). *Power Encounters: Reclaiming spiritual warfare.* Grand Rapids: Baker

NOTES for Chapter 24 (David's Sermon)

1. Matzat, D. (1992). "A Better Way: Christ Is My Worth." In M. S. Horton (Ed.), *Power Religion*. Chicago: Moody.
2. Bulkley, E. (1993). *Why Christians Can't Trust Psychology*. Eugene, OR: Harvest House. (p. 31).
3. Ibid.
4. Ibid (p. 143).
5. Chambers, O. (1992). "The Right Kind of Help." *My Utmost for His Highest*. Grand Rapids: Discovery House. (12/20).
6. Blackaby, H. & Brandt, H. (1997). *The Power of the Call*. Nashville: Broadman & Holman. (pp. 207-208).
7. Ibid (p. 82).
8. Powlison, D. (1997). "Does Biblical counseling really work?" In H. Eyrich & E. Hindson, (Eds.), *Totally Sufficient*. Eugene, OR: Harvest House. (p. 72).
9. Furendi, F. (cited in Benton, J. (2003). *What's Going on Out There?* Webster, NY: Evangelical Press. (p. 9).
10. American Psychiatric Association: (1994). *Diagnostic and statistical Manual of Mental Disorders* (4th Ed.). Washington, DC.
11. Blackaby, H. & Brandt, H. (1997). *The Power of the Call*. Nashville: Broadman & Holman. (p. 209).
12. Breggin, P. (1991). *Toxic Psychiatry*. NY: St. Martin's Press. (p. 276).
13. Caplan, P. (1995). *They Say You're Crazy*. NY: Addison-Wesley Publishing. (p. 144).
14. Breggin, P. & Breggin, G. (1994). *Talking Back to Prozac: What Doctors Aren't Telling You about Today's Most Controversial Drug*. NY: St. Martin's Press. (pp.34-35).
15. Ibid. (p. 33).
16. Welch, E. (1998). *Blame It on the Brain: Distinguishing Chemical Imbalances, Brain Disorders, and Disobedience*. Philipsburg, NJ: Presbyterian & Reformed. (p. 58).
17. Powlison, D. (1999). "Biological Psychiatry." *The Journal of Biblical Counseling*, V.27, #3, (2-8).
18. MacArthur, J., Jr. (1991). *Our Sufficiency in Christ*. Dallas: Word. (p. 89).
19. Blackaby, H. & Brandt, H. (1997). *The Power of the Call*. Nashville: Broadman & Holman. (p. 60).

20. Brandt, H. & Skinner, K. (1995). *The Word for the Wise*. Nashville: Broadman & Holman. (p. 230; 232).
21. Ibid. (p. 37).
22. Ankerberg, J. & Weldon, J. (1995). *The Facts on Self-Esteem, Psychology, and the Recovery Movement.* Eugene, OR: Harvest House. (p. 38; 41).
23. Boyd, J. (19997). "An Insider's Effort to Blow Up Psychiatry." *The Journal of Biblical Counseling,* V. 15, #3, 21-31. (p. 21).
24. Ibid. (pp. 25-26).
25. Guinness, Os. (1992). America's Last Men and Their Magnificent Talking Cure. In O. Guinness & J. Seel (Eds.). *No god but God* (p 126).
26. Guinness, Os. (1992). More Victimized than Thou. In O. Guiness & J. Seel, (Eds.), *No God but God*. Chicago: Moody. (pp. 131-132).
27. Blackaby, H. & Brandt, H. (1997). *The Power of the Call*. Nashville: Broadman & Holman. (pp. 232-233).
28. "Interview with Tullian Tchividjian" by Jeremy Lelek: "Rediscovering the Power of the Cross: The Gospel Revolution." The Association of Christian Counselors. (Mar. 27, 2010, at www.christiancounseling.com).